Introduction to Arabic
Natural Language Processing

Introduction to Arabic Natural Language Processing

Nizar Y. Habash

ISBN: 978-3-031-01011-8   paperback
ISBN: 978-3-031-02139-8   ebook

DOI 10.1007/978-3-031-02139-8

A Publication in the Springer series
SYNTHESIS LECTURES ON ADVANCES IN AUTOMOTIVE TECHNOLOGY

Lecture #10
Series Editor: Graeme Hirst, *University of Toronto*
Series ISSN
Synthesis Lectures on Human Language Technologies
Print 1947-4040   Electronic 1947-4059

Synthesis Lectures on Human Language Technologies

Editor

Graeme Hirst, *University of Toronto*

Synthesis Lectures on Human Language Technologies is edited by Graeme Hirst of the University of Toronto. The series consists of 50- to 150-page monographs on topics relating to natural language processing, computational linguistics, information retrieval, and spoken language understanding. Emphasis is on important new techniques, on new applications, and on topics that combine two or more HLT subfields.

Introduction to Arabic Natural Language Processing
Nizar Y. Habash
2010

Cross-Language Information Retrieval
Jian-Yun Nie
2010

Automated Grammatical Error Detection for Language Learners
Claudia Leacock, Martin Chodorow, Michael Gamon, and Joel Tetreault
2010

Data-Intensive Text Processing with MapReduce
Jimmy Lin and Chris Dyer
2010

Semantic Role Labeling
Martha Palmer, Daniel Gildea, and Nianwen Xue
2010

Spoken Dialogue Systems
Kristiina Jokinen and Michael McTear
2009

Introduction to Chinese Natural Language Processing
Kam-Fai Wong, Wenjie Li, Ruifeng Xu, and Zheng-sheng Zhang
2009

Introduction to Arabic
Natural Language Processing

Nizar Y. Habash
Columbia University

SYNTHESIS LECTURES ON HUMAN LANGUAGE TECHNOLOGIES #10

ABSTRACT

This book provides system developers and researchers in natural language processing and computational linguistics with the necessary background information for working with the Arabic language. The goal is to introduce Arabic linguistic phenomena and review the state-of-the-art in Arabic processing. The book discusses Arabic script, phonology, orthography, morphology, syntax and semantics, with a final chapter on machine translation issues. The chapter sizes correspond more or less to what is linguistically distinctive about Arabic, with morphology getting the lion's share, followed by Arabic script. No previous knowledge of Arabic is needed. This book is designed for computer scientists and linguists alike. The focus of the book is on Modern Standard Arabic; however, notes on practical issues related to Arabic dialects and languages written in the Arabic script are presented in different chapters.

KEYWORDS

Arabic, natural language processing, computational linguistics, script, phonology, orthography, morphology, syntax, semantics, machine translation

This book is dedicated to the memory of my father,
Sakher Habash, who opened my eyes to the beauty of language
and to the elegance of science.
I owe so much to his love, support and faith in me.

Contents

Preface

The Arabic language has recently become the focus of an increasing number of projects in natural language processing (NLP) and computational linguistics (CL). In this book, I try to provide NLP/CL system developers and researchers (computer scientists and linguists alike) with the necessary background information for working with Arabic. I discuss various Arabic linguistic phenomena and review the state-of-the-art in Arabic processing.

The content of this book initially appeared as a tutorial that became rather popular. Much of the style of the book reflects the tutorial and addresses the various kinds of questions I usually get from students, researchers and developers. As a general guideline for writing this book, I thought of my current doctoral students as my prime audience. I wanted them to have a resource that helps them catch up with the concepts and terminology in the field and avoid many of the confusing issues that could slow their progress.

Given the current and growing size of the area of Arabic NLP, this book is far from a complete reference. It is merely an introductory guide for the beginner.

Nizar Y. Habash
New York, August 2010

Acknowledgments

I would like to thank Owen Rambow, Mona Diab, Tim Buckwalter, Kareem Darwish, Otakar Smrž, Mohamed Maamouri, Ann Bies, Seth Kulick, Alon Lavie, Ryan Roth, Yassine Benajiba, Kristen Parton, Marine Carpuat, Mohamed Eltantawy, Sarah Alkuhlani, Ahmed El Kholy, Fadi Biadsy, Wael Abd-Almageed, Katrin Kirchhoff, Bonnie Dorr, Amy Weinberg, Mary El-Kadi, John P. Broderick, Janet Bing, and Robert Fradkin for helpful discussions and feedback. I would also like to thank Warren Churchill for his invaluable support and encouragement during the writing of this book.

Finally, I would like to thank all the researchers working on Arabic NLP and all the funding agencies that have supported research on Arabic NLP across the world.

Nizar Y. Habash
New York, August 2010

CHAPTER 1

What is "Arabic"?

In the context of this book, the label *Arabic* is used to refer to a language, a collection of dialects and a script.

1.1 ARABIC LANGUAGE AND ARABIC DIALECTS

The Arabic language is a collection of multiple variants among which one particular variant has a special status as the formal written standard of the media, culture and education across the Arab World.[1] The other variants are informal spoken dialects that are the media of communication for daily life. Of course, language exists in a natural continuum, both historically and geographically. The term language as opposed to dialect is only an expression of power and dominance of one group/ideology over another. In the Arab World, politics (primarily, Arab nationalism) and religion (primarily, Islam) are what shapes the view of what is the Arabic language and what is an Arabic dialect. This power relationship is similar to others that exist between languages and their dialects. However, two aspects of Arabic's linguistic situation sets it apart: (a) the high degree of difference between standard Arabic and its dialects and (b) the fact that standard Arabic is not any Arab's native language.[2]

Modern Standard Arabic (MSA, العربية/فصحى العصر [1]) is the official language of the Arab World. MSA is the primary language of the media and education. MSA is syntactically, morphologically and phonologically based on Classical Arabic (CA, العربية/فصحى التراث [1]), the language of the Qur'an (Islam's Holy Book). Lexically, however, MSA is much more modern. MSA is primarily written not spoken.

The Arabic dialects, in contrast, are the true native language forms. They are generally restricted in use for informal daily communication. They are not taught in schools or even standardized although there is a rich popular dialect culture of folktales, songs, movies, and TV shows. Dialects are primarily spoken not written. However, this is changing as more Arabs are gaining access to electronic media of communication such as emails and newsgroups. Arabic dialects are loosely related to Classical Arabic. They are the result of the interaction between different ancient dialects of Classical Arabic and other languages that existed in, neighbored and/or colonized what is today the

---

[1]The Arab World refers to the Arabic-speaking countries spread between the Atlantic Ocean and the Persian Gulf. These countries have a collective population of over 300 million people. The 22 members of the Arab League are Algeria, Bahrain, Comoros, Djibouti, Egypt, Iraq, Jordan, Kuwait, Lebanon, Libya, Mauritania, Morocco, Oman, Palestine, Qatar, Saudi Arabia, Somalia, Sudan, Syria, Tunisia, United Arab Emirates and Yemen. Arabic is an official language in three other countries: Chad, Eritrea and Israel. Iran, Pakistan, Afghanistan and Turkey are Muslim countries and close neighbors of the Arab World, but they are not Arabic speaking.

[2]Compare, for example, with High German, a living dialect that has standard status.

Arab World. For example, Algerian Arabic has a lot of influences from Berber as well as French. Arabic dialects substantially differ from MSA and each other in terms of phonology, morphology, lexical choice and syntax.

Arabic dialects vary on many dimensions – primarily, geography and social class. Geolinguistically, the Arab World can be divided in many different ways. The following is only one of many (and should not be taken to mean that all members of any dialect group are completely homogenous linguistically):

- Egyptian Arabic (EGY) covers the dialects of the Nile valley: Egypt and Sudan.

- Levantine (LEV) Arabic includes the dialects of Lebanon, Syria, Jordan, Palestine and Israel.

- Gulf Arabic (GLF) includes the dialects of Kuwait, United Arab Emirates, Bahrain, and Qatar. Saudi Arabia is typically included although there is a wide range of sub-dialects within it. Omani Arabic is included some times.

- North African (Maghrebi) Arabic (Mag) covers the dialects of Morocco, Algeria, Tunisia and Mauritania. Libyan Arabic is sometimes included.

- Iraqi Arabic (IRQ) has elements of both Levantine and Gulf.

- Yemenite Arabic (Yem) is often considered its own class.

- Maltese Arabic is not always considered an Arabic dialect. It is the only Arabic variant that is considered a separate language and is written with the Roman script.

Socially, it is common to distinguish three sub-dialects within each dialect region: city, rural and bedouin. The three degrees are often associated with a class hierarchy in which rich settled city dwellers are on top and bedouins are on bottom. Different social associations exist, as common in many other languages around the world. For example, the city dialect is considered less marked and more refined and prestigious; whereas the Bedouin dialect is considered less prestigious and more rough, yet pure to the origin of the language. Speakers are known to moderately alternate among variants in different social contexts [2].

The relationship between MSA and the dialect in a specific region is rather complex. Arabs do not think of these two as separate languages. This particular perception leads to a special kind of coexistence between two forms of language that serve different purposes. This kind of situation is what linguists term *diglossia* [3]. Although the two variants have clear domains of prevalence: formal written (MSA) versus informal spoken (dialect), there is a large gray area in between that is often filled with a mix of the two forms [1, 2].

1.2   ARABIC SCRIPT

Arabic, the language, is written using Arabic, the script, which is also used to write many languages around the world which are not related to Arabic such as Persian, Kurdish, Urdu and Pashto. In fact, some of these languages are closer to English than to Arabic: e.g., Persian is an Indo-European language, a relative of English and French. Arabic dialects are by default written in Arabic script although there are no standard dialectal spelling systems. There have been calls at different times during the last century to exchange the Arabic script with the Roman script for MSA or at least its dialects. These calls parallel Ataturk's successful romanization program in Turkey where the Arabic script was used to write Turkish under Ottoman rule. Political and religious opposition to such calls have preserved the use of Arabic script in the Arab World. Currently, even calls for spelling standardization in the dialects in Arabic script are sometimes perceived as a challenge to MSA hegemony.

1.3   THIS BOOK

This book consists of eight chapters including this introductory chapter. Of the different variants of Arabic, we discuss MSA primarily and may occasionally refer to CA or Arabic dialects. As this book is focused on a language as opposed to a specific Natural Language Processing (NLP) area of research, it trades depth for breadth in its discussion of NLP problems. Each chapter has a linguistic component followed or intersected with discussions of NLP tasks. NLP tasks are defined and exemplified, and pointers to previous and ongoing research are provided. Being an introductory text, this book is only intended to provide a stepping stone to accessing the more detailed work on different NLP tasks. This book is designed for computer scientists and linguists alike. No previous knowledge of Arabic is needed.

In Chapter 2, we present the Arabic script and its peculiarities. We also discuss issues of encoding choices, transliteration and optical character recognition. We briefly point out issues relevant to languages other than Arabic that use the Arabic script. Basic skills for handling Arabic text, even when illiterate in Arabic script, are discussed.

In Chapter 3, we discuss Arabic phonology and orthography (how the Arabic script is used to represent the Arabic language). We also discuss the NLP problems of proper name transliteration, diacritization, automatic speech recognition and speech synthesis.

In Chapter 4, we discuss Arabic's rich morphology. This chapter focuses on terminology and provides a sketch of Arabic morphology.

In Chapter 5, we discuss the NLP tasks of morphological analysis and generation, morphological disambiguation, POS tagging and tokenization.

Chapter 6 is about Arabic syntax. We present a sketch of Arabic syntactic issues and discuss existing resources for research on Arabic syntax and parsing.

Chapter 7 is a brief note on Arabic computational semantics, primarily describing some of the available resources for research in that area.

In Chapter 8, we present a brief note on Arabic machine translation.

The chapter sizes correspond more or less to what is linguistically distinctive about Arabic, with morphology getting the lion's share, followed by Arabic script.

The book ends with four appendices consisting of pointers to resources and tools relevant to Arabic NLP.

A note on Arabic transliteration and transcription We use the Habash-Soudi-Buckwalter transliteration scheme [4] for representing Arabic orthography and phonology. This scheme is discussed in Chapter 2.

CHAPTER 2

Arabic Script

In this chapter, we discuss the Arabic script primarily as used to write Modern Standard Arabic (MSA). We start with a linguistic description of Arabic script elements and follow it with a discussion of computer encodings and text input and display. We also discuss common practices in NLP for handling peculiarities of the Arabic script and briefly introduce four script-related computational tasks: orthographic transliteration, orthographic normalization, handwriting recognition and automatic diacritization. The transliteration used for romanizing the Arabic script is discussed in Section 2.3.1.

2.1 ELEMENTS OF THE ARABIC SCRIPT

The Arabic script is an alphabet written from right to left. There are two types of symbols in the Arabic script for writing words: letters and diacritics. In addition to these symbols, we discuss digits, punctuation and other symbols in this section.

2.1.1 LETTERS

Arabic letters are written in cursive style in both print and script (handwriting). They typically consist of two parts: letter form (رسم *rasm*) and letter mark (إعجام *AiʕjAm*). The letter form is an essential component in every letter. There is a total of 19 letter forms. See Figure 2.1. The letter marks, also called consonantal diacritics, can be sub-classified into three types. See Figures 2.2. First are dots, also called points, of which there are five: one, two or three to go above the letter form and one or two to go below the letter form. Second is the short Kaf, which is used to mark specific letter shapes of the letter Kaf (see Figure 2.4). Third is the Hamza (همزة:ة *hamzah*) letter mark. The Hamza can appear above or below specific letter forms. The term Hamza is used for both the letter form (ء) and the letter mark, which appears with other letter forms such as أ *Â*, ؤ *ŵ*, and ئ *ŷ*. The Madda letter mark (مدة *mad~aħ*) is a Hamza variant.[1]

Figure 2.1: Letter forms are the basic graphic backbones of Arabic letters.

ء ا ب ح د ر س ص ط ع ف ق ل ل م ں ه و ى

Figure 2.2: Letter marks are necessary to distinguish different letters. The figure features five dots/points, the short Kaf, three Hamzas and the Madda.

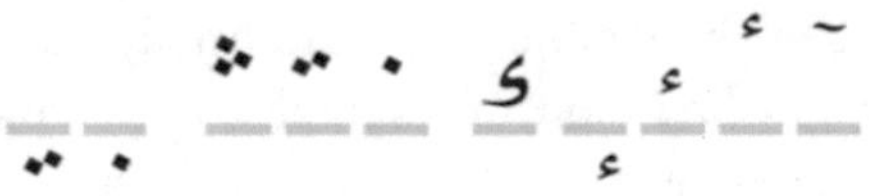

Specific combinations of letter forms and letter marks result in the 36 letters of the Arabic alphabet used to write MSA (see Table 2.1 at the end of this chapter). Some letters are created using letter forms only with no letter marks. Letter marks typically distinguish letters with different consonantal phonetic mappings although not always. See Figure 2.3. We discuss the question of sound-to-letter mapping in the next chapter.

Figure 2.3: Letter dots in the first and second clusters from the right create letters with distinct consonantal phonetic values. All the letters in the first cluster from the left are used for marking the glottal stop in different vocalic and graphic contexts.

ء ؤ ئ آ إ أ ا	س ش	ث ت ب
/'/	/š/ /s/	/θ/ /t/ /b/

---

[1] An additional less common letter mark related to *Hamza* is the Wasla, which only appears with the Alif letter form in Alif-Wasla/Hamzat-Wasl: ٱ *Ă*. This letter is so uncommon it is not part of some encodings of Arabic. We return to discuss this briefly in Section 3.2.1.

> **Terminology Alert** *Letter marks*, specifically *dots*, should not be confused with Hebrew Niqqud 'dots', which are optional diacritics comparable to Arabic diacritics (Section 2.1.2). Arabic dots and other letter marks are all obligatory. That said, among researchers in optical character recognition (OCR), the term *diacrtic* (i.e., consonantal diacritic) is often used to mean letter mark not diacritic in the sense used in this book and by most researchers in NLP. The Hamza letter mark in stem-initial positions tends to be perceived as a diacritic as opposed to stem-medial and stem-final positions [5]. See Section 2.1.2.

Figure 2.4: A sample of letters with their different letter shapes.

`	w	r	d	A	l	k	h	T	S	s	q	f	m	γ	j	y	n	b	
ء	و	ر	د	ا	ل	ك	ه	ط	ص	س	ق	ف	م	غ	ج	ي	ن	ب	Isolated
					ل	ك	ه	ط	ص	س	ق	ف	م	غ	ج	ي	ن	ب	Initial
	ـو	ـر	ـد	ـا	ل	ك	ه	ط	ص	س	ق	ف	م	غ	ج	ي	ن	ب	Medial
	ـو	ـر	ـد	ـا	ل	ك	ه	ط	ص	س	ق	ف	م	غ	ج	ي	ن	ب	Final

Letter Shapes

Arabic letters have different shapes depending on their position in a word: initial, medial, final or stand-alone. The letter shapes are used in both print and script, with no distinction. The letter shapes are also called *allographs*, and the letters *graphemes*, by analogy to allophones and phonemes (Section 3.1.1). Similarly, the context-based selection of letter shape is called *graphotactics*, by analogy to phonotactics. The terminology used in font and encoding design is different: letters are *characters* and shapes are *glyphs* (Section 2.2). The initial and medial shapes are typically similar and so are the final and stand-alone shapes. Most letter forms are written fully connected. However, a few letter forms are post-disconnective; they connect to preceding letters but not to following letters. All letter shapes following a post-disconnective letter form are either initial or stand-alone. One letter form, the Hamza (ء) is fully disconnective. See Figure 2.4.

Associated with disconnective letters are small white spaces that follow the letter creating visually isolated islands of connected letters, called word parts. In the example in Figure 2.5, there are two words and five word parts. These spaces make it harder for OCR systems to identify the boundary of a word correctly. The spaces also can lead to spelling errors that may not stand out visually: words split into word parts or multiple words attached with no real space. To some extent, this problem of identifying which word parts make up a word is similar to the Chinese word segmentation problem where a word is made up of one or more characters which can be words on their own [6].

Figure 2.5: Arabic words are mostly connected but may contain small spaces from disconnective letters.

Figure 2.6: Putting it all together: from letters to words. The two words exemplified here are كتب *ktb* and كتاب *ktAb*. Read from right to left. Short vowel diacritics are not shown.

كتب ← ب ت ك

كتب

batak   b t k

كتاب ← ب ا ت ك

bAtik   b A t k

Figure 2.6 shows how a word is constructed by putting all of its letters together. Remember that Arabic is written from right to left when you match up the transliterations with the letters. The letter Alif (*A* in green) is a disconnective letter, and as such, it breaks the second word into two word parts.

Although, in principle, the letter shape is tied to the letter form component, some letters, such as the Ta-Marbuta (ة *ħ*) and Alif-Maqsura (ى *ý*),[2] share only some of the letter shapes of their letter forms and are post-disconnective even though their letter forms are not. Moreover, some letter shapes, as in initial and medial Kaf, lose the letter mark which appears in the final and stand-alone shapes (See Figure 2.4 and 2.6).

---

[2]There are numerous possible romanizations for Arabic names, including Arabic letter names. See Section 3.3.1. In this book, we try to be internally consistent, but readers should be aware that they will encounter variant spellings, e.g., the Unicode standard names we display for reference in Table 2.1.

FAQ: How many letters does Arabic have?

There is some disagreement over the number of Arabic letters resulting from different classifications of what is a diacritic and from ignoring some of the letters. Most commonly, the Arabic alphabet is said to have 28 letters (basic 28, sometime substituting ا with أ) or 29 letters (basic 28 plus the Hamza-on-the-line letter constructed from the Hamza letter form). In these counts, the Hamza letter marks are considered diacritical. In other counts, the four Lam-Alif ligatures are added to the 36 Arabic letters (basic 28 + Hamza letters + Ta-Marbuta + Alif-Maqsura) leading to a count of 40. In this book, we follow the *common* use of standard computer encodings, which do not count Hamza letter marks as diacritics, count Ta-Marbuta and Alif-Maqsura as letters and not count Lam-Alif ligatures as separate letters. We discuss encoding issues in Section 2.2.

Ligatures

In addition to the shape variations, Arabic has a large set of common **ligatures**, different representations of two or even three letters. Ligatures typically involve vertical positioning of letters (Figure 2.7) and vary by font (Figure 2.13). All ligatures are optional and font dependent except for the Lam-Alif ligature which is obligatory: ا+ل is represented as لا (or medially as ﻼ) not لا . This post-disconnective ligature has three variants that include Hamzated Alifs and Alif with Madda: لأ, لإ and لآ. Ligatures pose an added challenge to encoding Arabic. We discuss this in Section 2.2.

Figure 2.7: Example of two optional ligatures in one font but not another. The second and third letters and the last two letters in the bottom example forge vertical ligatures but not in the top example.

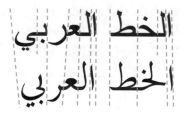

Different Types of Letters

The 36 Arabic letters used in MSA can be classified into the following subsets:

1. **The basic 28 letters** The basic letters of the Arabic alphabet corresponding to Arabic's 28 consonantal sounds. They are constructed using all letter forms except for the Hamza letter form. In all of these letters, the letter marks are fully discriminative distinguishing different consonants from each other.

2. **The Hamza letters** There are six. One is the ء Hamza-on-the-line, which is made of the Hamza letter form. The rest use the Hamza and Madda letter marks with other letter forms: (ء, آ, أ, ؤ, إ, ئ). When a Hamzated Alif (آ, أ, إ) follows a Lam, the obligatory Lam-Alif ligature

---

FAQ: What is Arabic's alphabetical sorting order?

There are two commonly used Arabic sorting orders. The shape-based order, also called ألفبائية *ÂlfbAŷyħ* (lit. 'alef-bet'), clusters letters of similar shapes together:

ي و ه ن م ل ك ق ف غ ع ظ ط ض ص ش س ز ر ذ د خ ح ج ث ت ب أ

Â b t θ j H x d ð r z s š S D T Ď ς γ f q k l m n h w y

The second order, called أبجدية *Âbjadiyaħ* 'Abjad', is loosely based on the ancient Phoenician alphabet order, still used in Hebrew, with six additional letters added at the end. This order is mostly used for enumeration of small lists, typically less than 10. Longer lists are enumerated with digits (Section 2.1.3). Traditional Arabic dictionaries typically list words in root-based clusters sorted in the Abjad order, although not all dictionaries do so. As in Hebrew Gematria, the Abjad order has associated numerical values (which we present below the letters):

غ ظ ض ذ خ ث ت ش ر ق ص ف ع س ن م ل ك ي ط ح ز و ه د ج ب أ

Â b j d H w z H T y k l m n s ς f S q r š t θ x ð D Ď γ

1 2 3 4 5 6 7 8 9 10 20 30 40 50 60 70 80 90 100 200 300 400 500 600 700 800 900 1000

Both of these orders only cover the basic 28 letters. Modern encodings of Arabic (see Section 2.2) are based on the shape-based order with insertions to accommodate the additional letters of MSA (see Tables 2.1 and 2.2). Non-MSA extensions are typically listed outside the range of the MSA order. So, for sorting in MSA shape-based order, we can rely on the character encoding value, but sorting with non-MSA extensions and sorting for Abjad order requires special routines.

---

takes on the letter mark too. These letters are not listed as part of the alphabet typically. The Hamza letters all represent one consonant: the glottal stop (see Section 3.1.2). The different Hamza forms are governed by a set of complex spelling rules that reflect vocalic context and neighboring letter forms [7, 8].

3. **The Ta-Marbuta** This letter is a special morphological marker typically marking a feminine ending. The Ta-Marbuta (ة *ħ*), literally 'tied Ta', is a hybrid letter merging the form of the letters Ha (ه *h*) and Ta (ت *t*). Ta-Marbuta only appears in word final positions. When the morpheme it represents is in word-medial position, it is written using the letter Ta (ت *t*). For example, مكتبة+هم mktbħ+hm 'library+their' is written as مكتبتهم mktbthm 'their library'. Although the letter form of the Ta-Marbuta is fully connective, the Ta-Marbuta letter is post-disconnective.

4. **The Alif-Maqsura** This letter is also a special morphological marker marking a range of morphological information from feminine endings to underlying word roots. The Alif-Maqsura (ى *ý*), literally 'shortened Alif', is a hybrid letter merging the forms of the letters Alif (ا *A*) and Ya (ي *y*). The Alif-Maqsura only appears in word-final positions as a dotless Ya. When the morpheme it represents is in word-medial position, it is written using the letters Alif (ا *A*) or Ya (ي *y*). For example, مستشفى+هم mstšfý+hm 'hospital+their' is written مستشفاهم mstšfAhm 'their hospital'; however, إلى+هم Ălý+hm 'to+them' is written إليهم Ălyhm 'to them'. Although the letter form of the Alif-Maqsura is fully connective, the Alif-Maqsura letter is post-disconnective.

There are few additional letters that are not officially part of the Arabic script for MSA. Most commonly seen are پ *p*, چ *c*, ڤ *v* and گ *g*. These are borrowings from other languages typically used to represent sounds not in MSA or the local dialect. See Section 2.1.5.

2.1.2 DIACRITICS

The second class of symbols in the Arabic script is the diacritics. Whereas letters are always written, diacritics are optional: written Arabic can be fully diacritized, partially diacritized, or entirely undiacritized. The NLP task of restoring diacritics, or simply *diacritization* is briefly introduced in Section 2.3.4. Typically, Arabic text is undiacritized except in religious texts, children educational texts, and some poetry. Some diacritics are indicated in modern written Arabic to help readers disambiguate certain words. In the Penn Arabic Treebank (part 3) [9], 1.6% of all words have at least one diacritic indicated by their author. Out of these, 99.3% are actually correct, as in they appear in the correct position in the word.

There are three types of diacritics: Vowel, Nunation, and Shadda. They are presented in Figure 2.8. Vowel diacritics represent Arabic's three short vowels (Fatha /a/, Damma /u/ and Kasra /i/) and the absence of any vowel (no vowel, Sukun). Nunation diacritics can only occur in word final positions in nominals (nouns, adjectives and adverbs), where they indicate indefiniteness (see Section 4.2.2). They are pronounced as a short vowel followed by an unwritten /n/ sound. For example, بٌ *bū* is pronounced /bun/. The Nunation diacritics look like a doubled version of their corresponding short vowels and are named in Arabic as such: Fathatan, Dammatan, Kasratan [lit. two Fathas, two Dammas, two Kasras, respectively]. This is simply an orthographic accident and has no linguistic significance. Shadda is a consonant doubling diacritic: بّ *b~* (/bb/). Shadda typically combines with a vowel or Nunation diacritic: بُّ *b~u* (/bbu/) or بٌّ *b~ū* (bbun). For example, the word عَبَّر *ʕab~ara* 'he expressed' is pronounced /ʕabbara/. More details on Arabic pronunciation are presented in Chapter 3. Figure 2.9 shows an example of fully diacritized words.

One other less commonly used diacritic is the Dagger Alif (الألف الخنجرية *á*), aka *small Alif* or *superscript Alif*, which is a diacritic representing a *long /a/ vowel* (/ā/). It appears in archaic spelling of a few words, e.g., الله *All~áh* 'Allah' and هٰذا *háðA* 'this'.

Figure 2.8: Types of Arabic diacritics.

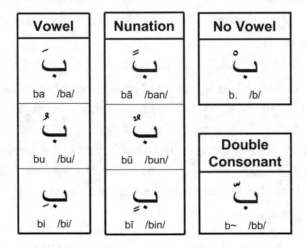

Figure 2.9: Example of fully diacritized words.

Quranic spelling makes use of a variety of additional diacritics as a guide to the reading of the Quran. We will not discuss Quranic Arabic here as it is a specialized form of Arabic that is rather different from MSA [10].

2.1.3   DIGITS

Arabic numbers are written in a decimal system. There are two sets of digits used for writing numbers in the Arab World. The *Arabic Numerals* commonly used in Europe, the Americas and most of the rest of the world, are only used in Western Arabic countries (Morocco, Algeria, Tunisia). Middle Eastern Arab countries (e.g., Egypt, Syria, Iraq, Saudi Arabia) use what is called Indo-Arabic numerals. Some

---

FAQ: Hamza: to be or not to be *a diacritic*?

As we mentioned earlier, the Hamza is a diacritic-like symbol that appears with a limited number of letter forms. The general consensus on encoding the Hamza is to consider it a letter mark (and as such part of the letter) as opposed to being a diacritic. Now, the fact that Arabic writers often ignore writing the Hamza (especially with stem-initial Alifs [5]) makes it de-facto optional and diacritic-like. In computational systems, one can discuss Hamza restoration as a variant problem that is or is not part of the Arabic diacritization problem [11, 12, 13]. The Hamzated Alif letters are often reductively normalized by brute force replacement with a bare Alif. Hamzas in letters other than Alif are usually kept as writers usually do not drop them. See Section 2.3.2.

---

non-Arab countries, such as Iran and Pakistan use a variant of the Indo-Arabic numeral set, which differs in the forms of digits 4, 5 and 6 only. The three digit sets are contrasted in Figure 2.10.

Figure 2.10: Three sets of digits used in the Arabic script.

Western Arabic *Tunisia, Morocco, etc.*	0	1	2	3	4	5	6	7	8	9
Indo-Arabic *Middle East*	٠	١	٢	٣	٤	٥	٦	٧	٨	٩
Eastern Indo-Arabic *Iran, Pakistan, etc.*	٠	١	٢	٣	۴	۵	۶	٧	٨	٩

Figure 2.11: Arabic digits are typed from left-to-right in right-to-left text.

استقلت الجزائر في سنة 1962 بعد 132 عاما من الاحتلال الفرنسي.

Although Arabic is written from right to left, the forms of multi-digit numbers in Arabic are the same as those used in European (left-to-right) languages. In typing, the multi-digit numbers are keyed from left-to-right. See Figure 2.11. In handwriting, two-digit number are written right-to-left but larger numbers start on the left and head rightward. This is a reflection of how Arabic numbers are commonly uttered in Arabic: in smaller numbers (up to 100), the smaller place-value digit is uttered (and written first), but in larger numbers, the highest place-value is uttered first. For example, a number such as ٢,٣٤٥ *2,345* is uttered as *two-thousand three-hundred five and forty*.[3] Mapping between digit and utterance is important for applications such as text-to-speech and also language modeling for Automatic Speech Recognition (ASR) [14].

2.1.4   PUNCTUATION AND OTHER SYMBOLS

Modern Arabic uses similar punctuation marks to those used in European languages, e.g., !, ., :, ", (, and). However, some punctuation marks look slightly different as a result of adjusting to the right-to-left aesthetics of Arabic, e.g., (؟ *?*), (، *,*) and (؛ *;*). The Arabic comma (،) is used as a decimal point. Although in some cases, the letter ر *r* is used for the same purpose: ١،٥ *1,5* or ١ر٥ *1r5* '1.5'.

A particularly unique Arabic symbol is the Tatweel (lit. 'elongation') or Kashida: ـ. The Tatweel is used to stretch words to indicate prominence or simply to force vertical justification. Since Arabic has no equivalent to capital letters, Tatweel serves a similar purpose to using capitals for prominence or emphasis. Here is a word with no Tatweel: قال *qAl* 'he said'. Here is the same word with one and two Tatweel characters, respectively: قـال and قــال. Obviously, Tatweel can only stretch connective letters in medial positions. Tatweel is sometimes used to force initial position of standalone letters, e.g., هـ *h_* '[abbreviation for] Hijri year'. Tatweel is almost always deleted to reduce sparsity as part of preprocessing Arabic text for NLP purposes, such as building a language model (Section 2.3.2).

2.1.5   ARABIC SCRIPT EXTENSIONS

The Arabic script is a versatile script that has been used to write many languages from different language families: Baluchi, Dari, Hausa, Kabyle, Kashmiri, Kazak, Kurdish, Kyrghyz, Malay, Morisco, Pashto, Persian/Farsi, Punjabi, Sindhi, Siraiki, Tatar, Ottoman Turkish, Uyghur, and Urdu. As with the Roman script, the extension of the Arabic script to languages other than Arabic included the addition of various letter marks and the redefinition of the phonetic value of some letters [15]. Since the focus of this book is on Arabic (the language, specifically MSA) in NLP/CL, the purpose of this section is to enable the reader to do rudimentary language identification, on the level of what many Roman script readers can do when faced with unfamiliar Roman-script text, i.e., be able to guess that some text is English, French, German or "some Scandinavian language."

All languages extending the Arabic script use the set of letters from MSA and add to it. The list of common extended letter marks and examples of extended letters appear in Figure 2.12. Some of the letter extensions include using dot clusters on letter forms in non-MSA combinations (such as three dots below a letter form or two dots over a form that does not get two dots in MSA). Some of the letter mark extensions are simply adding more dots (up to four dots) or changing the orientation of dots (such as two vertical dots). Some more striking letter mark extensions include the *Haft* (v), *ring* (o) and *small Ta* (ط).

---

[3]It should be noted that in Classical Arabic, the number is uttered completely from right to left, e.g., ٢,٣٤٥ *2,345* is *five and forty and three-hundred and two-thousand*.

Figure 2.12: Some of the additional letter marks not used in MSA are presented below. In the graph on the bottom, the inner circle contains MSA Arabic letters, which are used in all extended variants. The middle circle marked with a dotted border contains letters that infrequently appear in MSA as borrowed symbols. The outer circle contains non-MSA letters.

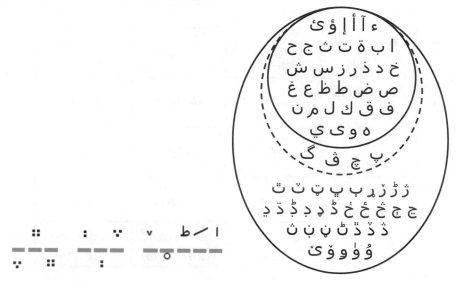

FAQ: **What are the most prominent differences between the Arabic and Roman scripts from the point of view of NLP?**

Some of the differences, such as script direction, letter-shaping and obligatory ligatures, are effectively abstracted away in computational applications (see Section 2.2) and, as such, are rendered irrelevant. The two most prominent differences are perhaps optionality of diacritics and lack of capitalization. Diacritics, or precisely the fact that they are almost never written, put a bigger load on human readers in a way that is much harder for machines to model compared to Roman-script languages. We discuss Arabic morphological disambiguation in Chapter 5. The lack of capital/small letter distinction, which is used in specific ways in different Roman script languages, makes some applications, such named entity recognition and part-of-speech tagging, more challenging in Arabic.

2.1.6   ARABIC TYPOGRAPHY

The Arabic script has a large and growing number of fonts and styles that vary widely. See Figure 2.13 for some examples of Arabic script use. Most current operating systems, Windows, MacOS and

Linux variants, support Arabic and varying sets of Arabic fonts. For editing Arabic in LATEX, we recommend the ArabTEX package [16], which was used in typesetting this book.

Figure 2.13: Examples of various Arabic fonts in print, handwriting, graffiti and calligraphy.

Traditional Arabic	عربي	محمد	الجبر
Simplified Arabic	عربي	محمد	الجبر
Tahoma Arabic	عربي	محمد	الجبر
Andalus	عربي	محمد	الجبر
	çarabiy~ *Arabic*	muHam~ad *Muhammad*	Aljabr *Algebra*

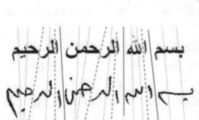

2.2   ARABIC ENCODING, INPUT AND DISPLAY

An *encoding*, aka character set, charset, character map or code page, is a systematic representation of the symbols in a script for the purpose of consistent storage and access (data entry and display) by machines. The representational choices made in an encoding must be synchronized with data entry and display tools. The Arabic script brings certain challenges to the question of encoding design and how it interacts with data storage and access. This is primarily a result of how Arabic script is different from European scripts, whose handling has been the historical default. The basic challenges are the right-to-left directionality, contextually variant letter shapes, ligatures, the use of diacritics and bidirectional handling of digits and Roman characters in Arabic contexts.

In the extreme, an encoding can represent each complex ligature and letter shape with different diacritics as a separate complex "symbol." The number of different symbols in the encoding becomes very large. On the other extreme, different letter marks can be encoded as separate symbols from letter forms and diacritics. Most commonly used encodings for Arabic, such as Unicode, CP-1256 and ISO-8859, encode Arabic as graphemes of letters and diacritics in *logical order* (first to last). Basically, the fact that Arabic is displayed in a different direction on the screen from Roman script is considered irrelevant to the encoding as are the issues of contextual shaping and diacritization. This encoding design choice makes Arabic storage efficient although it places the burden of correct entry and display on the operating system or the specific program processing Arabic.

2.2.1 ARABIC INPUT/OUTPUT SUPPORT

For a long time, Arabic support, beyond available fonts, was missing on many operating systems and editing programs. Most current operating systems provide Arabic support, but it has to be activated in some cases. Partial support of Arabic can be deceptive to those who do not read Arabic: the presence of an Arabic font may allow the characters to be identifiable, but the text is left-to-right or is not correctly shaped. See Figure 2.14.

Figure 2.14: An example of what a string of Arabic text looks like in memory and on the screen. In memory, letters are ordered logically (first-to-last). For display purposes, a basic algorithm for reorienting and shaping the text is used. However, special handling of multiple directions for Arabic digits and non-Arabic letters can make this a complex task.

Logical Order	→ÔÇÑßÊ ÝáÓØíä (Palestine) Ýí ÇæáãÈíÇÏ (Olympics) 2000 æ 2004. .4002 æ 0002)scipmylO(ÏÇíÈãáæÇ íÝ)enitselaP(äíØÓáÝÝ ÊßÑÇÔ ←
Visual Order	. 2004 و 2000 (Olympics) في اولمبياد (Palestine) شاركت فلسطين ← .2004 و 2000 (Olympics) في اولمبياد (Palestine) شاركت فلسطين ←

In the 1990s, several now-obsolete solutions were created to by-pass the lack of universal support for Arabic input an display. The basic idea was to encode Arabic *allographically* by not only assigning different symbol codes to different letter shapes and ligatures but also internally encoding Arabic in *visual order*. Visual order refers to encoding Arabic "backward" so that it appears from right-to-left when displayed by a system expecting a left-to-right script [17]. These encodings suffered from lots of problems and limitations. It is worth pointing out that visual encoding of digits can still be found in some texts and is a problem for NLP.[4]

---

[4]Try for example googling "1999 سنة" *snh 1999 'year 1999'* and compare it to googling "9991 سنة".

Figure 2.15: The standard Arabic keyboard layout for PCs. Mac machines have a slightly different keyboard layout. The keyboard is based on letters, although it also contains Lam-Alif keys which have the effect of striking Lam then Alif. The person typing strikes the keys in logical order, and the text is displayed from right-to-left with correct shapes and ligatures.

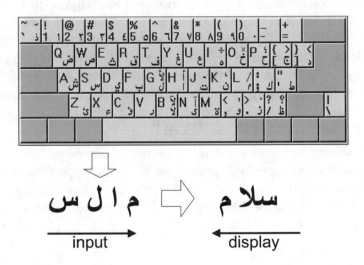

Before computers, typewriters and print press machines had different type bars (the equivalent of symbols) for different ligatures and letter shapes. Typing on a typewriter required specifying the correct letter shape to produce. This is a more complex version of specifying capitals and small letters in Roman script. The encoding choice used with modern computers provides a major simplification to Arabic data entry via keyboards. Arabic is simply entered graphemically in logical order. See Figure 2.15.

We discuss next some of the most commonly used encodings for Arabic.

2.2.2   ARABIC ENCODINGS

Many different "standard" encodings have been developed for Arabic over the years. We only discuss here the three most commonly used encodings, which are all well supported for input and output on different platforms. Tables 2.1 and 2.2 present the different code values used for MSA Arabic symbols in multiple encodings side-by-side. For additional discussions of Arabic encoding standards, see [18, 19].

Figure 2.16: Comparing the correct and incorrect decoding of various Arabic encodings.

		Display Encoding			
		CP-1256	**ISO-8859**	**Unicode**	**Western**
Actual Encoding	**CP-1256**	تدشين منطقة حرة في دبي للتجارة الالكترونية	ة حرة□تدشيل كلظ ترنلة□دب ففتجارة افاف	ϒ ɠ ɠ□ ψ□□Ŏɠãã□Λ	ÊÏÔíá ãäØÞÉ ÍÑÉ Ýí ÏÈí ááÊÌÇÑÉ ÇáÇáÊÈÑÑÑæäíÉ
	ISO-8859	ة حرة â □×و هو ê□تدش ننتجارة ê□دب ê□ ة ê□ و ê□انانمتر	تدشين منطقة حرة في دبي للتجارة الالكترونية	ϒ□柔既 ɠ ɠ□ ψ ㊑親ɠ	ÊÏÔêæ åæ×âÉ ÍÑÉ áê ÏÈê ääÊÌÇÑÉ ÇäÇäÊÑÑÑèæêÉ
	Unicode	┐ط┣ط†□ظ□ظ ┐رۡظ...ظ□ط┣†-ظ□ط┣ط□ط ظ□ظك┐ط┐ط□ظ ظ□ط┣ط┣§┐ط┣ط□ط ظ„ظ§ظك┐رۡف ظ„ظ§┐ط┣ط†□ط□ط©	┐ظ□□ط؟┐┐ظ ؛؟ء؟ ┐ط□□ط ┐┐ظ ┐ط□ظ εε ┐ط┐ظ-┐□□ط εε εε ┐ط□□ظ εε ┐┐ظ ┐ط□□ط, ┐ط□□ط εε ┐□□ط εε ┐ط□□ط, εε ┐┐ظ	تدشين منطقة حرة في دبي للتجارة الالكترونية	ï»¿Ø□ªØ¯Ø´ÙŠÙ† Ù„Ù†Ø·Ù‚Ø© Ø¯Ø±ØŠ Ù ÙŠ ÙˆØ¬ Ø§Ø³ØµÙ Ù„Ù„ØµÙ„¬ÙƒÙ Ø§Ø±±Ù ^Ù†ÙŠŠÙ©©

8-bit Encodings: ISO-8859-6 and CP-1256

ISO-8859-6 and CP-1256 are two of the most popular early encoding schemes of Arabic. ISO-8859-6, developed by the International Standards Organization (ISO), is identical to the ASMO-708 standard created by the Arab Standards and Metrology Organization (ASMO). CP-1256, (Code Page 1256), aka Arabic Windows encoding, was developed by Microsoft and made extremely popular through Windows. Both of these encodings use 1 byte (8-bits) to represent every single symbol (for a maximum of 256 characters). As in other encodings in their class for scripts/languages other than Arabic, the first 7-bits (or 128 characters) are reserved for English ASCII (American Standard Code for Information Interchange). The *other* script is represented in the other 128 characters. This allows the same encoding to be used for two scripts (or multiple languages) if needed. The Arabic portion in ASMO-708 and ISO-8859-6 is based on (compatible with but not identical to) an earlier 7-bit Arabic encoding (ASMO-449) [19].

In CP-1256, the Arabic characters are listed in order although with some gaps in between different sets of characters to allow for maintaining the code values for some European languages, particularly French, thus effectively producing a multilingual code page (Arabic, English, French). Both CP-1256 and ISO-8859-6 couldn't accommodate the full set of extended Arabic characters; however, characters from Persian are included. These encodings specify the graphemes only and rely on separate algorithms to display the correct font glyphs.

CP-1256 and ISO-8859 are not compatible although they agree on the first 22 characters. This simple fact means that words made up completely from characters in this overlapping set will look "correct" in either encoding. For example, see the word حرة in Figure 2.16. When verifying the encoding of a sorted list of words (as in a dictionary), it is wise to look beyond the first few words to avoid falling for this ambiguity.

Unicode

Unicode is the current de facto standard for encoding a large number of languages and scripts simultaneously. Unicode was originally designed to use two bytes of information (to code 65,536 unique symbols) and has been expanded since to cover over 1 million unique symbols. For Arabic, Unicode supports an extended Arabic character set. It also gives Arabic letter shapes and ligatures unique addresses under what it calls Presentation Forms A and B charts.[5] Because Unicode encodes so many more characters than ISO-8859-6 and CP-1256, conversion from these encodings into Unicode is possible, but the reverse may be lossy. Although Unicode provides an important solution to representing the extended Arabic script set, it introduces new challenges. In particular, it introduces multiple ways to represent the same looking symbol. For instance, the Indo-Arabic and Eastern Indo-Arabic numbers are all replicated. Similarly, some letters have shapes that may not be distinguished easily, e.g., ك (U+0643) *Arabic k* and ک (U+06A9) *Persian k*, which initially have a similar shape: ک. This confusion will typically arise when Arabic is typed on a Persian keyboard. Finally, the presence of presentation form charts allows incorrect allographic encoding that may not be easily detectable visually. All of these cases make it hard to match strings of text that on the screen look identical although they are encoded differently.

2.3   NLP TASKS

2.3.1   ORTHOGRAPHIC TRANSLITERATION

In addition to the standard encodings discussed above, many researchers in NLP use an orthographic transliteration, specifically a romanization, in their research on Arabic NLP. Here, we follow the definition of the terms *transcription* and *transliteration* given by Beesley [20]: the term transcription denotes an orthography that characterizes the phonology or morpho-phonology of a language, whereas the term transliteration denotes an orthography using carefully substituted orthographical symbols in a one-to-one, fully reversible mapping with that language's customary orthography. This specific definition of transliteration is sometimes called a "strict transliteration" or "orthographical transliteration."

The most popular orthographic transliteration scheme for Arabic NLP in the West is the Buckwalter transliteration [23] or one of its variants (Tables 2.1 and 2.2). The Buckwalter transliteration is a transliteration system that follows the standard encoding choices made for representing

---

[5]http://www.unicode.org/charts/PDF/U0600.pdf
 http://www.unicode.org/charts/PDF/UFB50.pdf
 http://www.unicode.org/charts/PDF/UFE70.pdf

Terminology Alert The term *transliteration* is used by many researchers to mean any kind of mapping from one script to another regardless of the type of mapping. This may include any type of transcription (strict or ad hoc) and may lead to multiple valid mappings. The most common variant of this is the task of Proper Name Transliteration, which explores the ways names are represented in different scripts [21, 22]. We discuss this task in Section 3.3.1.

Arabic characters for computers, e.g., Unicode. The Buckwalter transliteration has been used in many NLP publications and in resources developed at the Linguistic Data Consortium (LDC). The main advantages of the Buckwalter transliteration are that it is a strict transliteration (i.e., one-to-one) and that it is written in ASCII characters, i.e., easily reproducible without special fonts.

One of the common critiques of the Buckwalter transliteration is that it is not easy to read. In this book, we use the more intuitive Habash-Soudi-Buckwalter transliteration (HSB) [4] variant of the Buckwalter transliteration. A second critique of the Buckwalter transliteration is that it contains some characters that are reserved symbols in different computer programming languages such as Perl or C and representations such as XML, e.g., the curly brackets and dollar sign. To address this issue, several "safe" Buckwalter variants emerged, but they are not standardized. Since there are many variants of this encoding that are needed for different settings, special care is needed not to mix them up. Finally, the Buckwalter transliteration is also criticized for being monolingual since ASCII symbols cannot be used to represent English if they are used for Arabic. Some researchers address this by special markers to escape non-Arabic characters before converting into Buckwalter from a standard encoding.

2.3.2 ORTHOGRAPHIC NORMALIZATION

Orthographic normalization is a basic task that researchers working on Arabic NLP always apply with a common goal in mind: reducing noise and sparsity in the data. This is true regardless of the task: preparing parallel text for machine translation, documents for information retrieval or text for language modeling. Additional more sophisticated preprocessing techniques, such as tokenization (Section 5.3), lexical normalization for words spelled in different ways, and spelling correction, can also be applied, although usually after orthographic normalization.

There are many different types of orthographic normalization that can be applied separately or together to the text of interest. We only discuss Arabic script specific issues here. Tasks such as punctuation separation, which are applied to Roman script languages as well as Arabic, pose the same universal challenges.

- **Encoding cleanup**: Arabic encoding, in Unicode in particular, brings many challenges resulting from the many ways one can achieve the same displayed sequence of text with different underlying characters. First, there are multiple ways to encode seemingly similar characters,

---

FAQ: Buckwalter transliteration or Unicode?

Despite all the critiques of the Buckwalter transliterations, it continues to be used simply because it is easy to read and debug by non-Arabic-literate researchers. It has also been pointed out that despite its flaws, the Buckwalter transliteration can be more reliable in detecting encoding errors, which may go unnoticed in Unicode, such as representing letters allographically instead of graphemically.

FAQ: Why use a one-to-one transliteration?

One-to-one transliterations allow for simple non-lossy mapping from Arabic to Roman script and back. Some of the popular multi-character mappings may be fine to use only if the different sequences are marked to avoid any ambiguity. For example, the sequence *sh* often used for the letter (ش *š*) may be misinterpreted as the sequence (سه *sh*), e.g., compare أشم *Âašum~* 'I smell' and أسهم *Âashum* 'arrows'.

FAQ: How can I type Arabic text without an Arabic keyboard?

There are several tools online that allow their users to type in some form of a strict or loose romanization, e.g., `Yamli`, Google's `ta3reeb` and Microsoft's `Maren`. Some operating systems also provide a phonetic keyboard for Arabic.

---

such as the codes for Indo-Arabic and Eastern Indo-Arabic digits and various related forms of Arabic letters, e.g., Arabic and Persian Kafs (ك/ک *k*). Many similar looking punctuation marks appear in different charts under Unicode too. Cleaning up the encoding involves normalizing the variant symbols into a single form. Second, Arabic presentation forms can be encoded directly, which results in letter and letter shape ambiguity that cannot be detected easily on the screen. Complex ligature shapes also add to the problem. Proper normalization would convert these allographic characters into their graphemic form.

- **Tatweel removal**: The Tatweel symbol is simply removed from the text.

- **Diacritic removal**: Since diacritics occur so infrequently, they are considered noise by most researchers and are simply removed from the text.

- **Letter normalization**: There are four letters in Arabic that are so often misspelled using variants that researchers find it more helpful to completely make these variants ambiguous (normalized). The following are the four letters in order of most commonly normalized to least commonly normalized (the first two are what most researchers do by default, the last two are less commonly applied).

    1. The Hamzated forms of Alif (آ *Ā*, أ *Â*, إ *Ǎ*) are normalized to bare Alif (ا *A*).

    2. The Alif-Maqsura (ى *ý*) is normalized to a Ya (ي *y*). In Egypt, but not in other Arab countries necessarily, a final Ya is often written dotless (i.e., as an Alif-Maqsura). However,

more recently, the exact opposite can be seen: all Alif-Maqsuras are written as a dotted Yas.[6]

3. The Ta-Marbuta (ة ħ) is normalized to a Ha (ه h).

4. The non-Alif forms of Hamza (ؤ ŵ and ئ ŷ) are normalized to the Hamza letter (ء ').

2.3.3 HANDWRITING RECOGNITION

Handwriting Recognition (HR) is the task of converting handwritten or printed input text into digital text. HR can be classified into offline HR and online HR. In offline HR, the input is typically a digital image of written text obtained using either scanning or camera photocopying. Online HR refers to the task of automatic recognition of text input as a sequence of two-dimensional points (as with using a digital pen or stylus). Optical Character Recognition (OCR) is sometimes distinguished from offline HR in referring to printed text (as opposed to manually written text). That said, some researchers use the terms HR (specifically offline) and OCR interchangeably.

HR of handwritten Arabic is still an area of active research, in both offline and online modes, due to the innate difficulties of the task [24, 25, 26]. Printed Arabic OCR, where the uniformity of letter shape and other factors allow for easier recognition, is currently of less interest [25]. The Arabic script has several properties that make recognition, particularly of handwritten Arabic, challenging [27, 28, 25]. These properties include the cursive connected nature of the script complicated with the existence of disconnective letters, the use of floating letter marks and diacritics (which often shift horizontally in writing) and the use of vertical ligatures and Tatweel.

The connected script and the use of ligatures make it rather difficult for a machine to distinguish between individual characters. This is certainly not a property unique to Arabic; methods, such as Hidden Markov Models, developed for other cursive script languages can be applied successfully to Arabic [29, 30, 25, 31]. While Arabic disconnective letters may make it hard to determine word boundaries, they could plausibly contribute to reduced ambiguity of otherwise similar shapes. The floating nature of letter marks and diacritics poses different problem for online and offline HR. In offline HR, trace amounts of dust or dirt on the original document scan can be easily mistaken for these symbols [27]. Alternatively, these symbols may be too small, light or closely-spaced to be readily distinguished, causing the system to drop them entirely. For online HR, letter marks and diacritics, also called delayed strokes, have to be paired with the appropriate letter forms for correct recognition [24].

The DARPA-funded MADCAT[7] program, which targets machine translation of OCRed handwritten Arabic text, has led to the creation of many resources for training and evaluating Arabic HR [32]. The National Institute for Standards and Technology (NIST) has a public version of MADCAT's evaluation competition named Open HaRT (Open Handwriting Recognition and Transcription). For additional resources, see also Appendix C.

---

[6]See the page of the Egyptian daily newspaper Al-Ahram. It is hard to call such a spelling convention a spelling error given its relative regularity (at least within the same text).

[7]MADCAT stands for Multilingual Automatic Document Classification Analysis and Translation.

2.3.4 AUTOMATIC DIACRITIZATION

Diacritization, also called diacritic restoration, vocalization, vowelization and vowel restoration, is the process of recovering missing diacritics (short vowels, nunation, the marker of the absence of a short vowel, and the gemination marker). Diacritization is closely related to morphosyntactic disambiguation and to lemmatization (Section 5.1) since some of the diacritics vary depending on syntactic conditions (such as case-related diacritics) and some vary to indicate semantic differences.

The choice of the diacritic on the last written letter of the word (without the possessive or object clitic which may be attached) is particularly hard since it requires syntactic information: in imperfective verbs, this diacritic often expresses mood, and in nouns and adjectives, it expresses syntactic case. Thus, it is often common to define a simpler diacritization task which does not choose the word-final diacritic.

Much work has been done on Arabic automatic diacritization using a wide range of techniques [33, 11, 34, 12, 35].

2.4 FURTHER READINGS

The Arabic script may seem intimidating to those unfamiliar with it; however, it is rather easy to learn compared to, say, Chinese. There are numerous books on the market for teaching Arabic script reading and writing. Basic familiarity with the script is sure to demystify some of its peculiarities and is recommended for the researcher/developer working on Arabic (try, e.g., `http://books.google.com/books?q=arabic+script`).

Arabic	Unicode Letter Name	HSB	Buckwalter			CP-1256	ISO-8859-6	Unicode
			base	*xml*	*safe*			
ء	Hamza	'	'	'	C	C1	C1	0621
آ	Alef Madda Above	Ā	|	|	M	C2	C2	0622
أ	Alef Hamza Above	Â	>	O	O	C3	C3	0623
ؤ	Waw Hamza Above	ŵ	&	W	W	C4	C4	0624
إ	Alef Hamza Below	Ǎ	<	I	I	C5	C5	0625
ئ	Yeh Hamza Above	ŷ	}	}	Q	C6	C6	0626
ا	Alef	A	A	A	A	C7	C7	0627
ب	Beh	b	b	b	b	C8	C8	0628
ة	Teh Marbuta	ħ	p	p	p	C9	C9	0629
ت	Teh	t	t	t	t	CA	CA	062A
ث	Theh	θ	v	v	v	CB	CB	062B
ج	Jeem	j	j	j	j	CC	CC	062C
ح	Hah	H	H	H	H	CD	CD	062D
خ	Khah	x	x	x	x	CE	CE	062E
د	Dal	d	d	d	d	CF	CF	062F
ذ	Thal	ð	*	*	V	D0	D0	0630
ر	Reh	r	r	r	r	D1	D1	0631
ز	Zain	z	z	z	z	D2	D2	0632
س	Seen	s	s	s	s	D3	D3	0633
ش	Sheen	š	$	$	c	D4	D4	0634
ص	Sad	S	S	S	S	D5	D5	0635
ض	Dad	D	D	D	D	D6	D6	0636
ط	Tah	T	T	T	T	D8	D7	0637
ظ	Zah	Ď	Z	Z	Z	D9	D8	0638
ع	Ain	ς	E	E	E	DA	D9	0639
غ	Ghain	γ	g	g	g	DB	DA	063A
ف	Feh	f	f	f	f	DD	E1	0641
ق	Qaf	q	q	q	q	DE	E2	0642
ك	Kaf	k	k	k	k	DF	E3	0643
ل	Lam	l	l	l	l	E1	E4	0644
م	Meem	m	m	m	m	E3	E5	0645
ن	Noon	n	n	n	n	E4	E6	0646
ه	Heh	h	h	h	h	E5	E7	0647
و	Waw	w	w	w	w	E6	E8	0648
ى	Alef Maksura	ý	Y	Y	Y	EC	E9	0649
ي	Yeh	y	y	y	y	ED	EA	064A

Table 2.1: Arabic encodings contrasted: letters.

Table 2.2: Arabic encodings contrasted: diacritcs, punctuation and borrowed letters.

Arabic	Unicode Letter Name	HSB	Buckwalter base	Buckwalter xml	Buckwalter safe	CP-1256	ISO-8859-6	Unicode
ً	Fathatan	ã	F	F	F	F0	EB	064B
ٌ	Dammatan	ũ	N	N	N	F1	EC	064C
ٍ	Kasratan	ĩ	K	K	K	F2	ED	064D
َ	Fatha	a	a	a	a	F3	EE	064E
ُ	Damma	u	u	u	u	F5	EF	064F
ِ	Kasra	i	i	i	i	F6	F0	0650
ّ	Shadda	~	~	~	~	F8	F1	0651
ْ	Sukun	.	o	o	o	FA	F2	0652
ٰ	Dagger Alef	á	'	'	e			0670
ٱ	Alef Wasla	Ä	{	{	L			0671
ـ	Tatweel	_	_	_	_	DC	E0	0640
،	Comma	,	,	,	,	A1	AC	060C
	Soft Hyphen	-	-	-	-	AD	AD	00AD
؛	Semicolon	;	;	;	;	BA	BB	061B
؟	Question Mark	?	?	?	?	BF	BF	061F
پ	Peh	p	P	P	P	81		067E
چ	Tcheh	c	J	J	J	8D		0686
ڤ	Veh	v	V	V	B			06A4
گ	Gaf	g	G	G	G	90		06AF

CHAPTER 3

Arabic Phonology and Orthography

In this chapter, we present a brief description of MSA phonology and related concepts. This is followed by a description of how Arabic orthography, i.e., its spelling standard, is used to map phonology to/from the Arabic script. Then, we present four related computational tasks: proper name transliteration, spelling correction, speech recognition and speech synthesis.

3.1 ARABIC PHONOLOGY

This section presents a very brief introduction to Arabic phonology. Phonological terms are introduced only as needed. For further discussions of phonology in a computational setting, consider [36]. Although the focus of this book is on MSA, this chapter presents some dialectal issues since dialects are primarily spoken and they sometimes influence MSA pronunciation. Quranic Arabic has its own pronunciation and spelling rules that differ in many respects from MSA and dialectal Arabic. We will not discuss it here.

3.1.1 BASIC CONCEPTS

Phonology is the study of how sounds, or phones, are organized in natural languages [37]. A central concept in phonology is the *phoneme*, the smallest contrastive unit in the sound system of a language. Being contrastive means that the language in question has a *minimal pair* involving the phoneme: two words that have different meanings and that happen to differ phonologically in that phoneme only. For example, the MSA words قلب /qalb/ 'heart' and كلب /kalb/ 'dog' constitute a minimal pair for the phonemes /q/ and /k/. A phoneme can correspond to multiple *phones*, or basic sounds, that are distributed according to predictable rules, called phonotactics. The predictable phones associated with a phoneme are called its *allophones*. For example, while Arabic does not have a phoneme /p/, often causing the characteristically Arabic-accented p-b confusion in English speech, the phone [p] appears as an allophone of the phoneme /b/ in limited contexts, such as preceding a voiceless phone: the word دبس *dibs* 'molasses' is phonemically represented as /dibs/, but phonetically as [dips].[1]

---

[1]We follow the common practice of using '/.../' to indicate phonemic sequences and '[...]' phonetic sequences. We use the HSB transcription [4] with some extensions instead of the International Phonetic Alphabet (IPA) to minimize the number of representations used in this book.

> **Terminology Alert**: The use of terms like phoneme, phone and phonotactics in NLP areas such as Automatic Speech Recognition (ASR) may not be completely consistent with how linguists use them. For example, instead of explicit linguistic rules, *phonotactics* may just refer to n-gram sequences of phones/phonemes.

3.1.2   A SKETCH OF ARABIC PHONOLOGY

Figure 3.1: Arabic consonantal phonemic inventory. Rows represent the different *manners of articulation*, while columns represent the different *places of articulation*. Pairs of phonemes are plain and emphatic variants. Phonemes in gray are non-MSA (dialectal).

		Labial	Labio-dental	Interdental	Dental	Alveolar	Palatal	Velar	Uvular	Pharyngeal	Glotal
Stop	voiceless				t T			k	q		'
	voiced	b			d D			g	Q		
Fricative	voiceless		f	θ	s S	š		x		H	h
	voiced			ð Ď	z Z	ž		γ		ς	
Affricate	voiceless					č					
	voiced					j					
Glide		w					y				
Nasal		m				n					
Liquid					l	r					

Figure 3.2: Arabic vocalic phonemic inventory. Vowels are represented in terms of *height* and *backness* of the position of the tongue. Phonemes in gray are non-MSA (dialectal).

	Front	Central	Back
High	i ī		u ū
Mid	e ē		o ō
Low		a ā	

MSA's basic phonological profile includes 28 consonants, three short vowels and three long vowels. In addition, MSA has two diphthongs: /ay/ and /aw/. Figures 3.1 and 3.2 present the various consonantal and vocalic (respectively) phonemes in MSA in terms of their articulatory features (in consultation with [38, 39]). In Figure 3.1, the presence of a pair of phonemes in one cell, as in 't T', indicates that they are plain and emphatic, respectively. Emphasis (تفخيم *tafxiym*) is a bass effect giving an acoustic impression of hollow resonance to the basic sound [38]. Emphasis together with the presence of eight consonants in the velar and post-velar region is what gives Arabic pronunciation its distinctive guttural quality [38]. Vowel phoneme pairs in Figure 3.2 indicate length difference (short and long). The phonemes in gray in Figures 3.1 and 3.2 are not MSA, i.e., they are dialectal. More on this in Section 3.1.3. All of Arabic's consonants have direct comparables in English with the following exceptions:[2]

- /H/ sounds like an *h* with a hissing quality that can be approximated with the sound made when breathing on eyeglasses before wiping them clean.

- /ς/ is a voiced variant of /H/ that sounds like a sharp /a/.

- /x/ is similar to Scottish *loch* or Yiddish-English *chutzpa*.

- /r/ and /γ/ correspond to Spanish *r* and Parisian French *r*, respectively.

- The uvular stop /q/ sounds like a deep bass /k/.

- The glottal stop (Hamza) /'/ sounds like the English phone in the middle of *uh-oh*.

- The emphatics /D/, /T/, /S/ and /Ď/ have a bass quality added to their plain counterparts (/d/, /t/, /s/, /ð/, respectively).

Notice that the phonemes /š/ and /θ/ correspond to the same phonemes in English often written with the two-letter combinations *sh* and *th*, respectively.

MSA vowel phonemes are limited in number compared to English or French; however, there are many allophones to each of them depending on the consonantal context [38]. For instance, contrast the pronunciation of the vowel /ā/ in باس /bās/ 'he kissed' and باص /bāS/ 'bus', which can be approximated by the English words 'bass [the fish]' and 'boss', respectively. This phenomenon is called emphasis spread. It is a common phonotactic where vowels and consonants near an emphatic consonant become expressed as their emphatic allophones. Another interesting phenomenon in MSA vowel pronunciation is the optionality of dropping the final vowel marking syntactic case in words at the end of utterances (as in the end of a sentence or in citation). This is called *waqf* (وقف) '[lit. stopping/pause]' pronunciation.

There are numerous additional phonological variations that are limited to specific morpho-logical contexts, i.e., they are constrained morpho-phonemically as opposed to phonologically. Some of these phenomena are explicitly expressed in the orthography and some are not. We call cases that are expressed orthographically *morphological adjustments* and discuss them in the next chapter. For example, the phoneme /t/ in verbal pattern VIII becomes voiced and is spelled (not just pronounced)

---

[2]We do not include additional emphatic phonemes that appear in a limited number of minimal pairs (such as emphatic /l/ and emphatic /b/) or phonemes in borrowed words from foreign languages (such as /p/ and /v/).

as a د *d* when adjacent to specific root consonants. On the other hand, we call cases that are not expressed orthographically, such as the phonological assimilation of the Arabic definite article +ال *Al*+ to some phonemes that follow it, *morpho-phonemic spelling*. We discuss these cases in Section 3.2.3. For a detailed discussion of MSA phonology, stress and syllabic structure, see [39, 38].

3.1.3   PHONOLOGICAL VARIATIONS AMONG ARABIC DIALECTS AND MSA

Arabic dialects vary phonologically from MSA and from each other. Some of the common variations include the following [38, 40, 41]:

- The MSA alveolar affricate ج /j/ is realized as /g/ in EGY, as /ž/ in LEV and as as /y/ in GLF. For example, جميل 'handsome' is pronounced /jamīl/ (MSA, IRQ), /gamīl/ (EGY), /žamīl/ (LEV) and /yamīl/ (GLF). The Levantine and Egyptian pronunciations are considered "standard MSA" in those regions.

- The MSA consonant ق /q/ is realized as a glottal stop /'/ in EGY and LEV and as /g/ in GLF and IRQ. For example, طريق 'road' appears as /Tarīq/ (MSA), /Tarī'/ (EGY and LEV) and /Tarīg/ (GLF and IRQ). Other variants are also found in some sub-dialects such as /k/ in rural Palestinian (LEV), /j/ in Emirati (GLF) and /Q/ (voiced /q/) in Sudanese (EGY). These changes do not apply to modern and religious borrowings from MSA. For instance, قرآن 'Quran' is never pronounced anything but /qur'ān/.

- The MSA consonant (ك /k/) is generally realized as /k/ in Arabic dialects with the exception of GLF, IRQ and the Palestinian rural sub-dialect of LEV, which allow a /č/ pronunciation in certain contexts. For example, سمك 'fish' is /samak/ in MSA, EGY and most of LEV but /simač/ in IRQ and GLF.

- The MSA consonant ث /θ/ is pronounced as /t/ in LEV and EGY (or /s/ in more recent borrowings from MSA), e.g., ثلاثة 'three' is pronounced /θalāθa/ in MSA versus /talāta/ in EGY.

- The MSA consonant ذ /ð/ is pronounced as /d/ in LEV and EGY (or /z/ in more recent borrowings from MSA), e.g., هذا 'this' is pronounced /hāða/ in MSA versus /hāda/ (LEV) and /da/ EGY.

- The MSA consonants ض /D/ (emphatic d) and ظ /Ď/ (emphatic /ð/) are both normalized to /D/ in EGY and LEV and to /Ď/ in GLF and IRQ. For example, ظل يضرب 'he continued to hit' is pronounced /Ďalla yaDrubu/ in MSA versus /Dall yuĎrub/ (LEV) and /Ďall yuĎrub/ (GLF). In modern borrowings from MSA, /Ď/ is pronounced /Z/ (emphatic z) in EGY and LEV. For instance, ظابط 'police officer' is /ĎābiT/ in MSA but /ZābiT/ in EGY and LEV.

- Vocalic changes include: (a) change in or complete drop of short vowels: يكتب 'he writes' is pronounced /yaktubu/ MSA versus /yiktib/ (EGY and IRQ) or /yoktob/ (LEV); (b) shortening of final and unstressed long vowels in some dialects: مطارات 'airports' is /maTārāt/ (MSA) versus /maTarāt/ (LEV and EGY); and (c) the MSA diphthongs /aw/ and /ay/ have mostly become /ō/ and /ē/, respectively, in some dialects: بيت 'house' is /bayt/ (MSA) but /bēt/ (LEV and EGY).

- In some dialects, a loss of emphasis for some MSA consonants occurs, e.g., لطيف 'pleasant' is pronounced /laTīf/ in MSA as opposed to /latīf/ in Lebanese city sub-dialect of LEV.

3.2 ARABIC ORTHOGRAPHY

An orthography is a specification of how the sounds of a language are mapped to/from a particular script. In this section, we present an account of standard MSA orthography using the Arabic script. The correspondence between writing and pronunciation in MSA falls somewhere between that of languages such as Spanish and Finnish, which have an almost one-to-one mapping between letters and sounds, and languages such as English and French, which exhibit a more complex letter-to-sound mapping [42].

Figure 3.3: Mapping Arabic letters to sounds.

MSA has 34 phonemes (28 consonants, 3 long vowels and 3 short vowels). The Arabic script has 36 letters and 9 diacritics (including the Dagger Alif). Most Arabic letters have a one-to-one mapping to an MSA phoneme (Figure 3.3). However, there are some common important exceptions [4, 42], which we summarize next.

3.2.1 OPTIONAL DIACRITICS

Arabic script diacritics are mapped to the following sounds:

- The three short-vowel diacritics, ـَ a, ـُ u, and ـِ i, represent the vowels /a/, /u/ and /i/, respectively. The short vowel diacritics ـُ u and ـِ i are used together with the glide consonants letters و w and ي y to denote the long vowels /ū/ (as uw) and /ī/ (iy). The long vowel /ā/ is most commonly written as a combination of the short-vowel diacritic ˛ *a* and the letter ا *A*.[3] This makes these three letters ambiguous.

- The three *nunation* diacritics ˛ ã, ˛ ũ and ˛ ĩ represent a combination of a short vowel and the nominal indefiniteness marker /n/ in MSA: /an/, /un/ and /in/, respectively.

- The consonant lengthening diacritic Shadda ˛ ∼ repeats/elongates the previous consonant, e.g., كتّب *kat∼ab* is pronounced /kattab/.[4]

- The Sukun ˛. diacritic marks when there is no vowel.

- The long-vowel diacritic, Dagger Alif ˛ á, represents the long vowel /ā/ in a small number of words.

Arabic diacritics can only appear after a letter. As such, word-initial short vowels are represented with an extra silent Alif, also called Alif-Wasla or Hamzat-Wasl, ٱ *Ä* (often simply written as ا *A*). Sentence/utterance initial Hamzat-Wasl is pronounced like a glottal stop preceding the short vowel; however, the sentence medial Hamzat-Wasl is silent. For example, انكتب كتاب *Ainkataba kitAbũ* 'a book was written' is pronounced /'inkataba kitābun/ but كتاب انكتب 'a book was written' *kitAbũ Ainkataba* is pronounced /kitābun inkataba/. A real Hamza is always pronounced as a glottal stop. The Hamzat-Wasl appears most commonly as the Alif of the definite article *Al*. It also appears in specific words and word classes such as relative pronouns, e.g., *Alðy* 'who' and verbs in Form VII (see Chapter 4).

The most problematic aspect of diacritics is their optionality. This is not so much of a problem when mapping from phonology to script, but it is in the other direction. Diacritics are largely restricted to religious texts and Arabic language school textbooks. In other texts, around 1.5% of the words contain a diacritic. Some diacritics are lexical (where word meaning varies) and others are inflectional (where nominal case or verbal mood varies). Inflectional diacritics are typically word final. Since nominal case, verbal mood and nunation have all disappeared in spoken dialectal Arabic, Arabic speakers do not always produce these inflections correctly or even at all. Notable exceptions are frequent formulaic expressions such as السلام عليكم *AlslAm ςlykm* 'Hello ([lit.] Peace be upon you)' /'assalāmu ςalaykum/.

3.2.2   HAMZA SPELLING

As discussed in the last chapter, the consonant Hamza (glottal stop /'/) has multiple forms in Arabic script: ء ', آ *Ā*, أ *Â*, ؤ *ŵ*, إ *Ă* and ئ *ŷ*. There are complex rules for Hamza spelling that primarily depend on its vocalic and morphological context [8]. For example, consider the different Hamza forms in

---

[3]Some Arabic NLP resources, most notably the Buckwalter Arabic Morphological Analyzer [23], drop the diacritic *a* before the letter *A* as a convention.
[4]Make sure to pronounce the two /t/s separately as if saying /kat/ and /tab/ very quickly.

the following word meaning 'his glory' when its case marker changes: بهاءه *bahA'ahu* /bahā'ahu/ (accusative), بهاؤه *bahAŵuhu* /bahā'uhu/ (nominative), and بهائه *bahAŷihi* /bahā'ihi/ (genitive).

Hamza spelling is further complicated by the fact that Arabic writers often replace hamzated letters with the un-hamzated form, e.g., أ *Â* ⇔ ا *A*, or through two-letter spelling, e.g., ئ *ŷ* ⇔ ءى *y'*. These common variations do not always add ambiguity, especially when they are stem-initial: اول/أول *Âwl/Awl* 'first'. When they add ambiguity, typically in stem-medial and stem-final positions, they are often avoided: بدا *bdA* 'he appeared' and بدأ *bdÂ* 'he started'. It's been observed that Hamzas in stem-initial Hamzated Alifs are typically perceived by Arab writers as diacritical and optional compared to stem-medial and stem-final cases, which are more than not considered obligatory [5].

3.2.3 MORPHO-PHONEMIC SPELLING

The Arabic script contains a small number of morphemic/lexical spellings, some of which are very common:

- **Ta-Marbuta** The Ta-Marbuta (ة *ħ*) is typically a feminine ending. It can only appear at the end of a word and can only be followed by a diacritic. In MSA, it is pronounced as /t/ unless it is not followed by a vowel (as in *waqf*), in which case it is silent. For example, المكتبة *Almaktabaħu* 'the library' is pronounced /'almaktabatu/ (normal) or /'almaktaba/ (waqf).

- **Alif-Maqsura** The Alif-Maqsura (ى *ý*) is a silent derivational marker, which always follows a short vowel /a/ at the end of a word. For example, both عصى *ςaSaý* 'to disobey' and عصا *ςaSaA* 'a stick' are pronounced /ςaSa/.[5]

- **Definite Article** The Arabic definite article is a proclitic that assimilates to the first consonant in the noun or adjective it modifies if this consonant is an alveolar, dental or inter-dental phoneme (except for /j/).[6] This set of 14 consonants is called *the Sun Letters*. They are ت *t*, ث θ, د *d*, ذ *ð*, ر *r*, ز *z*, س *s*, ش *š*, ص *S*, ض *D*, ط *T*, ظ *Ď*, ل *l*, and ن *n*. For example, the word الشمس *Al+šams* 'the sun' is pronounced /'aššams/ not */'alšams/.[7] The rest of the consonants are called the *Moon Letters*; the definite article is not assimilated with them. For example, the word القمر *Al+qamar* 'the moon' is pronounced /'alqamar/ not */'aqqamar/. Arabic spelling rules require the addition of a Shadda diacritic on the Sun letter to indicate assimilation without deleting the assimilating *l*, e.g., الشّمس *Alš~ams*.

---

[5]The unstressed word-final vowel in عصا *ςaSaA* 'a stick' is shortened.

[6]Another classification is that all of these consonants are coronal, i.e., articulated with the flexible front part of the mouth [39]. The exceptionality of /j/ is often attributed to that phoneme's likely pre-Classical Arabic pronunciation as a (non-coronal) palatal [38] or voiced velar stop (/g/) [39]. The situation in dialectal Arabic is similar to MSA, although with some differences [39].

[7]The star symbol (*) preceding an example is a linguistic marker that indicates the example is **incorrect**. This star has nothing to do with the Kleene star used in regular expressions, the Buckwalter transliteration of the letter ذ *ð*, or the star used to mark the selected in-context analysis in the Penn Arabic Treebank.

- **Nunation** The indefiniteness morpheme spelling with diacritics is another example of morpho-phonemic spelling that is already mentioned in the discussion of diacritics above.

- **Silent Letters** A silent Alif appears in the morpheme واو+ +*uwA* /ū/ (واو الجماعة *wAw AljamAςaħ*), which indicates a masculine plural conjugation in verbs. Another silent Alif appears word finally with some nunated nouns (before or after the diacritic), e.g., كتابا *ki-taAbAā* or *kitaAbāA* /kitāban/. In some poetic readings, this Alif can be produced as the long vowel /ā/: /kitābā/. Finally, a common odd spelling is that of the proper name عمرو *ςamrw* /ςamr/ 'Amr' where the final و *w* is silent.

3.2.4   STANDARDIZATION ISSUES

MSA orthography has largely been standardized for a long time now. However, few variations persist across and within different Arab countries. For example, there are two common spellings for some proper names of geographic entities ending with an /a/ vowel: /sūrya/ 'Syria' appears as سوريا *swryA* and سورية *swryħ*, and /'afrīqya/ 'Africa' appears as أفريقيا *ÂfryqyA* and أفريقية *Âfryqyħ*. Hamza spelling rules may have some exceptions also. For example: /mas'ūl/ 'official/responsible' appears as مسؤول *msŵwl* (common in the Levant) and مسئول *msŷwl* (common in Egypt). Additional examples involve spelling of vowels in loan words: e.g., أوربا *ÂrwbA* or أوروبا *ÂwrwbA* 'Europe' (both pronounced /'urubba/ with stress on the second vowel), and فلم *flm* or فيلم *fylm* 'film' (pronounced /film/). As for Arabic dialects, there are no standard orthographies. As a result, there is not as much consistency in dialectal writing as in MSA writing.

FAQ: How true is "Arabic has no vowels"?

This is a common statement made about Arabic. It is laughably wrong. A weaker variant, suggesting that **"Arabic does not write vowels,"** exemplifies to English readers what Arabs read using a sentence like: *ths s wht n rbc txt lks lk wth n vwls* (a de-voweled form of '*this is what an Arabic text looks like with no vowels*'). This statement is also not true. As we have seen, even with dropping all optional diacritics, Arabic orthography still represents some vowels: (a.) all long vowels are indicated with the letters *A*, *w*, and *y*; (b.) all initial vowels are indicated with a stand-in Alif ا*A*; and (c.) some final vowels are indicated with morpho-phonemic spelling symbols such as Ta-Marbuta and Alif-Maqsura. A more appropriate analogy is the following de-voweled form of the English example above: *ths is wht an arbc txt lks lik wth no vwls*. Interestingly, this looks a lot like English text messages. Perhaps, some of the approaches to Arabic diacritization and disambiguation could be used for voweling text-message English.

3.3   NLP TASKS

3.3.1   PROPER NAME TRANSLITERATION

Proper name transliteration is a specific sub-problem of machine translation focusing on mapping/approximating the phonetic value of proper names from one language to another and typically across scripts. In the context of mapping from Arabic to/from English, we face several challenges:

- Arabic optional diacritics;

- Arabic consonants with no exact match in the Roman script such as /H/ and /ʕ/;

- Dialectal variants on the pronunciation of Arabic names;

- English consonants foreign to Arabic such as /p/ (approximated as ب /b/) and /v/ (approximated as ف /f/);

- Names in English from other European languages also written in Roman script bringing their own particular orthographic and phonological challenges, such as French pronunciations which drop final consonants and the many ways to write the same phoneme, e.g., /š/: *sh, sch* and *ch* among others.

There are many instantiations of the proper name transliteration problem. Here are a few examples.

- The *Qaddafi problem* refers to cases where one spelling in Arabic corresponds to many spellings in English. Whereas the Libyan leader's name is spelled قذافي *qað~Afiy* in Arabic, there are numerous English spellings: Qadafi, Qaddafi, Gaddafi, Kaddafi, Kadafy, etc.

- The *Schwarzenegger problem* refers to cases where one spelling in English corresponds to multiple spelling in Arabic. Here, the single correct spelling for the California governor can appear in Arabic as شوارتزنجر *šwArznyγr*, شوارزنغر *šwArznyγr*, شوارزنيجر *šwArznyjr*, or شوارزنيغر *šwArtznjr*, among others. A variant on this problem is the *Mozart* case, where a couple of spellings that preserve particular pronunciations appear in Arabic: موزارت *mwzArt* (Anglophonic) and موزار *mwzAr* (Francophonic).

- The *Hassan problem* refers to cases where distinct spellings in Arabic of different names collapse in English. The name *Hassan* can be a transliteration of حسن *Hasan* /Hasan/ or حسان *Has~An* /Hassān/. The ambiguity added here is a result of the lack of a method to indicate gemination in English spelling, especially when s-doubling is used to force an /s/ pronunciation (as opposed to /z/). A more complex example is the name *Salem*, which can be an Anglophonic transliteration of the Arabic name سالم *sAlim* /sālim/ or a Francophonic transliteration of the Arabic name سلام *salAm* /salēm/ (as pronounced in Tunisia).

- The *Mary/Mari/Marie problem* refers to cases where distinct spellings in Roman script are collapsed in Arabic. The three names *Mary, Mari,* and *Marie* often appear in Arabic spelled as ماري *mAry*. This can also happen to some Arabic names, whose spelling is ambiguous, e.g., Salim, Seleem and Slim are three Roman script spellings of the *historically same* Arabic name سليم *slym* influenced by how it is commonly pronounced in the Levant, Egypt and Morocco, respectively. In a way, this is related to the Qaddafi problem except in that the various Roman spellings here are distinctive in their reference to different individuals.

- The *Urshalim/Alquds problem* refers to cases that do not have a phonetic match or whose phonetic similarity is partial. For example, the Arabic name for *Jerusalem* is القدس *Alquds.* The Hebraic name for the city in Arabic, اورشليم *Awršlym* bears more resemblance to *Jerusalem* since the English name comes from Hebrew.

It is important to remember that errors of name transliteration can have major consequences on the lives of the name bearers, e.g., by unjustly confusing them with suspected individuals. The problem of proper name transliteration has received a lot of attention in NLP and has been addressed in a wide range of solutions [21, 43, 44, 45, 22].

3.3.2   SPELLING CORRECTION

Spelling correction is often thought of as a preprocessing step that addresses the presence of spelling errors. Spelling errors can cause NLP models to be less effective and can add an often irrecoverable error margin from the first step in a system. Spelling errors can be hard to identify if the misspelled form happens to be a valid word that is contextually incorrect morphologically or semantically [46].

As was mentioned in Chapter 2, the most common spelling errors in Arabic involve Hamzated Alifs and Alif-Maqsura/Ya confusion. These errors affect 11% of all words (or 4.5 errors per sentence) in the Penn Arabic Treebank (PATB) [47]. Other forms of errors including misplaced dots, joint/split words near disconnective letters, or misplaced letters occur less frequently – 0.3% of all words (at least once in around 12% of all sentences). This is still non-trivial since a single spelling error can wreak havoc on the processing of the whole sentence.

Examples of efforts towards automatic spelling correction or handling spelling errors for other NLP applications include [48, 49, 46, 50]. Automatic generation of alternative correct Hamzated Alif and Alif-Maqsura forms is done as part of some morphological analyzers out of context, e.g., [23]. The Morphological Analysis and Disambiguation for Arabic (MADA) toolkit [51] automatically chooses the appropriate Hamzated Alif and Alif-Maqsura form in context as part of a general morphological disambiguation approach. It is reported to be successful at 99.4% in this task [13].

It is important to point out that since Arabic dialects are not standardized, their orthography is not always consistent. As such any approach to handling dialects needs an internal convention to use as standard spelling [52, 53, 54].

3.3.3   SPEECH RECOGNITION AND SYNTHESIS

Speech Recognition (aka Automatic Speech Recognition – ASR; Speech-to-Text – STT) is the task of mapping an acoustic speech signal to its corresponding string of words. Inversely, Speech Synthesis (aka Text-to-Speech – TTS) is the task of producing an acoustic signal from an input word string. Much research has been done in both areas [55, 56, 33, 57, 58, 41, 59, 42]. There are also lots of resources for system training and testing (see Appendix C). Most of the techniques used for ASR and TTS are language independent once an appropriate level of representation is defined for the language of interest. For Arabic, the big challenge is bridging the gap between Arabic phonology and its orthography, since typically the more complex and lossy the orthography, the more difficult a language is for ASR or TTS.

As such, a central task for work on ASR and TTS for Arabic involves producing the phonemic or phonetic form of the Arabic text. It's been noted that diacritization alone does not predict actual pronunciation in MSA [41]. Different researchers have described different sets of pronunciation/phonotization rules based on MSA phonology which extend a diacritized word to a set of possible pronunciations. Some of these rules attempt to accommodate pronunciation variants to handle common failures to produce "proper" pronunciation according to Arabic syntax and phonology even by MSA-trained speakers [42, 58, 41].

Another challenge is Arabic's complex and rich morphology, which results in a very large vocabulary to cover. Arabic is noted to have 2.5 times the vocabulary growth rate of English and to have 10 times the out-of-vocabulary (OOV) rate (on a 64K dictionary) [60, 61]. This issue is addressed through introducing morphological models to reduce vocabulary size and OOV rates [60, 61].

As for dialectal variations, the general convention in the field and by language technology developers is that ASR should be robust enough to handle MSA, any dialect and code-switching of MSA and dialects. However, TTS should only focus on MSA production. One exception is the work done on English ⇔ Iraqi speech-to-speech machine translation in the DARPA-funded TRANSTAC[8] project [62] http://www.darpa.mil/IPTO/programs/transtac/transtac.asp.

3.4   FURTHER READINGS

There is a growing number of publications in the area of automatic dialect identification, where the task is to identify Arabic dialects from acoustic signals [63, 64, 65]. There is also some very interesting work on the automatic identification of emotional aspects of speech (in Arabic among other languages), specifically charisma and how it is perceived differently across cultures [66].

---

[8]TRANSTAC stands for Spoken Language Communication and Translation System for Tactical Use.

CHAPTER 4

Arabic Morphology

Morphology is central in working on Arabic NLP because of its important interactions with both orthography and syntax. Arabic's rich morphology is perhaps the most studied and written about aspect of Arabic. As a result, there is a wealth of terminology, some of it inconsistent, that may intimidate and confuse new researchers. In this chapter, we start with a review of different terms used in discussing Arabic morphology issues. This is followed by a brief sketch of of Arabic morphology. The next chapter discusses a few important computational problems of Arabic morphology and reviews their solutions.

4.1 BASIC CONCEPTS

Morphology is the study of internal word structure. We distinguish two types of approaches to morphology: *form-based morphology* and *functional morphology*. Form-based morphology is about the form of units making up a word, their interactions with each other and how they relate to the word's overall form. By contrast, functional morphology is about the the function of units inside a word and how they affect its overall behavior syntactically and semantically.[1]

A chart of the various morphological terms discussed in this section is presented in Figure 4.1.

4.1.1 FORM-BASED MORPHOLOGY

A central concept in form-based morphology is the *morpheme*, the smallest meaningful unit in a language. A distinguishing feature of Arabic (in fact, Semitic) morphology is the presence of *templatic* morphemes in addition to *concatenative* morphemes. Concatenative morphemes participate in forming the word via a sequential concatenation process, whereas templatic morpheme are interleaved (interdigitated, merged).

Concatenative Morphology

There are three types of concatenative morphemes: stems, affixes and clitics. At the core of concatenative morphology is the *stem*, which is necessary for every word. *Affixes* attach to the stem. There are three types of affixes: (a.) *prefixes* attach before the stem, e.g., +ن *n+* 'first person plural of imperfective verbs'; (b.) *suffixes* attach after the stem, e.g., ون+ *+wn* 'nominative definite masculine sound plural'; and (c.) *circumfixes* surround the stem, e.g., ين++ت *t++yn* 'second person feminine

---

[1]Our classification is influenced by [67], who distinguishes between *illusory* (our form-based) and *functional* morphology. The additional classification of *functional* morphology into *logical* and *formal* is not discussed explicitly in this book although the phenomena they address are presented.

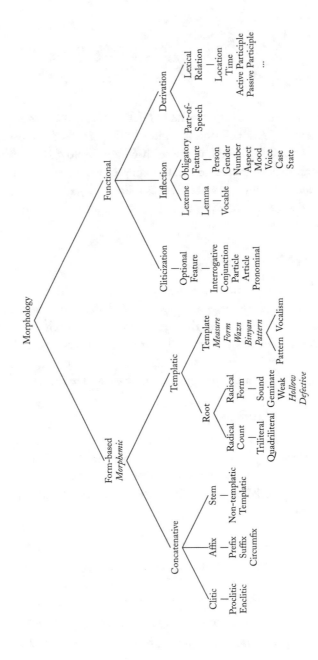

Figure 4.1: A chart of some related morphological terms.

singular of imperfective indicative verbs'. Circumfixes can be considered a coordinated prefix-suffix pair. MSA has no pure prefixes that act with no coordination with a suffix.

Clitics attach to the stem after affixes. A clitic is a morpheme that has the syntactic characteristics of a word but shows evidence of being phonologically bound to another word [37]. In this respect, a clitic is distinctly different from an affix, which is phonologically and syntactically part of the word. *Proclitics* are clitics that precede the word (like a prefix), e.g., the conjunction +و *w+* 'and' or the definite article +ال *Al+* 'the'. *Enclitics* are clitics that follow the word (like a suffix), e.g., the object pronoun هم+ *+hm* 'them'.

Multiple affixes and clitics can appear in a word. For example, the word وسيكتبونها *wasayaktubuwnahA* has two proclitics, one circumfix and one enclitic:

(4.1) wasayaktubuwnahA

wa+	*sa+*	*y+*	*aktub*	*+uwna*	*+hA*
and	will	3person	write	masculine-plural	it

'and they will write it'

For more examples, see Figure 4.2.

Terminology Alert The terms prefix and suffix are sometimes used to refer to proclitics and enclitics, respectively. Prefix and suffix have also been used to refer to the whole sequence of affixes and clitics attaching to a stem, e.g., in the databases of the Buckwalter Arabic Morphological Analyzer (BAMA) [23], which treats Arabic words as containing three components: prefix+stem+suffix. For instance, the example above would be broken up as such in BAMA: و سي+كتب+ونها *wasaya+ktub+uwnhA*. The stem-initial vowel in this example is considered part of the prefix *ya+* in BAMA. This highlights the problem with stem definition, which can be ad hoc and implementation dependent.

The stem can be *templatic* or *non-templatic*. Templatic stems are stems that can be formed using templatic morphemes (next section), whereas non-templatic word stems (NTWS) are not derivable from templatic morphemes. NTWSes tend to be foreign names and borrowed nominal terms (but never verbs), e.g., واشنطن *wAšinTun* 'Washington'. NTWS can take nominal affixational and cliticization morphemes, e.g., والواشنطنيون *wa+Al+wAšinTun+iy~+uwna* 'and the Washingtonians'.

Templatic Morphology

Templatic morphemes come in three types that are equally needed to create a word templatic stem: roots, patterns and vocalisms. The *root* morpheme is a sequence of (mostly) three, (less so) four, or very rarely five consonants (termed *radicals*).[2] The root signifies some abstract meaning shared by all

---

[2]Roots are classified based on the number of their radicals into triliteral (three radicals), quadriliteral (four radicals) and quintiliteral (five radicals) roots. Some researchers posit that triliteral and other roots were created from biconsonantal roots called etymons (an earlier form of a word in an ancestor language) [68].

Figure 4.2: Morphological representations of Arabic words. This figure compares different ways of representing Arabic words morphologically. Row 1 shows three ambiguous undiacritized words. Row 2 shows two disambiguated diacritized readings for each word in Row 1 (among others). Rows 3 and 4 show allomorphs (stems, affixes and clitics) and morphemes (root, pattern, affixes and clitics), respectively. Row 5 shows the Lexeme and (some of the) feature-value pairs. *n/a* means a features is not applicable (for the particular part-of-speech of the lexeme). Row 6 contains an English gloss for reference.

1	وكتبه wktbh		كاتبته kAtbth		للكتاب llktAb	
2	wakatabahu	wakutubihi	kAtabathu	kAtibatuhu	lilkitAbi	lilkut~Abi
3	wa+katab+a+hu	wa+kutub+i+hi	kAtab+at+hu	kAtib+at+u+hu	li+l+kitAb+i	li+l+kut~Ab+i
4	wa+$\frac{ktb}{1a2a3}$+a+hu	wa+$\frac{ktb}{1u2u3}$+i+hu	$\frac{ktb}{1A2a3}$+at+hu	$\frac{ktb}{1A2i3}$+aħ+u+hu	li+Al+$\frac{ktb}{1i2A3}$+i	li+Al+$\frac{ktb}{1u22A3}$+i
5	|katab|$_{Verb}$ conjunction:wa particle:ø article:*n/a* person:3rd gender:masc number:sing case:*n/a* aspect:perfect object:3MS	|kitAb|$_{Noun}$ conjunction:wa particle:ø article:ø person:*n/a* gender:masc number:plur case:gen aspect:*n/a* possessive:3MS	|kAtab|$_{Verb}$ conjunction:ø particle:*n/a* article:*n/a* person:3rd gender:fem number:sing case:*n/a* aspect:perfect object:3MS	|kAtib|$_{Noun}$ conjunction:ø particle:ø article:ø person:*n/a* gender:fem number:sing case:nom aspect:*n/a* possessive:3MS	|kitAb|$_{Noun}$ conjunction:ø particle:li article:Al person:*n/a* gender:masc number:sing case:gen aspect:*n/a* possessive:ø	|kAtib|$_{Noun}$ conjunction:ø particle:li article:Al person:*n/a* gender:masc number:plur case:gen aspect:*n/a* possessive:ø
6	*and he wrote it*	*and his books [genitive]*	*she corresponded with him*	*his writer [female]*	*for the book*	*for the writers*

its derivations. For example, the words كتب *katab* 'to write', كاتب *kAtib* 'writer', مكتوب *maktuwb* 'written' and all the words in Figure 4.2 share the root morpheme ك-ت-ب *k-t-b* 'writing-related'. For this reason, roots are used traditionally for organizing dictionaries and thesauri. That said, root semantics is often idiosyncratic. For example, the words لحم *laHm* 'meat', لحم *laHam* 'to solder', لحّام *laH~Am* 'butcher/solderer' and ملحمة *malHamaħ* 'epic/fierce battle/massacre' are all said to have the same root ل-ح-م *l-H-m* whose meaning is left to the reader to imagine.

Not all consonantal combinations are possible in a root. For instance, no roots where all radicals are copies of the same consonant are allowed, e.g., ب-ب-ب *b-b-b*. Second and third radicals can be identical, or *geminate*, e.g., ر-د-د *r-d-d* 'repeating-related', but they cannot be homo-organic, i.e., produced in the same articulation point [38]. Some roots have one or two *weak* radicals (the consonants و *w* or ي *y*). For example, و-ز-ن *w-z-n* 'measure-related', ق-و-ل *q-w-l* 'voice-related', or ر-م-ي *r-m-y* 'throwing-related'. Middle-weak roots are called *hollow* roots. Final weak roots are called *defective* roots.

Terminology Alert Roots are *bound* morphemes, i.e., they cannot appear on their own unlike *words*. They are also not pronounceable unlike *words* and *stems*. However, the notion of *root* in Arabic is sometimes confused by researchers with the notions of *word* and *stem* for a variety of reasons. One reason is that the notion of *root* in English and other European languages (all non-templatic) is closer to that of *stem* in Arabic. Researchers of Arab background make a similar error possibly because of Arabic orthography's optional diacritics which cause some undiacritized words to look like a sequence of root radicals, e.g., the word كتب *ktb [kataba]* 'he wrote' and its root ك-ت-ب *k-t-b*. Although Arabic speakers recognize that roots are not vocalized, they are often pronounced with the stock pattern *1a2a3a*, which, being identical to a verb template, adds to the confusion. Finally, the closeness of the Arabic terms for *root* جذر (*jaðr*) and *stem* جذع (*jiðς*) may also contribute to this confusion.

The *pattern* morpheme is an abstract template in which roots and vocalisms are inserted. We represent the pattern as a string of letters including special symbols to mark where root radicals and vocalisms are inserted. We use the numbers *1, 2, 3, 4, or 5* to indicate radical position[3] and the symbol *V* is used to indicate the position of the vocalism. For example, the pattern *1V22V3* indicates that the second root radical is to be doubled. A pattern can include letters for additional consonants and vowels, e.g., the verbal pattern *V1tV2V3*.

The *vocalism* morpheme specifies the short vowels to use with a pattern. Traditional accounts of Arabic morphology collapse the vocalism into the pattern [69]. The separation of vocalisms was introduced with the emergence of more sophisticated models that abstract certain inflectional features that consistently vary across complex patterns, such as voice (passive versus active) [70].

Terminology Alert There are many terms used to refer to the concept "template." In addition to *template* and *pattern*, researchers may encounter *wazn* (from Arabic grammar), *binyan* (from Hebrew grammar), *Form* and *Measure*. The term *pattern* is used ambiguously to include or exclude vocalisms, i.e., *vocalism-specified pattern* and *vocalism-free pattern*.

A word stem is constructed by interleaving (aka interdigitating) the three types of templatic morphemes. For example, the word stem كتب *katab* 'to write' is constructed from the root ك-ت-ب *k-t-b*, the pattern *1V2V3* and the vocalism *aa*.

---

[3]Often in the literature, radical position is indicated with *C* with no position distinction. Some researchers make the distinction using particular letters such as FCL or FML for 123, and KRDS or FMLR for 1234. This pays homage to the long Arabic and Hebrew grammarian tradition of referring to the radicals using the letters of the root for *doing-related*: ف-ع-ل *f-ς-l*. So, for example, the عين ςayn of the root ك-ت-ب *k-t-b* is ت *t*.

Form Adjustments

The process of combining morphemes can involve a number of phonological, morphological and orthographic rules that modify the form of the created word; it is not always a simple interleaving and concatenation of its morphemic components. These rules complicate the process of analyzing and generating Arabic words. One example is the feminine morpheme, ة+ +*ħ* (*Ta-Marbuta, [lit. tied T]*), which is turned into ت+ +*t* (also called *Ta-Maftuha [lit., open T]*) when followed by a possessive clitic: أميرة+هم *Âamiyraħu+hum* 'princess+their' is realized as أميرتهم *Âamiyratuhum* 'their princess'. We refer to the ت+ +*t* form of the morpheme ة+ +*ħ*, as its *allomorph*. Similarly, by analogy to allophones and phonotactics, we can talk about *morphotactics*, as the contextual conditions that cause a morpheme to realize as one of its allomorphs. More examples of such rules are discussed in Section 4.2.

4.1.2   FUNCTIONAL MORPHOLOGY

In functional morphology, we study words in terms of their morpho-syntactic and morpho-semantic behavior as opposed to the form of the morphemes they are constructed from. We distinguish three functional operations: *derivation*, *inflection* and *cliticization*. The distinction between these three operations in Arabic is similar to that in other languages. This is not surprising since functional morphology tends to be a more language-independent way of characterizing words. The next four sections discuss derivational, inflectional and cliticization morphology in addition to the central concept of the *lexeme*.

Derivational Morphology

Derivational morphology is concerned with creating new words from other words, a process in which the core meaning of the word is modified. For example, the Arabic كاتب *kAtib* 'writer' can be seen as derived from the verb كتب *to write katab* the same way the English *writer* can be seen as a derivation from *write*. Derivational morphology usually involves a change in part-of-speech (POS). The derived variants in Arabic typically come from a set of relatively well-defined *lexical relations*, e.g., *location* (اسم مكان), *time* (اسم زمان), *actor/doer/active participle* (اسم فاعل) and *actee/object/passive participle* (اسم مفعول) among many others. The derivation of one form from another typically involves a pattern switch. In the example above, the verb كتب *katab* has the root ك-ت-ب *k-t-b* and the pattern *1a2a3*; to derive the active participle of the verb, we switch in the pattern *1A2i3* to produce the form كاتب *kAtib* 'writer'.

Although compositional aspects of derivations do exist, the derived meaning is often idiosyncratic. For example, the *masculine* noun مكتب *maktab* 'office/bureau/agency' and the *feminine* noun مكتبة *maktabaħ* 'library/bookstore' are derived from the root ك-ت-ب *k-t-b* 'writing-related' with the pattern+vocalism *ma12a3*, which indicates location. The exact type of the location is thus idiosyncratic, and it is not clear how the nominal gender difference can account for the semantic difference.

Inflectional Morphology

On the other hand, in inflectional morphology, the core meaning and POS of the word remain intact and the extensions are always predictable and limited to a set of possible features. Each feature has a finite set of associated values. For example, in row (5) column (3) from the left in Figure 4.2, the feature-value pairs *number:plur* and *case:gen*, indicate that that particular analysis of the word وكتبه *wakutubihi* is plural in number and genitive in case, respectively. Inflectional features are all obligatory and must have a specific (non-nil) value for every word. Some features have POS restrictions. In Arabic, there are eight inflectional features. *Aspect*, *mood*, *person* and *voice* only apply to verbs, while *case* and *state* only apply to nouns/adjectives. *Gender* and *number* apply to both verbs and nouns/adjectives.

Cliticization Morphology

Cliticization is closely related to inflectional morphology. Similar to inflection, cliticization does not change the core meaning of the word. However, unlike inflectional features, which are all obligatory, clitics (i.e., clitic features) are all optional. Moreover, while inflectional morphology is expressed using both templatic and concatenative morphology (i.e., using patterns, vocalisms and affixes), cliticization is only expressed using concatenative morphology (i.e., using affix-like clitics).

The Lexeme

The *core meaning* of a word in functional morphology is often referred to using a variety of terms, such as the *lexeme*, the *lemma* or the *vocable*. These terms are not equal. A *lexeme* is a lexicographic abstraction: it is the *set* of all word forms that share a core meaning and differ only in inflection and cliticization. For example, the lexeme بيت$_1$ *bayt$_1$* 'house' includes بيت *bayt* 'house', للبيت *lilbayti* 'for the house' and بيوت *buyuwt* 'houses' among others; while the lexeme بيت$_2$ *bayt$_2$* 'verse' includes to بيت *bayt* 'verse', للبيت *lilbayti* 'for the verse' and أبيات *ÂabyAt* 'verses' among others. Note that the singulars in the two lexemes are *homonyms*[4] but the plurals are not. This is called *partial paradigm homonymy*. Sometimes, two lexemes share the full inflectional paradigm but only differ in their meaning (*full paradigm homonymy*). For example, the lexemes for قاعدة$_1$ *qAςidaħ$_1$* 'rule' and قاعدة$_2$ *qAςidaħ$_2$* 'base'. A lexeme can be referred to uniquely by supplementing the lemma with an index (as above), with additional forms that are necessary to distinguish the lexeme (such as the plural form) and/or with a gloss in another language.

By contrast, the *lemma* (also called the *citation form*) is a conventionalized choice of one of the word forms to stand for the set. For instance, the lemma of a verb is the third person masculine singular perfective form; while the lemma for a noun is the masculine singular form (or feminine

---

[4]See Section 7.1 for more on homonymy.

singular if no masculine is possible). Lemmas typically are without any clitics and without any sense/meaning indices. For the examples above, the lemmas are بيت *bayt* and قاعدة *qAʕidaħ*, both of which collapse/ignore semantic differences and morphological differences. Lexemes are commonly represented using sense-indexed lemmas (as we saw above).

The term *vocable* is a purely morphological characterization of a set of word forms without semantic distinctions. Words with partial paradigm homonymy are represented with two vocables (e.g., بيت₁ *bayt*₁ 'house' and بيت₂ *bayt*₂ 'verse'); however, words with full paradigm homonymy are represented with one vocable (e.g., قاعدة *qAʕidaħ* 'rule/base').

Terminology Alert The terms for *root* and *stem* are sometimes confused with *lemma*, *lexeme* and *vocable*.

4.1.3   FORM-FUNCTION INDEPENDENCE

Morphological form and function are rather independent in Arabic. This independence is realized in two ways.

First, templatic morphemes can function derivationally or inflectionally, with the exception of the roots, which are always derivational. For example, the semantic relationship between كاتب *kAtib* 'writer' and كتّاب *kut~Ab* 'writers' maintains the sense of the kind of person described, but only varies the number. The inflectional change in the number feature in this example is accomplished using templatic morphemes (pattern and vocalism change). This form of plural construction in Arabic is often called "broken plural" to distinguish it from the strictly affixational "sound plural" (e.g., كاتب+ات *kAtib+At* 'writers [fem]'). Although the majority of affixational morphemes are inflectional, one exception is the derivational suffix Ya of Nisba '[lit.] Ya of relatedness' (ـِيّ+ *iy~*).

This suffix maps nouns to adjectives related to them, e.g., كتبيّ *kutubiy~* 'book-related' is derived from the noun كتب *kutub* 'books'. Clitics' form and function are consistent (i.e., not independent).

Second, the values of different functional features are not necessarily consistent with their form-based/morphemic realization. Although the term *features* is primarily associated with functional morphology, we can also refer to form-based features, which are used to abstract away from morphemes, e.g., ات+ *+At* is feminine and plural and ة+ *+aħ* is feminine and singular. In this setting, form-function independence refers to the fact that the values of the form-based features and their corresponding functional features are not necessarily coordinated. For example, there are numerous cases of functionally masculine and plural nouns with feminine singular morphology (typically broken plurals), e.g., كتبة *katab+aħ* 'scribes [masc.pl.]'; or with feminine plural morphology, e.g., احتفالات *AiHtifAl+At* 'celebrations [masc.pl.]'. More examples appear in Section 4.2.2. This is a different issue yet from Arabic's complex agreement rules (see Chapter 6).

4.2   A SKETCH OF ARABIC WORD MORPHOLOGY

In this section, we present a general sketch of the most important phenomena in Arabic morphology. The section is divided into four subsections pertaining to cliticization, inflection, derivation and various form adjustments. We focus here on the different morphological variants and less on what constrains them, such as syntactic agreement (see Chapter 6).

4.2.1   CLITICIZATION MORPHOLOGY

Arabic clitics attach to the inflected base word (see Section 4.2.2) in a strict order that can be represented as follows using general class names:

[QST+ [CNJ+ [PRT+ [DET+ BASE +PRO]]]]

Since all clitics are optional, the inflected base word is valid as is. At the deepest level of cliticization, we find DET, the determiner (aka, the definite article) +الـ Al+, and PRO, a member of the class of pronominal clitics. Pronominal enclitics can attach to nouns (as possessives) or verbs and prepositions (as objects). The determiner Al+ doesn't attach to verbs or prepositions. Possessive pronominal clitics and the determiner do not co-exist on nouns. Next comes PRT, the class of particle proclitics. Depending on their POS, some of these clitics will only attach to verbs, e.g., the future particle +سـ s+. Prepositional particle proclitics such as +بـ b+ and +كـ k+ will typically attach to nouns, adjectives and some particles such as أنّ Ân~a but never to verbs. One attachment level shallower is the class CNJ, where we find the conjunctions +و w+ and +فـ f+. They can attach to any POS. Finally, the shallowest level of clitic attachment, QST (question), is preserved for the interrogative particle +أ Â+, which attaches to the first word in any sentence turning it into a question. The following are examples of how some clitics are used.

(4.2) أوبالقلمِ سيحاربهم؟

Âa+wa+bi+Al+qalami   sa+yuHAriba+hum   ?
question+and+with+the+pen   will+he-fight+them   ?
'Will he fight them with the pen?'

(4.3) وأما بالنسبة لأخي فهو يدرس الموسيقى

wa+Âam~A bi+Al+nisbaħi li+Âax+iy   fa+huwa yadrusu Al+muwsiqaý
and+as-for   in+the+regard   to+brother+my   then+he   studies   the+music
'As for my brother, he studies music'

A list of the most prominent Arabic proclitics and enclitics is presented in Figures 4.3 and 4.4, respectively. These figures also provide the various Penn Arabic Treebank (PATB) POS tags [23, 71] assignable to different clitics and their corresponding cliticization class and English translation. Note that the proclitic +و wa+ has multiple homonyms that can occupy two different positions.

Figure 4.3: Arabic proclitics. The most important clitics are presented with their order class, POS tag, function and English gloss.

Clitics	Class	PATB POS Tag	Function	English
+أ Â+	QST	INTERROG_PART	interrogative همزة الإستفهام	*yes/no question*
+و wa+	CNJ	CONJ	coordination واو العطف	and
			connection واو الربط	and
		SUB_CONJ	circumstantial واو الحال	while
	PRT	PREP	oath واو القسم	by
			accompaniment واو المعية	with
+ف fa+	CNJ	CONJ	conjunction فاء العطف	and, so
		CONNEC_PART	connection فاء الربط	and, so
		RC_PART	response conditional فاء الجزاء	so, then
		SUB_CONJ	subordinating conjunction فاء السببية	so that
+ب bi+	PRT	PREP	preposition حرف جر	by, with, in
+ك ka+	PRT	PREP	preposition حرف جر	such as, like
+ل li+	PRT	PREP	preposition حرف جر	to, for
+ل la+	PRT	EMPHATIC_PART	emphasis لام التوكيد	will certainly
		RC_PART	response conditional اسمها	so, then
+س sa+	PRT	FUT_PART	future particle سين المستقبل	will
+ال Al+	DET	DET	definite article ال التعريف	the

Clitics are usually attached to the word they are adjacent to; however, there are exceptions that allow them to be separated. For example, the determiner +ال *Al+* and prepositional proclitics can appear unattached when the word is quoted or written in a foreign script, e.g., "اعترافاته"ـل *li "Ǎiς irAfAtihi"* 'for his-confessions' or iPod الـ *Al iPod* 'the iPod'. The clitic in these cases is usually followed by the Tatweel/Kashida symbol to maintain a connected letter shape (although not necessarily: iPod ال *Al iPod* 'the iPod').

The prepositional proclitics can have pronominal objects, which may lead to what appears to be a proclitic followed by an enclitic and no word base, e.g., لهم *la+hum* 'for them'. In these cases, the prepositions are typically considered the base word.

Other Clitics   In addition to the clitics described above, there are few other clitics that are less frequent or more lexically constrained than the clitics discussed so far. These clitics are nonetheless decliticized in the Arabic treebanks (see Chapter 6), and as such they should not be simply ignored. The following is a brief description of these clitics.

- The negative particles ما *mA* and لا *lA* (PATB POS tag NEG_PART) and the vocative particle يا *yA* (PATB POS tag VOC_PART) are sometimes treated like proclitics although

Figure 4.4: Pronominal enclitics. All pronominal enclitics appear in cliticization class PRO. The PATB POS tag form is derived from the specific person-gender-number information of the pronoun; e.g., the tag of the 2nd person masculine plural possessive pronoun كم+ *+kum* is POSS_PRON_2MP.

		Pronominal Enclitics		
PATB POS Tags		[1]POSS_PRON_*PerGenNum* (nominal possessive) [2][PIC]VSUFF_DO: *PerGenNum* (verbal direct object) [3]PRON_*PerGenNum* (prepositional object)		
		Number		
Person	**Gender**	**Singular**	**Dual**	**Plural**
1st		[1,3] ي+ *+iy* [2] ني+ *+niy*		نا+ *+nA*
2nd	Masc	ك+ *+ka*	كما+ *+kumA*	كم+ *+kum*
	Fem	ك+ *+ki*		كن+ *+kun~a*
3rd	Masc	ه+ *+hu*	هما+	هم+ *+hum*
	Fem	ها+ *+hA*	*+humA*	هن+ *+hun~a*

their cliticization is actually a very common spelling error resulting from these particles ending with a disconnective letter. For example, the quoted sequence يزال لا *lA yzAl* 'continue [lit. not cease]' is six times more frequent on the web than its cliticized version لايزال *lA+yzAl*.[5]

- The special preposition ت+ *ta+*, often called القسم تاء *Ta of Oath*, is almost never used outside the phrase تالله *taAll~ahi* 'by God'.

- The definite article ال+ *Al+* has a homonym that acts almost exactly the same way in terms of cliticization but is a relative pronoun.

- The word ما *mA*, which can be an interrogative pronoun 'what', a relative pronoun 'which, that' or a subordination conjunction 'that' (PATB POS tags INTERROG_PRON, REL_PRON and SUB_CONJ, respectively), can be cliticized to a closed class of words such as عندما *ʕindamA* 'when [lit. at-which]' and بينما *baynamA* 'while [lit. between-which]'. In two cases, the attaching word experiences a change of spelling resulting from assimilation: ممّا *mim~A* 'from which' is actually من+ما *min+mA*; and عمّا *ʕam~A* 'about which' is actually عن+ما *ʕan+mA*. In these two cases and only these two cases, the enclitic ما+ *+mA* is sometimes reduced to م+ *ma*: ممّ *mim~a*.

[5]"يزال لا" *lA yzAl* got 763,000 hits as opposed to 132,000 hits for "لايزال" *lA+yzAl* on Google [July 15, 2009].

- The word من *man*, which can be an interrogative or relative pronoun 'who, whom' (PATB POS tags INTERROG_PRON, REL_PRON), can be cliticized to the prepositions من *min* 'from' and عن *ɛan* 'about'. The cliticization leads to a change of spelling similar to the case described above with ما *mA*: ممّن *mim~an* 'from whom' is actually من+من *min+man*; and عمّن *ɛam~an* 'about whom' is actually عن+من *ɛan+man*.

- The negative particle لا *lA* (PATB POS tag NEG_PART) appears as an enclitic to the subordinating conjunction أن *Âan*, which experiences a spelling change resulting from assimilation: ألّا *Âal~a* 'that not' is actually أن+لا *Âan+lA*. When the prepositional proclitic ل+ *li+* attaches to this word, it experiences yet another spelling change: لئلّا *liÂal~a* 'so that not' is actually ل+أن+لا *li+Âan+lA*.

- Arabic dialects introduce several additional clitics, some with new functionality that does not exist in MSA. For example, a verbal progressive particle, which has no correspondence in MSA, appears as ب+ *bi+* in Egyptian and Levantine Arabic, as د+ *da+* in Iraqi Arabic and ك+ *ka+* in Moroccan Arabic. The Egyptian and Levantine Arabic progressive clitic ب+ *bi+* is a homograph with the preposition *bi+* 'in/with', which is also present in these dialects. The MSA future proclitic س+ *sa+* is replaced by ح+ *Ha+* in Levantine and Egyptian (appearing also as ه+ *ha+* occasionally in Egyptian) and غ+ *ɣa* in Moroccan. Levantine, Iraqi and Gulf Arabic have a demonstrative proclitic ه+ *ha+*, which strictly precedes with the definite article ال+ *Al+*. Several dialects include the proclitic ع+ *ɛa+*, a reduced form of the preposition على *ɛalaý* 'on/upon/about/to'. Also, several dialect include the non MSA circum-clitic ما+ +ش *mA+* +*š*, which is used to mark negation. Iraqi Arabic has a contraction of the dialectal question word شنو *šinuw* 'what' that appears as ش+ *š+*. For more information on Arabic dialects, see [72, 73, 74, 75].

4.2.2   INFLECTIONAL MORPHOLOGY

In the next two subsections, we discuss aspects of Arabic verbal and nominal morphology.

Verbal Morphology

Arabic verbal morphology is often described as a very regular, almost mathematical, system with hardly any exceptions. Verbs inflect for aspect, mood, voice and subject (person, gender and number).

Verbal Forms   Arabic verbs have a limited number of patterns: ten basic triliteral patterns and two basic quadriliteral patterns. The very few additional rare patterns are not discussed here. In western tradition, verbal patterns are also called Forms (and given a Roman numeral). Figure 4.5 lists the different basic verbal patterns and their general meaning associations. As mentioned earlier, pattern meaning is mostly idiosyncratic although observations have been made on shared semantics [38]. Form I (triliteral pattern 1V2V3) and Form QI (quadriliteral pattern 1V23V4) are considered the most basic patterns (مجرد *mujar~ad*) as opposed to other patterns which are described as augmented [38] or derived [76] (مزيد *maziyd*).

Figure 4.5: Arabic verb forms. Patterns for perfective (PV) and imperfective (IV) aspect are provided in the active and passive voice. Passive voice patterns are in parentheses. All patterns and examples are conjugated in the 3rd person masculine singular. Form I has six subtypes that vary in the perfective/imperfective stem vowel (marked as V_p and V_i, respectively); however, Form I has only one passive voice form per aspect (regardless of subtype).

Form	PV-Pattern	IV-Pattern	Meaning	Example	Gloss
I-$V_p V_i$	1a2V_p3 (1u2i3)	a12V_i3 (u12a3)	Basic sense of root	-	-
I-aa	1a2a3	a12a3	-	*fataH, y+aftaH*	open
I-au	1a2a3	a12u3	-	*katab, y+aktub*	write
I-ai	1a2a3	a12i3	-	*jalas, y+ajlis*	sit
I-ia	1a2i3	a12a3	-	*γaDib, y+aγDab*	be angry
I-ii	1a2i3	a12i3	-	*Hasib, y+aHsib*	consider
I-uu	1a2u3	a12u3	-	*Hasun, y+aHsun*	be beautiful
II	1a22a3 (1u22i3)	u1a22i3 (u1a22a3)	Intensification, causation	*kat~ab, y+ukat~ib*	dictate
III	1A2a3 (1uw2i3)	u1A2i3 (u1A2a3)	Interaction	*kAtab, y+ukAtib*	correspond with
IV	'a12a3 ('u12i3)	u12i3 (u12a3)	Causation	*Áajlas, y+ujlis*	seat
V	ta1a22a3 (tu1u22i3)	ata1a22a3 (uta1a22a3)	Reflexive of Form II	*taEal~am, y+ataEal~am*	learn
VI	ta1A2a3 (tu1uw2i3)	ata1A2a3 (uta1A2a3)	Reflexive of Form III	*takAtab, y+atakAtab*	correspond
VII	in1a2a3 (in1u2i3)	an1a2i3 (un1a2a3)	Passive of Form I	*Ainkatab, y+ankatib*	subscribe
VIII	i1ta2a3 (i1tu2i3)	a1ta2i3 (u1ta2a3)	Acquiescence, exaggeration	*Aiktatab, y+aktatib*	register
IX	i12a3i3 (i12u3i3)	a12a3i3 (u12a3a3)	Transformation	*AiHmar~, y+aHmar~*	turn red, blush
X	ista12a3 (istu12i3)	asta12i3 (usta12a3)	Requirement	*Aistaktab, y+astaktib*	make write
QI	1a23a4 (1u23i4)	u1a23i4 (u1a23a4)	Basic sense of root	*zaxraf, y+uzaxrif*	ornament
QII	ta1a23a4 (tu1u23i4)	a1a2a3a4 (uta1a23a4)	Reflexive or unaccusative of QI	*tazaxraf, y+atazaxraf*	be ornamented

Verbal Subject, Aspect, Mood and Voice   The verbal subject is specified using three features: person, gender and number. Person has three values: 1st (speaker, متكلم *mutakal~im*), 2nd (addressee, مخاطب *muxATab*) 3rd (other, غائب *γAŷib*). Gender has two values: masculine or feminine. And number has three values: singular, dual or plural. The verbal subject is indicated through affixations, whose form is constrained by verbal aspect and mood. See Figure 4.6 for a list of all the verbal subject affixes. The subjects conjugated with the perfective aspect are only suffixes, while the subjects conjugated with the imperfective are circumfixes.

Arabic verbs have three aspects: perfective (ماضي *mADiy*), imperfective (مضارع *muDAriς*) and imperative (أمر *Âamr*).[6] The perfective indicates that actions described are completed (perfect) as opposed to the imperfective which does not specify any such information. The imperative is the command form of the verb. Aspect is indicated only templatically through pattern and vocalism combination. In all forms, except for Form I, pattern and vocalism specification are regular. Form I vocalism has six idiosyncratic variants that share a common pattern. See Figure 4.5. Some verbs can have more than one variant with no meaning change, e.g., لمس *lamas* 'touch' can have two imperfective forms: *y+almis* and *y+almus*. In other cases, a change in pattern vowels has different meanings, e.g., حسب/يحسب *Hasab/y+aHsub* 'compute', *Hasib/y+aHsib* 'regard', and *Hasub/y+aHsub* 'be esteemed'.

Terminology Alert The perfective / imperfective aspect stems are sometimes called *s-stem* (suffixing-stem) / *p-stem* (prefixing-stem) [38], where *p-stem* refers to the imperfective, not the perfective.

Arabic has three common moods that only vary for the imperfective aspect: indicative (مرفوع *marfuwς*), subjunctive (منصوب *manSuwb*), and jussive (مجزوم *majzuwm*). One additional archaic mood is called the energetic. The perfective aspect does not vary by mood, although the value of the mood feature with the perfective aspect is typically defaulted to *indicative*. The indicative mood is also the default mood with the imperfective aspect indicating present or incomplete actions. The other moods are restricted in their use with particular verb particles. The subjunctive is used after conjunction particles such as كي *kay* 'in order to' and the future-negation particle لن *lan* 'will not'.

The jussive most commonly appears after the past-negation particle لم *lam* 'did not'. There are no specific morphemes in Arabic corresponding to tense, such as past, present or future. Instead, these various tense values are expressed though a combination of aspect, mood and supporting particles. For instance, in addition to the two temporally marking particles exemplified above, the particle سوف *sawfa* 'will,' and its clitic form س+ *sa+* are used to indicate the future tense by appearing with indicative imperfective verbs.

Voice can be passive or active. It is only indicated though a change in vocalism. See Figure 4.5 for examples of aspect and voice templatic morpheme combinations.

Nominal Morphology

In this section, we discuss the morphology of nouns, adjectives and proper nouns, henceforth, collectively "nominals." In comparison to verbs, nominal morphology is far more complex and

---

[6]Some consider the imperative a mood rather than an aspect [77].

Figure 4.6: Arabic verb subject affixations.

	Perfective			Imperfective (Indicative, Subjunctive, Jussive)		
	Singular	Dual	Plural	Singular	Dual	Plural
1	+tu	+nA		'+ +(u,a,.)	n+ +(u,a,.)	
2	+ta	+tumA	+tum	t+ +(u,a,.)	t+ +(Ani,A,A)	t+ +(uwna,uwA,uwA)
	+ti		+tun~a	t+ +(iyn,iy,iy)		t+ +na
3	+a	+A	+uwA	y+ +(u,a,.)	y+ +(Ani,A,A)	y+ +(uwna,uwA,uwA)
	+at	+atA	+na	t+ +(u,a,.)	t+ +(Ani,A,A)	y+ +na

idiosyncratic. Arabic nominals inflect for gender, number, state and case. Figure 4.7 presents the different affixational morphemes associated with different combinations of these features.

Gender and Number   In functional morphology terms, Arabic has two gender values: masculine and feminine; and three number values: singular, dual and plural. However, in terms their form, the story is more complex. First, these two features are commonly expressed using shared morphemes that represent some number and some gender combination. This is not atypical compared to other languages. Second, there is a disconnect between the markers of morphemic and functional gender and number. In around 80% of nominals[7], functional and morphemic genders agree, e.g., مدرس *mudar~is* 'teacher [m.s.]', مدرسة *mudar~is+aħ* 'teacher [f.s.]', مدرسون *mudar~is+uwna* 'teachers [m.p.]', and مدرسات *mudar~is+At* 'teachers [f.p.]'. Plurals that agree functionally and morphemically are called sound plurals (الجمع السالم). However, in the other 20%, functional gender and number do not match morphemic gender and number. The following are some of the most common patterns of form-function disagreement.

- **Broken Plural** The most common case of function-form disagreement is broken (irregular) plural (جمع التكسير) where functional plurals are expressed using a pattern change with singular affixation. For example, the plural of مكتب *maktab* 'office' is مكاتب *makAtib* 'offices' (not **مكتبون* *maktabuwn*). Broken plurals make up around half of all plurals in Arabic. See Figure 4.8 for a list of common singular-plural pattern pairs. The pairing of singulars and plurals is basically idiosyncratic, but there are some very common pairs. Some of the plural patterns appear with singulars also: the words كتاب *kitAb* 'book' (singular) and رجال *rijAl* 'men' (broken plural) share the pattern *1i2A3*; and similarly, the words كتب *kutub* 'books' (broken plural) and عنق *ɛunuq* 'neck' (singular) share the pattern *1u2u3*. Finally, some nouns have multiple plurals

---

[7]Analyzed in a sample from the Penn Arabic Treebank [9].

Figure 4.7: Arabic nominal affixations.

Class	Gender	Number	Case	State	Morpheme
Triptote	Masc	Sg	Nom	Def/Con	+u
				InDef	+ū
			Acc	Def/Con	+a
				InDef	+A+ā
			Gen	Def/Con	+i
				InDef	+ī
	Fem	Sg	Nom	Def/Con	+aħ+u
				InDef	+aħ+ū
			Acc	Def/Con	+aħ+a
				InDef	+aħ+ā
			Gen	Def/Con	+aħ+i
				InDef	+aħ+ī
Diptote	Masc	Sg	Nom	Def/Con/InDef	+u
			Acc	Def/Con/InDef	+a
			Gen	Def/Con	+i
				InDef	+a
	Fem	Sg	Nom	Def/Con/InDef	+aħ+u
			Acc	Def/Con/InDef	+aħ+a
			Gen	Def/Con	+aħ+i
				InDef	+aħ+a
Indeclinable	Masc	Sg	Nom/Acc/Gen	Def/Con	+a
				InDef	+ā
Invariable	Masc	Sg	Nom/Acc/Gen	Def/Con/InDef	+ϕ
Sound Dual	Masc	Du	Nom	Con	+A
				Def/InDef	+A+ni
			Acc/Gen	Con	+ay
				Def/InDef	+ay+ni
	Fem	Du	Nom	Con	+at+A
				Def/InDef	+at+A+ni
			Acc/Gen	Con	+at+ay
				Def/InDef	+at+ay+ni
Sound Plural	Masc	Pl	Nom	Def/InDef	+uw+na
				Con	+uw
			Acc/Gen	Def/InDef	+iy+na
				Con	+iy
	Fem	Pl	Nom	Def/Con	+At+u
				InDef	+At+ū
			Acc/Gen	Def/Con	+At+i
				InDef	+At+ī

some with subtle distinctions that do not exist any more in MSA.[8] The multiple plurals can
be all broken or a mixture of broken and sound.

- **Broken Feminine** The most common way for deriving the feminine form of a masculine noun
  or adjective is using the feminine suffix ة+ +*ħ*. However, there are three stable masculine-
  feminine pattern pairs that we call Broken Feminine:[9]

  – Color/Deformity Adjective: 'a12a3-1a23A': أزرق *Âazraq* 'blue [m.]' ⇒ زرقاء *zarqA*'blue
    [f.]'

  – Superlatives: 'a12a3-1u23aY: أكبر *Âakbar* 'greatest [m.]' ⇒ كبرى *kubraý* 'greatest [f.]'

  – Other: 1a23An-1a23aY: سكران *sakrAn* 'drunk [m.]' - سكرى *sakraý* 'drunk [f.]'

- **Basic Gender Mismatch** Some of the nouns, particularly those that do not vary for gender (i.e.,
  inherently masculine or feminine), have inconsistent morphemic morphology. The following
  are some common examples: عين *ᶜayn* 'eye' and حامل *HAmil* 'pregnant' are masculine by
  form but feminine by function; and خليفة *xaliyfaħ* 'caliph' is feminine by form but masculine
  by function. A few of these nouns can be both feminine and masculine functionally, e.g.,
  طريق *Tariyq* 'road'. In other cases, the singular form may be correctly masculine, but it takes a
  feminine plural suffix (although it remains functionally masculine): تهديد *tahdiyd* 'threat [m.s.]'
  and باص *bAS* 'bus [m.s.]' have the plurals تهديدات *tahdiydAt* 'threats [m.p.]' and باصات *bASAt*
  'buses [m.p.]', respectively.

- **Singular Collective Plurals** It is important to also distinguish cases of Arabic nouns that
  semantically express plurality but are for all intents and purposes singular as far as Arabic
  morphology and syntax are concerned. The most common form of these nouns is collective
  nouns (اسم الجنس), which often are the uncountable form of some countable nouns. For
  example, the word تمر *tamr* 'dates' is a singular uncountable collective noun in Arabic, which
  cannot be modified with a number quantifier unlike the countable singular form تمرة *tamraħ*
  'date' and its countable plural تمرات *tamarAt*.[10] The collective تمر *tamr* 'dates' has its own plural
  form تمور *tumuwr* 'types of dates'.

- **Complex Disagreement** The disagreement in form and function can involve both gender and
  number. For example, the masculine plural كتبة *katabaħ* 'scribes' is morphemically feminine
  singular; and the feminine plural حوامل *HawAmil* 'pregnant women' is morphemically singular
  and masculine.

---

[8]A good example is the distinction of plural of paucity (جمع القلة) and plural of plenty/abundance (جمع الكثرة), which we do not
discuss here [78].

[9]A few feminine nouns have plurals that are different in pattern yet also use sound plural affixation. We call these semi-sound
nouns: the plural of تمرة *tamr+aħ* 'palm date' is تمرات *tamar+At* 'palm dates' (not **tamr+At*).

[10]The countable counterpart of a collective noun is called its unit noun (اسم الوحدة). We consider this a derivational relationship.

Figure 4.8: Common pairs of singular and broken plural patterns.

Pattern Pair		Example	
Singular	Plural	Singular	Plural
1a2a3	'a12A3	ولد *walad* 'boy'	أولاد *ÂawlAd* 'boys'
1a2i3	'a12A3	كتف *katif* 'shoulder'	أكتاف *ÂaktAf* 'shoulders'
1u2u3	'a12A3	عنق *ʕunuq* 'neck'	أعناق *AaʕnAq* 'necks'
1a2i3	1u2uw3	ملك *malik* 'king'	ملوك *muluwk* 'kings'
1a23	1u2uw3	طير *Tayr* 'bird'	طيور *Tuyuwr* 'birds'
1u23	1u2uw3	برج *burj* 'tower'	بروج *buruwj* 'towers'
1a2u3	1i2A3	رجل *rajul* 'man'	رجال *rijAl* 'men'
1a2a3	1i2A3	جمل *jamal* 'camel'	جمال *jimAl* 'camels'
1a23	1i2A3	كلب *kalb* 'dog'	كلاب *kilAb* 'dogs'
1u23	1i2A3	رمح *rumH* 'spear'	رماح *rimAH* 'spears'
1a23An	1i2A3	عطشان *ʕaTšAn* 'thirsty'	عطاش *ʕiTAš* 'thirsty'
1a2iy3	1i2A3	كبير *kabiyr* 'big'	كبار *kibAr* 'big'
1a2iy3	1u2u3	جديد *jadiyd* 'new'	جدد *judud* 'new'
1i2A3	1u2u3	كتاب *kitAb* 'book'	كتب *kutub* 'books'
1a2iy3	1u2a3A'	وزير *waziyr* 'minister'	وزراء *wuzarA'* 'ministers'
1a2iy3	'a12i3A'	صديق *Sadiyq* 'friend'	أصدقاء *ÂaSdiqA'* 'friends'
1a2iy3	1a23aY	مريض *mariyD* 'patient'	مرضى *marDaý* 'patients'
1a23A'	1a2A3aY	صحراء *SaHrA'* 'desert'	صحارى *SaHAraý* 'deserts'
'a12a3	1u23	أزرق *Âazraq* 'blue'	زرق *zurq* 'blue'
1A2i3	1u22A3	كاتب *kAtib* 'writer'	كتّاب *kut~Ab* 'writers'
1A2i3	1awA2i3	جانب *jAnib* 'side'	جوانب *jawAnib* 'sides'

Definiteness and Construct State Arabic nouns inflect for *state*, which has three values: definite, indefinite and construct. The definite state is the nominal form that appears most typically with the definite article and direct addressing with the vocative particle يا *yA*. For example, الكتاب *Al+kitAb+u*. The indefinite state is used to mark an unspecified instance of a noun, e.g., كتاب *kitAbū* 'a book'.

The construct state indicates that the noun is the head of an *Idafa* construction, i.e., it is the first word (or مضاف *muDAf*) that is possessed by the noun phrase that follows it, e.g., the word كتاب *kitAbu* 'book' in كتاب الطالب *kitAbu AlTAlibi* '[lit. book the-student] the book of the student'. For some nouns, like كتاب *kitAb*, the definite and construct state forms are identical. However, this is not true for all nouns affix combinations. Sound masculine plural nouns have identical definite and indefinite state forms but different construct state: الكاتبون *Al+kAtib+uwna* 'the writers', and كاتبون *kAtib+uwna* 'some writers', but كاتبو *kAtib+uw* 'writers of ...'. See Figure 4.7 for more such cases.

Case   All Arabic nominals inflect for case, which has three values in Arabic: nominative (NOM مرفوع *marfuwς*), accusative (ACC منصوب *manSuwb*) or genitive (GEN مجرور *majruwr*). The realization of nominal case in Arabic is complicated by its orthography, which uses optional diacritics to indicate short vowel case morphemes, and by its morphology, which does not always distinguish between all cases. Additionally, case realization in Arabic interacts heavily with the realization of state, leading to different realizations depending on whether the nominal is indefinite, i.e., receiving *nunation* (تنوين *tanwiyn*), definite or in construct state. See Figure 4.7.

Eight different classes of nominal case expression have been described in the literature [77, 79]. We briefly review them here:

We first discuss the realization of case in morphemically (form-wise) singular nouns (including broken plurals). *Triptotes* are the basic class which expresses the three cases in the singular using the three short vowels of Arabic: NOM is $\acute{}$ +*u*, ACC is $\grave{}$ +*a*, and GEN is $\_$ +*i*. The corresponding nunated forms for these three diacritics are: $\acute{}$ +*ū* for NOM, $\grave{}$ +*ā* for ACC, and $\_$ +*ī* for GEN. Nominals not ending with Ta-Marbuta (ة *ħ*) or Alif Hamza (اء *A'*) receive an extra Alif in the accusative indefinite case (e.g, كِتابًا *kitAbАā* 'book' versus كِتابَةً *kitAbaħā* 'writing').

Diptotes are like triptotes except that when they are indefinite: (a.) they do not express nunation and (b.) they use the $\grave{}$ +*a* suffix for both ACC and GEN. The class of diptotes is lexically specific. It includes nominals with specific meanings or morphological patterns (colors, elatives, specific broken plurals, some proper names with Ta Marbuta ending or location names devoid of the definite article). Examples include بيروت *bayruwt* 'Beirut' and أزرق *Âazraq* 'blue'.

The next three classes are less common. The *invariables* show no case in the singular (e.g., nominals ending in long vowels: سوريا *suwryA* 'Syria' or ذكرى *ðikraý* 'memoir'). The *indeclinables* always use the $\grave{}$ +*a* suffix to express case in the singular and allow for nunation (معنًى *maςnaýā* 'meaning'). The *defective* nominals, which are derived from roots with a final weak radical (*y* or *w*), look like triptotes except that they collapse NOM and GEN into the GEN form, which also includes loosing their final glide: قاضٍ *qADī* (NOM,GEN) versus قاضيًا *qADiyAā* (ACC) 'a judge'.

For the dual and sound plurals, the situation is simpler, as there are no lexical exceptions. The dual and masculine sound plural (the sixth and seventh classes) express number, case and state jointly in morphemes that are identifiable even if undiacritized: كاتبونَ *kAtib+uwna* 'writers [m.p.]' (NOM), كاتبانِ *kAtib+Ani* 'writers [m.d.]' (NOM), كاتبتانِ *kAtib+atAni* 'writers [f.d.]' (NOM). The dual and masculine sound plural do not express nunation. On the other hand, the feminine sound plural (the eighth class) marks nunation explicitly, and all of its case morphemes are written only as diacritics, e.g., كاتِبَاتٌ *kAtib+At+ū* 'writers [f.p.]' (NOM). For all duals and sound plurals, the ACC and GEN forms are identical, e.g., كاتِبينَ *kAtib+iyna* 'writers [m.p.]' (ACC, GEN) and كاتِبَاتٍ *kAtib+At+ī* 'writers [f.p.]' (ACC, GEN) (see Figure 4.7).

4.2.3   DERIVATIONAL MORPHOLOGY

There are many types of derivational relations between words in Arabic. Some of these cross POS categories, e.g., the deverbal nouns derived from verb forms. But others preserve the POS, e.g., the different semantically related verb forms (as in form II being the causative of form I). Most of the derivations involve pattern change, but some include affixation too. We describe below some of the common derivations in Arabic.

- Masdar (مصدر) also called the *infinitive* or the *(de)verbal noun*. There are no rules for deriving the masdar of verbal Form I: نام *nAm* 'sleep [v.]' → نوم *nawm* 'sleep [n.]', كتب *katab* 'write [v.]' → كتابة *kitAbah* 'writing [n.]', and دخل *daxal* 'enter [v.]' → دخول *duxuwl* 'entry [n.]'. The rest of the verbal forms are regular providing one pattern for each form, e.g., the masdar of Form II (1a22a3) is *ta12iy3*: كسّر *kas~ar* 'break [v.]' → تكسير *taksiyr* 'breaking'.

- The active participle (اسم الفاعل) and passive participle (اسم المفعول) both have unique pattern mappings for every verb form. For example, Form I active and passive participles are *1A2i3* and *ma12uw3*, respectively: كاتب *kAtib* 'writer' and مكتوب *maktuwb* 'written'. The corresponding patterns for Form X are *musta12i3* and *musta12a3*: the participles of the verb استخدم *Aistaxdam* 'use' are مستخدِم *mustaxdim* 'user' and مستخدَم *mustaxdam* 'used'.

- The patterns *ma12a3* and *ma12i3* are used to indicate nouns of place and time (أسماء المكان والزمان), e.g., مكتب *maktab* 'office' from كتب *katab* 'write' and مجلس *majlis* 'council' from جلس *jalas* 'sit'.

- There are several nominal patterns that denote instruments (اسم الآلة) used for the verb they are derived from. For example, *mi12A3* is used to derived مفتاح *miftAH* 'key' from فتح *fataH* 'open' and منشار *minšAr* 'saw [n.]' from نشر *našar* 'saw [v.]'. Other patterns include *1a22A3ah*, e.g., كسّارة *kas~Arah* 'nutcracker' from كسّر *kassar* 'smash [v.]'; and *1A2uw3*, e.g., حاسوب *HAsuwb* 'computer' from حسب *Hasab* 'compute'. These forms are rather idiosyncratic in their formation.

- The pattern *1u2ay3* among others is used to derive the diminutive form (اسم التصغير) of another noun, e.g., شجيرة *šujayrah* 'shrub' is the diminutive of شجرة *šajarah* 'tree'.

- The Ya of Nisba '[lit.] Ya of relatedness' is a derivational suffix (ي +‏ *iy~*) that maps nouns to adjectives related to them. It is quite productive compared to other examples of derivational morphology. Examples include أردنّ *Âurdun~* 'Jordan' → أردنّي *Âurdun~iy~* 'Jordanian', سياسة *siyAsaħ* 'politics' → سياسيّ *siyAsiy~* 'political' and ملك *malik* 'king' → ملكي *malakiy~* 'royal'. The last two examples illustrate how Ya of Nisba derivation can include dropping suffixes (such as the feminine ending) or changing the pattern and/or vocalism. These interaction are rather ad hoc.

- The countable counterpart of a collective noun is called its unit noun (اسم الوحدة). It is often derived through a feminine singular suffix, e.g., تمر *tamr* 'dates (collective)' تمرة *tamraħ* 'date (singular)'.

4.2.4   MORPHOPHONEMIC AND ORTHOGRAPHIC ADJUSTMENTS

Putting together all of the templatic, affixational and clitic morphemes is not simply a process of interdigitation and concatenation. There are numerous morphophonemic and orthographic rewrite/adjustment rules that apply, causing the word form to be sometimes radically different from its components (see [38, 80, 8] among others). We separate next between the discussion of rules applying with roots, patterns and affixes from those applying with clitics for the purpose of clarity (although at a cost of minor duplication).

Root-Pattern-Affix Interactions

Morphophonemic Rules   There is a large number of morphophonemic rules. We consider three common sets.

   Form VIII Rules The pattern consonant ت *t* in verbal Form VIII (افتعل *i1ta2a3*) changes to د *d* when the first root radical is ز *z*, د *d* or ذ *ð*. Similarly, the same pattern consonant changes to ط *T* when the first root radical is an emphatic consonant (ص *S*, ض *D*, ط *T* or ظ *Ď*). For example, compare the following verbs, all of which are in Form VIII: استلم *Astlm* 'he received' (root *s-l-m*, default case), ازدهر *Azdhr* 'he flourished' (root *z-h-r*) and اصطبر *ASTbr* 'he endured' (root *S-b-r*).

   Weak Radical Rules Weak root radicals (و *w*, ي *y*) change into a vowel or are deleted depending on their vocalic environment. There are several rules with different conditions. The following are some examples with the root ق-و-ل *q-w-l* and various patterns and affixes: قال *qAla* 'he said' (not *qawala*), يقول *yaquwlu* 'he says' (not *yaqwulu*), قيل *qiyla* 'it is said' (not *quwila*) and قلت *qultu* 'I said' (not *qawaltu*). Arabic has a small number of exceptions where a weak radical behaves like a regular consonant, leading often to two contrastive forms with the same root and pattern but different word form. One example is the pair استجاب *AistajAba* 'he complied' and استجوب *Aistajwaba* 'he interrogated' both of which are derived from the root ج-و-ب *j-w-b* and the pattern *ista12a3*. The common practice in the field is to handle the second (non-weak) as coming from a different root that has a *hard w*.

Geminate Radical Rules Roots with geminate radicals, e.g., م-د-د *m-d-d*, also interact with short vowels in the pattern but only under certain suffix conditions. For example, the following two examples use the same template (*1a2a3*) but different suffixes: مدت *mad~at* /maddat/ 'she extended' (not madad+at), but مددت *madadtu* 'I extended'.[11]

Orthographic Rules Some of these rules are lexical, meaning that they are conditioned on specific morphemes or morpheme boundaries; while others are non-lexical referring only to phonemes or letters. The majority of orthographic rules are non-lexical. The few exceptions include the spelling of Alif-Maqsura and Ta-Marbuta.

Alif-Maqsura The rule to write an Alif-Maqsura applies when a third radical ي *y* (defective root) is turned into a vowel in word final position: the root ر-م-ي *r-m-y* and pattern-affix *1a2a3+a* phonologically realize as /rama/ (not *ramaya*), which orthographically realizes as رمى *ramaý* 'he threw'.

Ta- Marbuta The Ta -Marbuta spelling is also dependent on the affix that follows it. Although in MSA, the Ta -Marbuta is always pronounced as /t/, it is only written as ة *ħ* when followed by an affix devoid of an orthographic letter. For example, مَكْتَبَةٌ *maktabaħū* /maktabat+un/ 'library' is spelled with a Ta-Marbuta because the nunnation suffix /un/ is written with a diacritic.

The rest of this section presents some of the more common non-lexical orthographic rules pertaining to diacritization and Hamza spelling.

Diacritization Appropriate modifications to spell with diacritics are applied regardless of whether the diacritics are kept in the final word form or not. These include (i.) spelling long vowels as a combination of a diacritical short vowel and a compatible consonant: /ī/ is ي *iy* and /ū/ is و *uw*, (ii.) adding sukuns (no-vowel diacritics) between adjacent consonants, (iii.) adding an Alif word-initially to words starting with vowel diacritics (the case of Hamzat-Wasl discussed in Chapter 3) and (vi.) replacing a repeated consonant with a Shadda. The Shadda rule leads to deleting some letters from stems and affixes. For example, the phonological word /bayyan+na/ 'they [fem] explained' (root ب-ي-ن *b-y-n* and pattern-affix 1a22a3+na) is written as بَيَّنَّ *bay~an~a*. With deleted diacritics, this eight-phoneme word is written with three letters.

Hamza Spelling The Hamza (glottal stop phoneme) is written using seven orthographic symbols depending on the Hamza's orthographic and phonological context. Some of the numerous rules include the following. A word-initial Hamza is written with Alif Hamza below (إ *Ă*) when followed by /i/ and with Alif Hamza above (أ *Â*), otherwise. Another common rule is that a Hamza between two vowels is written using a character compatible with the higher ranking vowel in the

---

[11] Arabic dialects share some rules with MSA but not others. For example, the geminate radical example used above for مدت *madadtu* 'I extended' is realized in Levantine Arabic as مدّيت /maddēt/. This changed form deletes the stem vowel and adds a long vowel before the suffix *t*.

order (high to low) /i/ > /u/ > /a/. For example, the Hamza of سئل *suŷila* /su'ila/ 'he was asked' is written with a hamzated Ya because /i/ outranks /u/, as opposed to the Hamza of سؤال *suŵAl* /su'āl/ 'question', which is written with a hamzated waw because /u/ outranks /ā/. For more Hamza spelling rules and examples, see [77].

Clitic-Word Interactions

The inflected form of a word interacts morpho-syntactically with the clitics attached to it. For example, nouns followed by the possessive pronouns must be in construct state, nouns following prepositional proclitics must be in the genitive case and verbs following the future proclitic must be in the imperfective aspect with indicative mood (see Section 4.2.2). That said, most clitics simply attach to the inflected word with little or no change in spelling or pronunciation. However, there are a few important exceptions with consequences to the tasks of tokenization, detokenization, diacritization and POS tagging. The most complicated cases involve pronominal clitics and the definite article.

Pronominal Clitics

- The *u* vowel in the +*hu*- pronominal enclitics, ه+ +*hu*, هما+ +*humA*, هم+ +*hum*, and هن+ +*hun~a*, undergoes phonological assimilation to *i* when following a word that ends with *i* as in the nominal genitive case. For example, كتابه 'his book' can be diacritized as 'kitAbu+hu', kitAba+hu' or 'kitAbi+hi'.

- The 1st person singular pronominal enclitic ي+ +*iy* has an allomorph +*ya* with words ending with the letters Alif, Ya or Alif-Maqsura: مولاي عيناي ع *aynAya* 'my eyes'(عينا+ي ع *aynA+iy*), *mawlAya* 'my lord' (مولى+ي ع *mawlaŷ+iy*), فيّ *fiy~a* 'in me' (في+ي ع *fiy+iy*), and عليّ ع *alay~a* 'on me' (على+ي ع *alaŷ+iy*). Note that in the case of words ending with Ya or with an Alif-Maqsura that turns into a Ya (last two examples above), the assimilation is orthographically represented with a Shadda, which means the undiacritized word (with or without the pronominal enclitic) is not distinguishable in the case of Ya and minimally different in the case of an Alif-Maqsura.

- The 1st person singular pronoun ي+ +*iy* overrides the word-final case marker effectively normalizing case for such words: كتابي *kitAbiy* 'my book' can be underlyingly *kitAbu+iy*, *kitAba+iy* or *kitAbi+iy* (nominative, accusative or genitive, respectively).

- When pronominal enclitics other than ي+ +*iy* attach to the preposition ل+ *li*+, the form of the preposition is changed to *la*+. However, this is not the case with the preposition ب+ *bi*+: compare لكم *la+kum* 'for you', لهم *la+hum* 'for them' (hu-/hi- assimilation averted), بكم *bi+kum* 'by you' and بهم *bi+him* 'by them' (with hu-/hi- assimilation).

- When followed by a pronominal enclitic, word-final Ta-Marbuta is rewritten as Ta: مكتبة+نا *mktbħ+nA* becomes مكتبتنا *mktbtnA* 'our library'. The resulting word spelling can be ambiguous with words not originally containing a Ta-Marbuta: كاتبتنا can be كاتبت+نا *kAtabat+nA* 'she corresponded with us' or كاتبة+نا *kAtibaħu+nA* 'our [female] writer'.

- When followed by a pronominal enclitic, Alif-Maqsura becomes Alif or Ya (lexically determined): مستشفى+هم *mstšfý+hm* becomes مستشفاهم *mstšfAhm* 'their hospital', and على+هم *ςlý+hm* becomes عليهم *ςlyhm* 'on them'.

- When followed by a pronominal enclitic, the silent Alif in the verbal suffix وا+ *+uwA* (واو الجماعة, 'Waw of Plurality') is deleted: كتبوا+ها *katabuwA+hA* 'they wrote it' becomes كتبوها *katabuwhA*.

- When followed by a pronominal enclitic, the verbal suffix تم+ *+tum* is rewritten as تمو+ *+tumuw*: كتبتم+ها *katabtum+hA* 'you wrote it' becomes كتبتموها *katabtumuwhA*.

- Some word-final Hamzas become case-variant when followed by a pronominal clitic: بهاء+ه *bahA'+hu* 'his glory' becomes بهاؤه/بهاءه/بهائه *bahAẅuhu/bahA'ahu/bahAẏihi* 'his glory' (Nom/Acc/Gen)'.

Definite Article

- The Lam of the definite article ال+ *Al+* phonologically assimilates if followed by a so-called Sun letter (see Section 3.2.3). Assimilation is indicated by doubling the first letter of the word (with a Shadda) and counterintuitively not deleting the assimilating letter in the definite article (to preserve the word's morphemic spelling). No diacritic is provided on the Lam of the definite article. For example, ال+شمس *Al+šamsu* 'the sun' is written as الشّمس *Alš~amsu*; however, ال+قمر *Al+qamaru* 'the moon' is written as القمر *Alqamaru*.

- The Alif of the definite article ال+ *Al+* is deleted when preceded by the prepositional proclitic ل+ *li+*: ل+الكتاب *li+AlkitAbi* 'for the-book' becomes للكتاب *lilkitAbi*. A similar case of phonological elision occurs with the prepositional proclitic ب+ *bi+*, but without the spelling change: ب+الكتاب *bi+AlkitAbi* 'by the-book' remains بالكتاب *biAlkitAbi*.

- The interaction between the definite article and nominals starting with the letter ل *l* is complex. The letter ل *l* is considered a Sun Letter and as such the definite article is not deleted (although considered silent) and the first letter of the word is geminated: اللّغة *All~uɣaħ* (ال+لغة *Al+luɣaħ*) 'the language'. However, when the Alif of the definite article is deleted following the prepositional proclitic ل+ *li+*, the special status of the silent Lam of the definite article is revoked (only with Lam-initial nominals!). The result is an ambiguity for the whole class of Lam-initial nominals of whether the definite article is present or not following the prepositional proclitic +ل *li+*: للغة *llγħ* can be *liluγaħ* (لغة+ل *li+luγaħ*) 'for a language', or *lil~uγaħ* (لغة+ال+ل *li+Al+luγaħ*) 'for the language'.

4.3   FURTHER READINGS

In this chapter, we presented a general sketch of Arabic word morphology. For further details, consider some of the numerous available references and manuals [78, 77, 7, 38, 76, 81, 82].

CHAPTER 5

Computational Morphology Tasks

In this chapter, we discuss a set of common computational morphology tasks and the various approaches to address them. Most of these tasks are not an end in themselves, e.g., part-of-speech (POS) tagging or root extraction. They are support (enabling) technologies that are crucial for higher order applications such as machine translation (MT), information retrieval (IR) or automatic speech recognition (ASR). A few serve both roles (an end and a mean), in particular automatic diacritization, which can be seen as a standalone application that allows users to transform undiacritized text into diacritized text and as a tool to enable text to speech.

In the following section, we define a number of these tasks and relate them to each other. In the next three sections, we discuss in more detail three sets of tasks: morphological analysis/generation, tokenization and part-of-speech tagging. In the last section in this chapter, we compare and contrast in detail two commonly used tools for Arabic processing that handle different subsets of these tasks.

5.1 BASIC CONCEPTS

In this section, we first present some of the most commonly researched computational morphology tasks and enabling technologies. Then we discuss some common themes that go across them.

Morphological analysis refers to the process by which a word (typically defined orthographically) has all of its possible morphological analyses determined. Each analysis also includes a single choice of core part-of-speech (such as noun or verb; the exact set is a matter of choice). A morphological analysis can be either *form-based*, in which case we divide a word into all of its constituent morphemes, or *functional*, in which case we also interpret these morphemes. For example, in broken (i.e., irregular) plurals, a form-based analysis may not identify the fact that the word is a plural since it lacks the usual plural morpheme while a functional analysis would.

Morphological generation is essentially the reverse of morphological analysis. It is the process in which we map from an underlying representation of a word to a surface form (whether orthographic or phonological). The big question for generation is what representation to map from. The shallower the representation, the easier the task. Some representation may be less constrained than others and as such lead to multiple valid realizations. Functional representations are often thought of as the prototypical strating point for generation.

Morphological disambiguation refers to the choosing of a morphological analysis in context. This task for English is referred to as *POS tagging* since the standard POS tag set, though only comprising 46 tags, completely disambiguates English morphologically. In Arabic, the corresponding tag set may comprise upwards of 330,000 theoretically possible tags [51], so the task is much harder. Reduced tag sets have been proposed for Arabic, in which certain morphological differences are conflated, making the morphological disambiguation task easier. The term **POS tagging** is usually used for Arabic with respect to some of the smaller tag sets.

Tokenization (also sometimes called *segmentation*) refers to the division of a word into clusters of consecutive morphemes, one of which typically corresponds to the word stem, usually including inflectional morphemes. Tokenization involves two kinds of decisions that define a *tokenization scheme* [83]. First, we need to choose which types of morphemes to segment. There is no single correct segmentation. Second, we need to decide whether after separating some morphemes, we regularize the orthography of the resulting segments since the concatenation of morphemes can lead to spelling changes on their boundaries. For example, the Ta-Marbuta (ة ħ) appears as a regular Ta (ت t) when followed by a pronominal enclitic; however, when we segment the enclitic, it may be desirable to return the Ta-Marbuta to its word-final form. Usually, the term **segmentation** is only used when no orthography regularization takes place. Orthography regularization is desirable in NLP because it reduces data sparseness, as does tokenization itself.

Lemmatization is the mapping of a word form to its corresponding lemma, the canonical representative of its lexeme. Lemmatization is a specific instantiation of the more general task of **lexeme identification** in which ambiguous lemmas are further resolved. Lemmatization should not be confused with **stemming**, which maps the word into its stem. Another related task is **root extraction**, which focuses on identifying the root of the word.

Diacritization is the process of recovering missing diacritics (short vowels, nunation, the marker of the absence of a short vowel, and the gemination marker). Diacritization is closely related to morphological disambiguation and to lemmatization: for an undiacritized word form, different morphological feature values and different lemmas can both lead to different diacritizations. See Section 2.3.4.

The different tasks and subtasks discussed so far can be further qualified in the following terms:

- **Context**: Some tasks are non-contextual (out-of-context) and others are contextual (in-context). Out-of-context tasks focus on describing the set of possible values (such as POS tags, diacritizations, lemmas, roots, etc.) associated with a particular word, in general. In contrast, in-context tasks focus on selecting the context-appropriate values (again, whether it is a diacritization, POS tag, lemma, root, etc.). Morphological analysis and morphological disambiguation are the prototypical out-of-context / in-context tasks, respectively. Every task can be defined in these two modes. For example, out-of-context tokenization is a task to determine for a word all the possible tokenizations it can have. The most common form of tokenization is to select a specific choice in-context. Different computational approaches to tokenization may (or may not) explicitly or implicitly represent the out-of-context choices internally.

- **Richness**: Some tasks differ in being shallow or deep, coarse or fine-grained. For example, there is a large number of POS tagging sets that can be based on form-based morphemic morphology (shallow) or functional morphology (deep); they can focus on the core tag of the main word (coarse) or extend to cover all the values of the inflectional features and clitics. Similarly, tokenization includes different ways of representing the word tokens including lemmas, stems, roots or even specific generated word forms; and diacritization can be full or partial.

- **Directionality**: Some tasks are primarily analytical, i.e., mapping from the surface form to a deeper form; others are generative, i.e., mapping from a deeper form to a shallower form. Morphological analysis and generation are the prototypical tasks of these two categories. Most tasks involving the selection of a subset of the word features, such as the lemma, root, etc., are analytical. Normalized tokenization, a task that focuses on producing a naturally occurring surface form is partly analytical and partly generative. The word is effectively analyzed to determine its components, but then a correct form of the tokenized word is generated. For example, the handling of Ta-Marbuta in words containing a pronominal enclitic necessitates rewriting the word form once the enclitic is segmented off.

5.2   MORPHOLOGICAL ANALYSIS AND GENERATION

Arabic morphological analysis and generation have been a focus of research in natural language processing for a long time due to the complexity of Arabic morphology.

There are certain desiderata that are generally expected from a morphological analysis/generation system for any language. These include (1) coverage of the language of interest in terms of both lexical coverage (large scale) and coverage of morphological and orthographic phenomena (robustness); (2) the surface forms are mapped to/from a deep level of representation that abstracts as much as possible over language-specific morphological and orthographic features; (3) full reversibility of the system so it can be used as an analyzer or a generator; (4) usability in a wide range of natural language processing applications such as MT or IR; and finally, (5) availability for the research community. These issues are essential in the design of any Arabic morphological analysis and generation system.

Numerous morphological analyzers have been built for a wide range of application areas from IR to MT in a variety of linguistic theoretical contexts [84, 85, 86, 87, 88, 23, 89, 90, 91, 92, 80, 93, 67] (among others). Published efforts that target morphological generation or handle it as part of a joint analysis/generation solution include [86, 92, 94, 95, 96, 97] (among others). There is a lot of work that we do not discuss here. We urge readers to consider some of the survey articles on the topic [85]. In this section, we first present dimensions of variation among the different solutions to Arabic morphology. We then discuss, in more detail, four specific solutions that contrast in interesting ways.

5.2.1   DIMENSIONS OF VARIATION

The following is a list of common aspects of variation among different approaches and solutions to Arabic morphological analysis and generation.

- **Lexicon and Rules** The lexicon and rules are the core knowledge base of any morphological analysis/generation system. The lexicon typically holds all the specific lexical knowledge that can include allowed root-pattern combinations (open class information), affixations (closed class information), word inflectional classes (morphological order and compatibility information), and even additional useful information such as entry glosses in another language (this is not necessary for analysis/generation). Rules, on the other hand, are typically generalizations addressing lexically independent phenomena, such as Ta-Marbuta spelling among other things. In certain ways, the rules and the lexicon are on a continuum of generality of morphological information: the lexicon is essentially a long list of very specific rules. What information is represented in the lexicon versus the rules is completely up the designers of the system. Most cases are clear cut decisions, but some can go either way. Obviously, for a system to function correctly, the lexicon and rules should be in synch. This is why it is often hard (or not straightforward) to reuse lexicons or rules from one system in another. Rules and lexicon can be either manually created or automatically/semi-automatically learned. As the knowledge base of the system, lexicons and rules contrast with the analysis/generation engine that uses them to accomplish the task. In certain language specific implementation, this distinction is lost and the engine may contain hard-coded rules. A very simple morphological analyzer can consist of nothing but a lexicon that lists all possible word variations and their corresponding analyses. One example of this is the Egyptian Colloquial Arabic lexicon [52]. Some analyzers may allow rule-based back-off output that does not appear in their lexicon. For example, the Buckwalter Arabic Morphological Analyzer [23] typically produces additional proper noun readings not in its lexicon.

- **External Representation** Another difference among systems is their external (input/output) representation. For analysis, this is the representation target in the output of the system. Analyses can be shallow or deep. For example, targeting undiacritized morphemes is a form of shallow morphological analysis, while targeting lexeme and functional features is a form of deep analysis. Analyzers can also be selective or comprehensive (at either shallow or deep levels): a selective analyzer focuses on one or more specific morphological features, such as the identification of roots or the conjunction *wa+*. A comprehensive analyzer will attempt to capture all the different morphological information at the targeted depth. Selective analyzers are extremely useful tools for specific tasks, such as IR [89] or statistical MT [98]. They typically trade richer target with efficiency and even accuracy. For generation, the external representation includes both the input/source representation to be generated from and the output/target to generate into. Either can be deep or shallow, selective or comprehensive, with the output being shallower than the input. The most typical generation output is surface text, although other representations can be used inside a larger system that uses generation as an internal component (see TOKAN in Section 5.5.1). By contrast, the most typical generation input is quite deep, e.g., lexeme and features [95, 96]. An example of generation from shallow representations appears in statistical systems targeting Arabic, such as statistical machine translation into Arabic or language modeling of Arabic. Such systems may use some tokenization of Arabic that helps their models; however, the tokenized Arabic output needs to be *recombined* (generated) into surface untokenized form [61, 99, 13].

- **Internal Representation**

  The internal representation of lexicon and rules varies widely among different systems. For instance, some approaches use a simple prefix-stem-suffix representation [23, 96] as opposed to roots, patterns and affixations [86, 80]. Even the use of patterns can vary: morphemic patterns that require rules to be fully inflected or allomorphic patterns that require more complex lexicon entries [67]. The internal representation can be to some degree independent of the external representation. For instance, a lexicon using stems as its internal representation for lookup and matching can have hard-coded root and pattern information associated with each stem. The internal representation is often than not a bound representation that is not valid outside the confines of the system that uses it. As such, it should not be used under different assumptions of validity. For example, using a stem lexicon as dictionary for say spelling correction is an invalid use of this resource as many of its entries are partial spellings of words that combine inside the analysis/generation system that use the lexicon.

- **Engine** A variety of frameworks and programming languages have been used for analysis and generation, with various degrees of sophistication, robustness and efficiency. Some of the more complex solutions, such as using finite state machinery [86, 80], trade elegance and reversibility with lower speed and large model sizes as opposed to simpler code-based solutions [23, 96, 67].

- **Directionality** Some systems are focused on analysis only or generation only as opposed to both. Certain techniques are inherently reversible such as finite state machinery, but others are not, such as code-based solutions. If the analysis target representation is very shallow, generation may not be hard or meaningful.

- **Extensibility** Different approaches to morphology vary in how easily extensible they are. The more hard-coded and merged the rules and lexicon are, the more complex the extension process. One particular challenge is extending systems for MSA to handle Arabic dialects, which require updates to both rules and lexicons.

- **Performance and Usability** There are numerous dimensions for judging performance and usability. Coverage, in terms of both lexical coverage and coverage of morphological phenomena, is an important metric. Both analysis and generation systems should only output correct analyses and realizations (generated forms), respectively, and nothing but those analyses and realizations. Lower precision[1] or lower recall[2] in the output is not desirable. Another aspect of performance is robustness to incorrect/misspelled input. Some of the better analyzers propose alternative corrections as part of the analysis. This is rather necessary for handling cases of common spelling errors, such as mis-hamzated Alif forms. Finally, the question of usability is really dependent on the application the analyzer/generator is used in. For some applications, a system with lower coverage but appropriate depth in external output is far more desirable than a system that has high coverage but shallow or inappropriate output.

5.2.2 BAMA: BUCKWALTER ARABIC MORPHOLOGICAL ANALYZER

The Buckwalter Arabic morphological analyzer (BAMA) uses a concatenative lexicon-driven approach where morphotactics and orthographic rules are built directly into the lexicon itself instead of being specified in terms of general rules that interact to realize the output [88, 23]. The system has three components: the lexicon, the compatibility tables and the analysis engine.

Lexicon   An Arabic word is viewed as a concatenation of three regions, a prefix region, a stem region and a suffix region. The prefix and suffix regions can be null. Prefix and suffix lexicon entries cover all possible concatenations of Arabic prefixes and suffixes, respectively. For every lexicon entry, a morphological compatibility category, an English gloss and occasional part-of-speech (POS) data are specified. Stem lexicon entries are clustered around their specific lexeme, which is not used in the analysis process. Figure 5.1 shows sample entries:[3] the first six in the left column are prefixes; the rest in that column are suffixes; the right column contains seven stems belonging to three lexemes. The stem entries also include English glosses, which allow the lexicon to function as a dictionary. However, the presence of inflected forms, such as passives and plurals among these glosses makes them less usable as English lexemic translations.

Compatibility Tables   Compatibility tables specify which morphological categories are allowed to co-occur. For example, the morphological category for the prefix conjunction و/wa *wa+* 'and', Pref-Wa, is compatible with all noun stem categories and perfect verb stem categories. However, Pref-Wa is not compatible with imperfective verb stems because BAMA imperfective prefixes must contain a subject prefix morpheme. Similarly, the stem كتاب/kitAb *kitAb* of the the lexeme 1_كتاب/kitAb_1 *kitAb* 'book' has the category (Ndu), which is not compatible with the category of the feminine marker ة/ap *aħ*: NSuff-ap. The same stem, كتاب/kitAb *kitAb*, appears as one of the stems of the lexeme 1_كتابة/kitAbap_1 *kitAbaħ* 'writing' with a category that *requires* a suffix with the feminine marker. Cases such as these are quite common and pose a challenge to the use of stems as tokens since they can add unnecessary ambiguity.

---

[1]In this context, the precision of a particular system is defined as the number of correct analyses/realizations produced by the system divided by the number of all analyses/realizations it produced.

[2]In this context, the recall of a particular system is defined as the number of correct analyses/realizations produced by the system divided by the number of all analyses/realizations in the evaluation reference.

[3]The Buckwalter transliteration is preserved in examples of Buckwalter lexicon entries (see Chapter 2).

Figure 5.1: Some Buckwalter mophological database lexical entries.

و /wa	Pref-Wa	and	;; 1_كتب /katab-u_1			
بـ /bi	NPref-Bi	by/with	كتب /katab	PV	write	
وبـ /wabi	NPref-Bi	and + by/with	كُتب /kotub	IV	write	
الـ /Al	NPref-Al	the	كُتب /kutib	PV_Pass	be written	
بالـ /biAl	NPref-BiAl	with/by + the	كُتب /kotab	IV_Pass_yu	be written	
وبالـ /wabiAl	NPref-BiAl	and + with/by the	;; 1_كتاب /kitAb_1			
ـة /ap	NSuff-ap	[fem.sg.]	كتاب /kitAb	Ndu	book	
ـتان /atAni	NSuff-atAn	two	كُتب /kutub	N	books	
ـتين /atayoni	NSuff-tayn	two	;; 1_كتابة /kitAbap_1			
ـتاه /atAhu	NSuff-atAh	his/its two	كتاب /kitAb	Nap	writing	
ـات /At	NSuff-At	[fem.pl.]				

Analysis Engine   The analysis algorithm is rather simple since all of the hard decisions are coded in the lexicon and the compatibility tables: Arabic words are segmented into all possible sets of prefix, stem and suffix strings. In a valid segmentation, the three strings exist in the lexicon and are three-way compatible (prefix-stem, stem-suffix and prefix-suffix). BAMA produces multiple analyses that are tuples of full diacritization, lemma, and morpheme analysis and morpheme tags (also called the Buckwalter POS tag; see Figure 5.4). For example, the word للكتب *llktb* 'for the books' would return an analysis specifying its diacritization as *lilkutubi*, its lemma as *kitAb_1*, and its morpheme analysis and tags as *li/PREP+Al/DET+kutub/NOUN+i/CASE_DEF_GEN*.

There are currently three version of BAMA: BAMA 1.0/1.2 are both publicly available. BAMA 2.0 and SAMA 3.0/3.1 (Standard Arabic Morphological Analyzer, essentially BAMA 3.0/3.1) are available through the LDC. See Appendix D for links to these resources.

5.2.3   ALMORGEANA: ARABIC LEXEME-BASED MORPHOLOGICAL GENERATION AND ANALYSIS

ALMORGEANA (or Almor for short) is a morphological analysis and generation system built on top of the BAMA/SAMA databases [88, 23].[4] Unlike BAMA, which focuses on analysis to a surfacy form-based representation, ALMORGEANA analyzes to, and generates from the functional (lexeme-and-feature) level of representation. Figure 5.2 lists the different features and their possible values.[5] To that effect, the ALMORGEANA lexicon extends the BAMA morphological databases with lexeme and

---

[4]A previous publication about ALMORGEANA focused on the generation component of the system which was named Aragen [96].

[5]It should be noted that ALMORGEANA's current version does not completely handle functional morphology. It rather has a mix of form-based and functional features.

feature keys, which are used in analysis and generation. This work on ALMORGEANA is close in spirit to the extensions to BAMA in the functional morphology system, ELIXIRFM [67] (Section 5.2.5).

Analysis   Analysis in ALMORGEANA is similar to BAMA: the word is segmented into prefix-stem-suffix triples, whose individual presence and bilateral compatibility is checked against the BAMA databases. The difference lies in an extra step that uses lexeme and feature keys associated with stem, prefix and suffix string sequences to construct the lexeme and feature output. For example, the word للكتب *llktb* 'for the books' returns the following analysis:[6]

(5.1) lilkutubi=[kitAb_1 POS:N l+ Al+ +PL +GEN]=books

Here, *lilkutubi* is the diacritized form of the word. Inside the square brackets, we find the nominal lexeme *kitAb_1* 'book', the proclitic preposition *l+* 'to/for', the definite article *Al+* 'the', the feature *+PL* 'plural' and the feature *+GEN* 'genitive case'. Most of the information in the feature set is directly derivable from the morpheme tags in the BAMA output for the same word: li/PREP+Al/DET+kutub/NOUN+i/CASE_DEF_GEN. However, the feature +PL indicating plurality is not. It is part of the extension done in ALMORGEANA in processing the BAMA databases.

Generation   In generation, the input is a lexeme and feature set. The generated output is a fully inflected and diacritized word. For example, [kitAb_1 POS:N l+ Al+ +PL +GEN] generates *lilkutubi*. The process of generating from lexeme and features is similar to analysis except that lexeme and feature keys used instead of string sequences. First, the feature set is expanded to include all forms of under-specified obligatory features, such as case, gender, number, etc. Next, all lexeme and feature keys in the ALMORGEANA lexicon that fully match any subset of the lexeme and expanded feature set are selected. All combinations of keys that completely cover the lexeme and expanded feature set are matched up in prefix-stem-suffix triples. Then, each key is converted to its corresponding prefix, stem or suffix string. The same compatibility tables used in analysis are used to accept or reject prefix-stem-suffix triples. Finally, all unique accepted triples are concatenated and output. In the case that no surface form is found, a back-off solution that attempts to regenerate after discarding one of the input features is explored.

See [97] for more details on ALMORGEANA and an evaluation of its performance. ALMORGEANA is the analyzer/generator used inside the MADA toolkit, which we discuss in detail in Section 5.5.

5.2.4   MAGEAD: MORPHOLOGICAL ANALYSIS AND GENERATION FOR ARABIC AND ITS DIALECTS

MAGEAD is a morphological analyzer and generator for the Arabic language family, by which we mean both MSA and the spoken dialects. MAGEAD relates (bidirectionally) a lexeme and a set of linguistic features to a surface word form through a sequence of transformations. In a generation perspective, the features are translated to abstract morphemes, which are then ordered, and expressed

---

[6]The example used in this book is based on ALMORGEANA version 2.0.

Figure 5.2: ALMORGEANA features and their possible values (version 2.0). Clitic features (such as conjunction and preposition) are optional; however, all other features are obligatory (although in some cases POS dependent, e.g., nouns do not take aspect or voice). *State* is handled using two features: definiteness and possession.

Feature Type	Values and Definitions	
Part-of-Speech	POS:N *Noun*, POS:PN *Proper Noun*, POS:V *Verb*, POS:AJ *Adjective*, POS:AV *Adverb*, POS:PRO *Pronoun*, POS:P *Preposition*, POS:D *Determiner*, POS:C *Conjunction*, POS:NEG *Negative particle*, POS:NUM *Number*, POS:AB *Abbreviation*, POS:IJ *Interjection*, and POS:PX *Punctuation*	
Conjunction	w+ *'and'*, f+ *'so'*	
Preposition	b+ *'by, with'*, k+ *'like'*, l+ *'for, to'*	
Verbal Particle	s+ *'will'*, l+ *so as to*	
Definite Article	Al+ *the*	
Gender	+FEM *Feminine*, +MASC *Masculine*	
Number	+SG *Singular*, +DU *Dual*, +PL *Plural*	
Case	+NOM *Nominative*, +ACC *Accusative*, +GEN *Genitive*	
Definiteness	+DEF *Definite*, +INDEF *Indefinite*	
Possession	+POSS *Construct state*, +NOPOSS *Not construct state*	
Verb Aspect	+PV *Perfective*, +IV *Imperfective*, +CV *Imperative*	
Voice	+ACT *Active*, +PASS *Passive*	
Mood	MOOD:I *Indicative*, MOOD:S *Subjunctive*, MOOD:J *Jussive*	
Subject	+S:PerGenNum	**Per**son = {1,2,3}
Object	+O:PerGenNum	**Gen**der = {M,F}
Possessive	+P:PerGenNum	**Num**ber = {S,D,P}

as concrete morphemes. The concrete templatic morphemes are interdigitated and affixes added. Separate morphophonemic and orthographic rewrite rules are applied. MAGEAD's implementation of rewrite rules follows [100] in using a multi-tape Finite-state transducer (FST) representation. This is similar to other FST-based implementations for Arabic morphology [86]. The use of explicit linguistic rules inside MAGEAD distinguishes it from other more opaque implementations such as BAMA and ALMORGEANA, in which the rules are effectively hard-coded in the form of the stem. This transparency makes MAGEAD a more complex system in certain ways, but it also makes it easier to extend to new dialects. The distinction between different levels of representation also allows using MAGEAD for a variety of tasks such as mapping from an orthographic form to a phonological form. In the rest of this section, we discuss MAGEAD's components in more detail using an illustrative example.

Lexeme and Features   MAGEAD's morphological analyses are represented in terms of a lexeme and features. MAGEAD defines the *lexeme* to be a triple consisting of a root, a *morphological behavior class* (MBC), and a meaning index. It is through this view of the lexeme that MAGEAD can both have a lexeme-based representation, and operate without a lexicon (as may be needed for dealing with a dialect). In fact, because lexemes have internal structure, MAGEAD can hypothesize lexemes on the fly without having to make wild guesses. For example, the word ازدهرت *Aizdaharat* 'she/it flourished' has the following lexeme-and-features analysis in MAGEAD:

(5.2) ROOT:zhr MBC:VERB-VIII POS:V PER:3 GEN:F NUM:SG ASPECT:PERF

Morphological Behavior Class   An MBC maps sets of linguistic feature-value pairs to sets of abstract morphemes. For example, MBC VERB-VIII maps the feature-value pair ASPECT:PERF to the abstract root morpheme [PAT_PV:VIII], which in MSA corresponds to the concrete root morpheme *V1tV2V3*, while the MBC VERB-II maps ASPECT:PERF to the abstract root morpheme [PAT_PV:II], which in MSA corresponds to the concrete root morpheme *1V22V3*. MBCs are defined using a hierarchical representation with non-monotonic inheritance. The hierarchy allows MAGEAD to specify only once those feature-to-morpheme mappings for all MBCs that share them. For example, the root node of the MBC hierarchy is a word, and all Arabic words share certain mappings, such as that from the linguistic feature CONJ:w to the clitic *w+*. This means that all Arabic words can take a cliticized conjunction. Similarly, the object pronominal clitics are the same for all transitive verbs, no matter what their templatic pattern is. The design of MAGEAD assumes that the MBC hierarchy is variant-independent, i.e., dialect/MSA independent. Although as more variants are added, some modifications may be needed.

Morphemes   To keep the MBC hierarchy variant-independent, MAGEAD uses a variant-independent representation of the morphemes that the MBC hierarchy maps to. These morphemes are referred to as *abstract morphemes* (AMs). The AMs are then ordered into the surface order of the corresponding concrete morphemes. The ordering of AMs is specified in a variant-independent context-free grammar. If we try to generate from the example (5.2), we get the following at this point:

(5.3) [Root:zhr][PAT_PV:VIII][VOC_PV:VIII-act] + [SUBJSUF_PV:3FS]

Note that as the root, pattern, and vocalism are not ordered with respect to each other, they are simply juxtaposed. The '+' sign indicates the ordering of affixival morphemes. Only now are the AMs translated to *concrete morphemes* (CMs), which are concatenated in the specified order. Our example becomes:

(5.4) <zhr,V1tV2V3,iaa> +at

Simple interdigitation of root, pattern and vocalism then yields the form *iztahar+at*. This form is incorrect since no morphological rules have been applied yet.

Rules   MAGEAD has two types of rules. *Morphophonemic/phonological rules* map from the morphemic representation to the phonological and orthographic representations. *Orthographic rules* rewrite only the orthographic representation. These include, for example, rules for using the *shadda* (consonant doubling diacritic). For our example, we get /izdaharat/ at the phonological level (see Section 4.2.4). Using standard MSA diacritized orthography, our example becomes *Aizdaharat* (in transliteration). Removing the diacritics turns this into the more familiar ازدهرت *Azdhrt*. Note that in analysis mode, MAGEAD hypothesizes all possible diacritics (a finite number, even in combination) and performs the analysis on the resulting multi-path automaton.

For a fuller discussion of MAGEAD, see [92, 80, 101].

5.2.5   ELIXIRFM: ELIXIR ARABIC FUNCTIONAL MORPHOLOGY

Elixir Functional Morphology (ELIXIRFM) is a high-level implementation of Arabic functional morphology [67, 102]. It was inspired by the methodology of Functional Morphology [103] and initially relied on a re-processed Buckwalter lexicon [88].

Morphotactics   In addition to using various morphophonemic rules at the boundaries of affixes (such as Ta-Marbuta alternations), one of the distinctive abstractions in ELIXIRFM is that word forms are encoded via carefully designed morphophonemic patterns that combine with roots or word stems. These patterns are mostly allomorphic, i.e., they encode the effect of root-type interaction with the morphemic template. For example, the root and pattern of the word ميزان *miyzAn* 'weight scales/measure/meter' is *wzn + MICAL* (in ELIXIRFM notation or *wzn + miy2A3* in a more surfacy notation) as opposed to the morphemic pattern indicating instruments *wzn + mi12A3*. By design, this avoids both (a) defining a rule to convert *miwzAn to *miyzAn* as in MAGEAD (Section 5.2.4) and (b) listing the surface forms for each lexical item as in BAMA (Section 5.2.2). In addition to such cases, there are some rules for handling regular root-pattern transformations in ELIXIRFM, e.g., *t*-assimilation of Form-VIII verbs (Section 4.2.4). For instance, the verb ازدهرت *Aizdaharat* used earlier would receive the following analysis in ELIXIRFM:

(5.5) ["prosper","flourish"]
```
      Verb  []   []   []   [VIII]
      izdahar  "z h r"  IFtaCaL
      VP-A-3FS--  izdaharat  "z h r"  IFtaCaL |<< "at"
```

The first line above is the English gloss. The second line summarizes the information of the lexical entry for the lexeme. In this case, the three bracket pairs after "Verb" would list any lexically dependent or exceptional perfective, imperfective, and imperative verb stems, but they are empty in our example because this information is inferred internally by the ELIXIRFM system. The final [VIII] indicates explicitly for the user that the pattern *IFtaCaL* belongs to the Form VIII derivational class. The third line indicates the lemma, root and lemma pattern (which happens to be the same as the pattern of the analyzed word in this example). The last line indicates the POS (See Section 5.4.5), the phonological form of the word, the root, the pattern and the suffix. Note that the pattern associated with the verb has the unassimilated *t* in it.

Phonology and Orthography Another unique feature of ELIXIRFM is that it internally represents its lexical items in a phonemic representation, which is then converted into a string of characters in the extended ArabTEX [16] notation. This notation can then be further converted into either Arabic orthography or phonetic transcription. This allows ELIXIRFM to avoid defining orthographic rules, and it basically separates phonology from orthography in a way similar to MAGEAD (Section 5.2.4).

Tokenization Finally, ELIXIRFM's external representation includes a basic tokenization decision that follows the conventions of the Penn Arabic Treebank and the Prague Arabic Dependency Treebank (Section 6.2). Each token receives its own POS tag and separate analysis. For example, the following is the ELIXIRFM analysis of للكتب *lilkutubi* 'for the books', which we discussed earlier:

```
(5.6) ["for","to"]
      Prep  []
      li  "l"  "li"

      ["book"]
      Noun  [FuCuL]  []
      kitAb  "k t b"  FiCAL

      li-al-kutubi

      P---------  li  "l"  "li"
      N------P2D  al-kutubi  "k t b"  al >| FuCuL |<< "i"
```

The core of ELIXIRFM is written in the functional programming language Haskell, while interfaces supporting lexicon editing and other interactions are written in Perl. See Appendix D for links to ELIXIRFM and its online interface.

5.3 TOKENIZATION

The common wisdom in NLP is that tokenization of Arabic words through decliticization and reductive orthographic normalization is helpful for many applications such as language modeling (LM), IR and statistical MT (SMT). Tokenization and normalization reduce sparsity and perplexity and decrease the number of out-of-vocabulary (OOV) words.

5.3.1 TOKENIZATION SCHEMES AND TECHNIQUES

We distinguish between tokenization schemes and tokenization techniques [83]. The scheme defines what the target tokenization is; whereas the technique is about how to implement it. Tokenization schemes vary along two dimensions: what to split (segmentation) and what form to represent the various split parts (regularization). There is a very large number of possible tokenization schemes.

In the context of IR, the form of tokenization often used is called *stemming* [104]. In *stemming* split clitics and other non-core morphemes are simply deleted.

Tokenization techniques can be as simple as a greedy regular expression or more complex involving morphological analysis and disambiguation (see Section 5.5). Since morphological ambiguity in Arabic is rampant, the more complex a scheme the harder it is to correctly tokenize in context. The more complex techniques have been shown helpful in that regard [83, 105]; however, it should be noted that in certain contexts *less is more*: e.g., phrase-based SMT only benefits from complex tokenizations with little training data where sparsity is a big problem. As more training data is introduced, complex tokenizations actually start to hurt compared to simpler tokenizations [83, 105].

5.3.2   DETOKENIZATION

In certain contexts, when Arabic is the output language, it is desirable to produce proper Arabic that is orthographically correct; i.e., tokenized and orthographically normalized words should be detokenized and enriched (orthographically corrected). As an example, the output of English-to-Arabic MT systems is reasonably expected to be proper Arabic regardless of the preprocessing used to optimize the MT performance. Anything less is comparable to producing all lower cased English or uncliticized and undiacritized French. Detokenization may not be a simple task because there are several morphological adjustments that should be applied in the process [99, 13, 106]. Obviously, the more complex the tokenization, the harder is detokenization.

5.3.3   VARIOUS TOKENIZATION SCHEMES

In discussing tokenization, it is important to remember that there is no single optimal tokenization. What is optimal for IR may not be true for SMT. Also, what is optimal for a specific SMT implementation may not be the same for another. Consistency within an implementation is desirable and it often puts constraints on what various components could be used. For example, most off-the-shelf syntactic parsers for Arabic use the Penn Arabic Treebank tokenization. A system for SMT using automatic parses needs to make sure its internal tokenization is consistent with the parser's or at least address the problem in some other way.

The following is a description of some commonly used tokenization schemes [83, 105, 107, 99, 13]. This is not a complete set. It is intended to illustrate variety. See Figure 5.3 for an example comparing these tokenizations.

• **ST**: Simple Tokenization is the baseline preprocessing scheme. It is limited to splitting off punctuation and numbers from words. For example, the last non-white-space string in the example sentence in Figure 5.3, "trkyA." is split into two tokens: "trkyA" and ".". An example of splitting numbers from words is the case of the conjunction +و w+ 'and,' which can prefix digits such as when a list of numbers is described: ١٥ و w15 'and 15'. This scheme requires no disambiguation. Any diacritics that appear in the input are typically removed in this scheme. This scheme is usually used as input to produce the other schemes. Sometimes this tokenization is referred to as **D0** (no decliticization).

- **ON**: Orthographic Normalization addresses the issue of sub-optimal spelling in Arabic by making consistent choices. Normalization is typically reductive (RED), i.e., it conflates multiple forms into one. Most typically, the various forms of Hamzated Alif and Alif-Maqsura/dotted Ya are normalized into bare Alif and dotted Ya, respectively. In enriched normalization (ENR), the contextually-appropriate form of these letters is determined [13]. An example of **ON** can be seen in the spelling of the last letter in the first and fifth words in the example in Figure 5.3 (wsynhý and Alý). Either type of normalization can in principle be applied to any tokenization scheme.

Figure 5.3: Example with different tokenization schemes: **ST/D0** simple tokenization, **ON**$_{Enr}$ (enriched orthographic normalization), **ON**$_{Red}$ (reduced orthographic normalization), **D1, D2, D3/S1** and **S2** (different degrees of decliticization), **WA** (wa+ decliticization), **TB** and **TB**$_{old}$ (new and old Arabic Treebank tokenization, respectively), **MR** (morphemes), **LEM** (lemmatization), **LEM+TB** (lemmatization with TB) and **ENX** (a tokenization equivalent to D3+LEM+POS with markers for verbal subject).

	وسينهى الرئيس جولته بزيارة الى تركيا.					
Input (ST/D0)	wsynhý	Alrýys	jwlth	bzyArħ	Alý	trkyA .
Gloss	and will finish	the president tour his	with visit	to	Turkey .
English	The president will finish his tour with a visit to Turkey.					
Scheme						
ON$_{Enr}$	wsynhy	Alrŷys	jwlth	bzyArħ	Âly	trkyA .
ON$_{Red}$	wsynhy	Alrŷys	jwlth	bzyArħ	Aly	trkyA .
D1	w+ synhy	Alrŷys	jwlth	bzyArħ	Âlý	trkyA .
D2	w+ s+ ynhy	Alrŷys	jwlth	b+ zyArħ	Âlý	trkyA .
D3/S1	w+ s+ ynhy	Al+ rŷys	jwlħ +h	b+ zyArħ	Âlý	trkyA .
S2	w+s+ ynhy	Al+ rŷys	jwlħ +h	b+ zyArħ	Âlý	trkyA .
WA	w+ synhy	Alrŷys	jwlth	bzyArħ	Âlý	trkyA .
TB	w+ s+ ynhy	Alrŷys	jwlħ +h	b+ zyArħ	Âlý	trkyA .
TB$_{old}$	w+ synhy	Alrŷys	jwlħ +h	b+ zyArħ	Âlý	trkyA .
MR	w+ s+ y+ nhy	Al+ rŷys	jwl +ħ +h	b+ zyAr +ħ	Âlý	trkyA .
LEM	Ânhý	rŷys	jwlħ	zyArħ	Âlý	trkyA .
LEM+TB	w+ s+ Ânhý	rŷys	jwlħ +h	b+ zyArħ	Âlý	trkyA .
ENX	w+ s+ Ânhý$_{VBP}$ +S3$_{MS}$ Al+ rŷys$_{NN}$	jwlħ$_{NN}$ +h b+ zyArħ$_{NN}$	Âlý$_{IN}$ trkyA$_{NNP}$.			

- **D1, D2, and D3**: Decliticization (degree 1, 2 and 3) are schemes that split off clitics. **D1** splits off the class of conjunction clitics (*w+* and *f+*) and the infrequent interrogative clitic. **D2** is the same as **D1** plus splitting off the class of particles (*l+*, *k+*, *b+* and *s+*). Finally, **D3** splits off what **D2** does in addition to the definite article *Al+* and all pronominal enclitics.

- **WA**: Decliticizing the conjunction *w+*. It is similar to D1, but without including *f+*. This simple tokenization is reported to be optimal for SMT with very large data sets [98].

- **TB**: Penn Arabic Treebank Tokenization. This is the same tokenization scheme used in the Arabic Treebank [9]. This is similar to **D3** but without the splitting off of the definite article *Al+*. An older version of **TB** did not split the future particle *s+*.
- **S1 and S2** are schemes used by [99]. S1 and S2 are essentially the same as D3. S2 joins the various proclitics in one string.
- **MR**: Morphemes. This scheme breaks up words into stem and affixival morphemes. It is identical to the initial tokenization used by [108].
- **LEM**: Lemmas. This scheme reduces every word to its lemma. Lemmas can also be used with other tokenization schemes where they are used for each split token; see **LEM+TB** in Figure 5.3.
- **ENX**: English-like tokenization used by [105]. This scheme is intended to minimize differences between Arabic and English. It decliticizes similarly to **D3** but uses Lemmas and POS tags instead of the regenerated words. The POS tag set used is the Bies reduced Arabic Treebank tag set (Section 5.4.2) [9, 109]. Additionally, the subject inflection is indicated explicitly as a separate token. Obviously, many other variations are possible here.

5.4   POS TAGGING

Part-of-Speech (POS) tagging is the task of assigning a contextually appropriate morpho-syntactic tag to every word in a sentence. The tags are selected from a tag set that in principle should be well defined and comprehensive. Because of its rich morphology, Arabic POS tag sets can be very large. Many researchers working on Arabic prefer to work with smaller reduced sets. The size (and granularity) of an Arabic POS tag set can vary wildly. On one end, the traditional Arabic grammar POS classification is a three-way distinction into noun, verb and particle (اسم ، فعل وحرف). This is a very coarse classification, and is often not used computationally. On the other end, the full-form (untokenized) Buckwalter tag set based on Arabic morphemes can hypothetically reach over 330,000 tags. The tag set size also interacts with whether the text is tokenized or not (and in which tokenization scheme). In principle, the POS tag of an untokenized word is equal to the stringing of the POS tags of its tokens.

Although the larger sets are more complete and can better help performance of higher order tasks (under gold/oracle conditions), they tend to be very hard to predict well [110]. Reduced tag sets can still be predicted accurately and have been shown useful for different NLP applications [111]. One reduced tag set, CATiB's, is argued for from the point of reducing manual treebanking annotation load [112]. There is no overall optimal POS tag set. Different applications and implementations will need different tag sets.

In the rest of this section, we present seven tag sets for Arabic with different degrees of granularity. These tag sets are used in different available resources. The tag sets are contrasted in one example in Figure 5.6. The ALMORGEANA analysis, which is used in MADA (Section 5.5.1) and which can be thought of as another POS tag, is included for comparison.

POS tagging techniques developed for other languages can be used for Arabic just the same. Much work has happened on this front [113, 109, 51, 114, 115, 116, 117]. We present two approaches in Section 5.5.

5.4.1   THE BUCKWALTER TAG SET

The Buckwalter tag set, developed by Tim Buckwalter, is a form-based tag set that can be used for tokenized and untokenized text. The untokenized tags are what is produced by BAMA (Section 5.2.2). The tokenized tags are used in the Penn Arabic Treebank (PATB) (Section 6.2.1). The tokenized variants are derived from the untokenized tags. Both set variants use the same basic 70 or so subtag symbols (such as DET 'determiner', NSUFF 'nominal suffix', ADJ 'adjective' and ACC 'accusative') [82]. See Figure 5.4.[7] These subtags are combined to form around 170 morpheme tags (135 in PATB 1v2.0 and 169 in PATB 3v3.1), such as NSUFF_FEM_SG 'feminine singular nominal suffix' and CASE_DEF_ACC 'accusative definite'. The word tags are constructed out of one or more morpheme tags, e.g., DET+ADJ+NSUFF_FEM_SG+CASE_DEF_ACC for the word الجميلة *Aljmylħ* 'the beautiful' in Figure 5.6.

Tokenized and untokenized tags differ in the number of subtags that can combine. For example, in the PATB Buckwalter tag set, the CONJ and PRON tags are not used in the token tags but are tags of their own. A Buckwalter untokenized tag set can reach thousands of tags and a Buckwalter tokenized tag set is around 500 tags or so. Several variants of this tag set are used in different versions of the BAMA/SAMA analyzer and in the different versions of the PATB.

5.4.2   REDUCED BUCKWALTER TAG SETS: BIES, KULICK, ERTS

The Buckwalter tag set is considered very rich for many computational problems and approaches. Several tag sets have been developed that reduce it to a "manageable" size. The CATiB tag set discussed earlier is an extreme form of reduction compared to the three tag sets we discuss here.

The Bies Tag Set

The Bies tag set was developed by Ann Bies and Dan Bikel as collapsed variant of Arabic tags into a smaller set (around 20+; [109] used a 24 tag variant) of tags inspired by the Penn English Treebank POS tag set [118]. Although this was an experimental set, it has been used widely for POS tagging Arabic [109, 51, 119]. The tag set is linguistically coarse as it ignores many distinctions

---

[7]Figure 5.4 contains some parameters which we define here:
  <PGN> *person-gender-number*, <GN> *gender-number*,
  person: 1 *first*, 2 *second*, 3 *third*, φ *unspecified*
  gender: M *masculine*, F *feminine*, φ *unspecified*
  number: S *singular* D *dual* P *plural* 0 unspecified
  <Mood>: I *indicative*, S *subjunctive*, J *jussive*, SJ *subjective/jussive*
  <Gen>: _MASC *masculine*, _FEM *feminine*
  <Num>: _SG *singular*, _DU *dual*, _PL *plural*
  <Cas>: _NOM *nominative*, _ACC *accusative*, _GEN *genitive*, _ACCGEN *accusative/genitive*, φ *unspecified*
  <Stt>: _POSS *construct/possessor*, φ *not construct*
  <Def>: _DEF *definite*, _INDEF *indefinite*

Figure 5.4: Buckwalter tag set components. See footnote 7.

Verbs	
VERB	verb
PSEUDO_VERB	pseudo-verb
PV	perfective verb
PV_PASS	perfective passive verb
PVSUFF_DO:<PGN>	direct object of perfective verb
PVSUFF_SUBJ:<PGN>	subject of perfective verb
IV	imperfective verb
IV_PASS	imperfective passive verb
IVSUFF_DO:<PGN>	imperfective verb direct object
IV<PGN>	imperfective verb prefix
IVSUFF_SUBJ:<PGN>	imperfective verb subject
_MOOD:<Mood>	and mood suffix
CV	imperative (command) verb
CVSUFF_DO:<PGN>	imperative verb object
CVSUFF_SUBJ:<PGN>	imperative verb subject

Particles	
PREP	preposition
CONJ	conjunction
SUB_CONJ	subordinating conjunction
PART	particle
CONNEC_PART	connective particle
EMPHATIC_PART	emphatic particle
FOCUS_PART	focus particle
FUT_PART	future particle
INTERROG_PART	interrogative particle
JUS_PART	jussive particle
NEG_PART	negative particle
RC_PART	response conditional particle
RESTRIC_PART	restrictive particle
VERB_PART	verb particle
VOC_PART	vocative particle

Nominals	
NOUN	noun
NOUN_NUM	nominal/cardinal number
NOUN_QUANT	quantifier noun
NOUN.VN	deverbal noun
NOUN_PROP	proper noun
ADJ	adjective
ADJ_COMP	comparative adjective
ADJ_NUM	adjectival/ordinal number
ADJ.VN	deverbal adjective
ADJ_PROP	proper adjective
ADV	adverb
REL_ADV	relative adverb
INTERROG_ADV	interrogative adverb
PRON	pronoun
PRON_<PGN>	personal pronoun
POSS_PRON_<PGN>	possessive personal pronoun
DEM_PRON_<GN>	demonstrative pronoun
REL_PRON	relative pronoun
INTERROG_PRON	interrogative pronoun
NSUFF<Gen><Num><Cas><Stt>	nominal suffix
CASE<Def><Cas>	
DET	determiner

Other	
PUNC	punctuation
ABBREV	abbreviation
INTERJ	interjection
LATIN	latin script
FOREIGN	foreign word
TYPO	typographical error
PARTIAL	partial word
DIALECT	dialectal word

in Arabic, e.g., JJ is used for all adjectives regardless of their inflections (the English tag, obviously, has no inflections). Of course, given Arabic's complex agreement rules (Section 6.1.3), this may be sufficient unless a much better model is used. Another example is the use of plural tags to mean both plural and dual. This tag set has also been referred to as the **Reduced Tag Set (RTS)** [120] and as the **PennPOS tag set**. The following are the tags in this set:

- **Nominals**:

    - **Nouns**: NN *singular common noun or abbreviation*, NNS *plural/dual common noun*, NNP *singular proper noun*, NNPS *plural/dual proper noun*

    - **Pronouns**: PRP *personal pronoun*, PRP$ *possessive personal pronoun*, WP *relative pronoun*

    - **Other**: JJ *adjective*, RB *adverb*, WRB *relative adverb*, CD *cardinal number*, FW *foreign word*

- **Particles**: CC *coordinating conjunction*, DT *determiner/demonstrative pronoun*, RP *particle*, IN *preposition or subordinating conjunction*

- **Verbs**: VBP *active imperfect verb*, VBN *passive imperfect/perfect verb*, VBD *active perfect verb*, VB *imperative verb*

- **Other**: UH *interjection*, PUNC *punctuation*,[8] NUMERIC_COMMA *the letter و r used as a comma*, NO_FUNC *unanalyzed word*

The Kulick Tag Set

The Kulick tag set was developed by Seth Kulick and shown to be beneficial for Arabic Parsing [119]. The Kulick tag set contains around 43 tags that extend the Bies tag set. The extensions can be classified into four categories:

- The following punctuation marks are given a tag that corresponds to their exact form: [,], [:], [.], ["], [-LRB-],[9] and [-RRB-].

- The following nouns and adjectives are marked explicitly: quantifier nouns (NOUN_QUANT), comparative adjectives (ADJ_COMP), adjectival/ordinal numbers (ADJ_NUM) and deverbals (DV).

- Demonstratives and definite article are distinguished as DEM and DT, respectively.

- The presence of a definite article (DT) is indicated in the tag, e.g., DT+NN, DT+ADJ_COMP, DT+CD, and DT+JJ.

---

[8]Although sometimes *comma*, *period* and *colon* can be POS tagged as themselves, e.g., the tag for the *comma* is [,].
[9]-LRB- is *left round bracket*; and -RRB- is *right round bracket*.

The Extended Reduced Tag Set (ERTS)

The Extended Reduced Tag Set (ERTS) is the base tag set used in the AMIRA system (see Section 5.5.2). ERTS has 72 tags. It is a subset of the full Buckwalter morphological set defined over tokenized text. ERTS is a superset of the Bies/RTS tag set. In addition to the information contained in the Bies tags, ERTS encodes additional morphological features such as number, gender, and definiteness on nominals only. Definiteness (or precisely here the presence of the definite article) is marked as a binary feature with D (for present article) or ϕ (nothing) for no article. Gender is marked with an F, an M or nothing, corresponding to *feminine*, *masculine* or the absence of gender marking, respectively. Number is marked with (Du) for *dual* or (S) for *plural*. The absence of any labels is used for singular. For example, while Bies nouns are tagged as either NN or NNS, indicating only number, ERTS nouns tags represent definiteness and gender in addition to number, e.g., DNNM is a definite (i.e., with article) singular masculine noun. A full description of ERTS is presented in [111]. The ERTS set was shown to be taggable at the same accuracy of the Bies tag set but adding much more value as learning features to a higher order computational task, Base Phrase Chunking [111].

5.4.3   THE CATIB POS TAG SET

The CATiB tag set was developed for the Columbia Arabic Treebank project (CATiB) [112, 121]. There are only six POS tags in CATiB. The simplicity of the POS tag set is intended to speed up human annotation yet maintain important distinctions.

- **VRB** is used for all verbs including the class of *incomplete verbs* (أفعال ناقصة), also known as *Kana and its sisters* (كان وأخواتها).

- **VRB-PASS** is used for passive-voice verbs.

- **NOM** is used for all nominals such as noun, adjective, adverb, active/passive participle, deverbal noun (مصدر *maSdar*), pronoun (personal, relative, demonstrative, interrogative), numbers (including digits), and interjections.

- **PROP** is used for proper nouns.

- **PRT** is used for all particles. This is a superset including several closed-classes, e.g., prepositions, conjunctions, negative particles, definite article, etc.

- **PNX** is used for all punctuation marks.

An automatically deterministically extended version of CATiB tag set, dubbed catibEx, has also been shown useful for parsing [110]. The extensions, which simply attach greedily-matched prefix/suffix sequences to the tag, increase the tag set size to 44. For example, the NOM tag of the world الكاتبون *AlkAtbwn* 'the writers' is extended to Al+NOM+wn. The CATiB tag set has also been shown to be easily extensible (given complete annotated trees) to the Kulick tag set at 98.5% accuracy [112].

5.4.4   THE KHOJA TAG SET

The Khoja tag set, developed by Shereen Khoja, is one of the earliest almost complete computational tag sets for Arabic [122, 113]. The tag set is functional (as opposed to form-based); however, it does not mark construct state (as opposed to definite/indefinite states), and it does not have complete coverage. For instance, proper nouns and pronouns are not marked for case. The tag set contains 177 tags: 103 nouns, 57 verbs, 9 particles, 7 residuals, and 1 punctuation. The tags are constructed by concatenating single and two letter markers in a specific sequences followed by specific attributes. See Figure 5.5. For example the tag NASgMNI stands for *singular masculine nominative indefinite adjective*; and the tag VIDu3FJ stands for *third-person dual feminine jussive imperfect verb*. The set is defined over non-cliticized words, but it can be used for cliticized word through simple concatenation with a separator. For example, بٱسمه *b+Asm+h* 'in his name' receives the tag PPr_NCSgMGI_NPrPSg3M.

5.4.5   THE PADT TAG SET

The PADT tag set, used in the ELIXIRFM analyzer (Section 5.2.5), was developed for use in the Prague Arabic Dependency Treebank [123, 114, 67]. The PADT tag set is defined for ATB tokenized Arabic. Each tag consists of two parts: *POS* and *Features*. The *POS* component consists of two characters:

- **VI** imperfect verb, **VP** perfect verb, **VC** imperative verb

- **N-** noun, **A-** adjective, **D-** adverb, **Z-** proper noun, **Y-** abbreviation

- **S-** pronoun, **SD** demonstrative pronoun, **SR** relative pronoun

- **F-** particle, **FI** interrogative particle, **FN** negative particle, **C-** conjunction, **P-** preposition, **I-** interjection

- **G-** graphical symbol, **Q-** number, **--** isolated definite article

The *Feature* part of the tag consists of seven character string. Each character efficiently encodes the value of the feature assigned to the character position:

- Mood: **I**ndicative, **S**ubjunctive, **J**ussive or **D** (if ambiguous between S and J)

- Voice: **A**ctive or **P**assive

- Person: **1** speaker, **2** addressee, **3** others

- Gender: **M**asculine or **F**eminine

- Number: **S**ingular, **D**ual or **P**lural

- Case: **1**=nominative, **2**=genitive or **4**=accusative

Figure 5.5:   The Khoja tag set.

- **N** *noun*

    - **+C** *common* + **Attribute:** *number-gender-case-definiteness*
    - **+P** *proper*
    - **+Pr** *pronoun*
        * **+P** *personal* + **Attribute:** *number-person-gender*
        * **+R** *relative*
            · **+S** *specific* + **Attribute:** *number-gender*
            · **+C** *common*
        * **+D** *demonstrative* + **Attribute:** *number-gender*
    - **+Nu** *numerical*
        * **+Ca** *cardinal* + **Attribute:** *[Sg]-gender*
        * **+O** *ordinal* + **Attribute:** *[Sg]-gender*
        * **+Na** *numerical adjective* + **Attribute:** *[Sg]-gender*
    - **+A** *adjective* + **Attribute:** *number-gender-case-definiteness*

- **V** *verb*

    - **+P** *perfective* + **Attribute:** *number-person-gender*
    - **+I** *imperfective* + **Attribute:** *number-person-gender-mood*
    - **+Iv** *imperative* + **Attribute:** *number-[2]-gender*

- **P** *particle*

    - **+Pr** *preposition*, **+A** *adverbial*, **+C** *conjunction*, **+I** *interjection*, **+E** *exception*, **+N** *negative*, **+A** *answers*, **+X** *explanations*, **+S** *subordinates*

- **R** *residual*

    - **+F** *foreign*, **+M** *mathematical*, **+N** *number*, **+D** *day of the week*, **+my** *month of the year*, **+A** *abbreviation*, **+O** *other*

- **PU** *punctuation*

- *Attributes*

    - Gender: M *masculine*, F *feminine*, N *neuter*
    - Number: Sg *singular*, Pl *plural*, Du *dual*
    - Person: 1 *first*, 2 *second*, 3 *third*
    - Case: N *nominative*, A *accusative*, G *genitive*
    - Definiteness: D *definite*, I *indefinite*
    - Mood: I *indicative*, S *subjunctive*, J *jussive*

• Definiteness: **I**ndefinite, **D**efinite, **R**educed or **C**omplex.

For example, the POS tag `VP-A-3MP--` represents a perfective verb with active voice and 3rd masculine plural subject. Note that the presence of the definite article proclitic is indicated only through the definiteness feature, which combines it with the feature state: in the PADT, Definite is equal to having the definite article and the definite state. The Reduced and Complex values of are both equal to the construct state. The difference is that Complex has the definite article (false Idafa; see Section 6.1.3).

5.5   TWO TOOL SUITES

In this section, we present with some degree of detail two rather different tool suites for computational processing of Arabic morphology: the MADA+TOKAN and AMIRA suites. These tools are publicly available and have been used by numerous academic and commercial research institutes around the world. We also compare and contrast them in terms of their design, functionality and performance in various NLP applications.

5.5.1   MADA+TOKAN

MADA (Morphological Analysis and Disambiguation for Arabic) is a utility that, given raw Arabic text, adds as much lexical and morphological information as possible by disambiguating, in one operation, part-of-speech tags, lexemes, diacritizations and full morphological analyses [51, 35, 116]. MADA's approach distinguishes between the problems of morphological analysis, which is handled by a morphological analyzer (ALMORGEANA), and morphological disambiguation. MADA is a morphological disambiguation system. Once a morphological analysis is chosen in context, so are its full POS tag, lemma and diacritization (all in a single step). Knowing the morphological analysis also allows for deterministic tokenization and stemming, which are handled by TOKAN once MADA has finished processing the text.

MADA   MADA operates in stages. First, it uses ALMORGEANA internally to produce a list of potential analyses for each word encountered in the text; at this point, word context is not considered. MADA then makes use of up to 19 features to rank the list of analyses. For each feature, a classifier is used to create a prediction for the value of that feature for each word in its context. Fourteen of the features use Support Vector Machine (SVM) classifiers; the remaining features capture information such as spelling variations and n-gram statistics. Each classifier prediction is weighted using a tuning set, and the collection of feature predictions is compared to the list of potential morphological analyses. Those analyses that more closely agree with the weighted set of feature predictions receive higher ranking scores than those which do not; the highest scoring analysis is flagged as the correct analysis for that word in that context. Since MADA selects a complete analysis from ALMORGEANA, all decisions regarding morphological ambiguity, lexical ambiguity, tokenization, diacritization and POS tagging in any possible POS tag set are made in one fell swoop. MADA has over 96% accuracy on lemmatization and on basic morphological choice (including tokenization but excluding syntactic

Figure 5.6: A comparison of several POS tag sets for the sentence خمسون ألف سائح زاروا مدينتنا الجميلة في أيلول الماضي '50 thousand tourists visited our beautiful city last September.'

xmsˈun Alf sAyˈH zArˈwA mdyntˈnA Aljmylˈh fy Aylˈul AlmˈADy '50 thousand tourists visited our beautiful city last September.'

Arabic	Gloss	Buckwalter/PATB	CATiB	Bies	Kulick	ERTS	Khoja	PADT	ALMORGEANA/MADA
خمسون xams+uwna	fifty	NOUN_NUM+NSUFF_MASC_PL_NOM	NOM	CD	CD	CD	NNuCaPlM	QL------1I	POS:NUM +MASC +PL +NOM
ألفا Âalf+a	thousand	NOUN_NUM+ CASE_DEF_ACC	NOM	CD	CD	CD	NNuCaSgM	QM------S4R	POS:NUM +DEF +ACC
سائح sÂyiH+i	tourist	NOUN+ CASE_INDEF_GEN	NOM	NN	NN	NNM	NCSgMGI	N------S2I	POS:N +INDEF +GEN
زاروا zAr+uwA	visited	PV+ PVSUFF_SUBJ:3MP	VRB	VBD	VBD	VBD	VPPl3M	VP-A-3MP--	POS:V +PV +S:3MS
مدينتنا madiyn+ah+a	city	NOUN+ NSUFF_FEM_SG+ CASE_DEF_ACC	NOM	NN	NN	NNF	NCSgFAI	N------S4R	POS:N +FEM +SG +DEF +ACC
نا +nA	our	POSS_PRON_1P	NOM	PRP$	PRP$	PRP$	NP+PPl1	S----1-P2-	+P:1P
الجميلة Al+jamiyl+ah+a	beautiful	DET+ADJ+ NSUFF_FEM_SG+ CASE_DEF_ACC	NOM	JJ	DT+JJ	DJJF	NASgFAD	A-----FS4D	POS:AJ Al+ +FEM +SG +DEF +ACC
في fiy	in	PREP	PRT	IN	IN	IN	PPr	P---------	POS:P
أيلول Âay.luwl+a	September	NOUN_PROP+ CASE_INDEF_GEN	PROP	NNP	NNP	NNPM	Rmy	N------S2I	POS:PN +INDEF +GEN
الماضي Al+mADiy	past	DET+ADJ	NOM	JJ	DT+JJ	DJJM	NASgMGD	A-----MS2D	POS:AJ Al+
.	.	PUNC	PNX	PUNC	.	PUNC	PU	G---------	POS:PX

case, mood, and state). MADA has over 86% accuracy in predicting full diacritization (including syntactic case and mood). Detailed comparative evaluations are provided in the following publications: [51, 35, 116] .

The operation of MADA is versatile and highly configurable. Starting with version 2.0, MADA applies weights to each of the 19 features it uses for better accuracy; these weights are determined on a tuning set and are optimized for different purposes, such as tokenization, diacritization, or POS tagging. These weight sets are included with the package and should be chosen by the user depending on how MADA will be used. However, users can also choose to set these weights directly themselves. By default, MADA attempts to rank complete analyses in terms of overall correctness. By choosing an alternative feature and weight set, it is possible to have MADA focus more specifically on getting a particular analysis aspect correct. For example, users can achieve a 0.4% absolute improvement in POS tagging accuracy if they use the weight set that was tuned for POS tagging, as opposed to the default set. However, the accuracy of the other MADA outputs (the lexeme prediction, for example) may suffer. MADA also includes a morphological back-off procedure, which can be turned on or off by the user.

TOKAN   TOKAN is a general tokenizer for Arabic that provides an easy-to-use resource for tokenizing MADA-disambiguated Arabic text into a large set of possibilities [83, 97]. The decision on whether an Arabic word has a conjunction or preposition clitic is made in MADA, but the actual tokenization of the clitics including handling various morphotactics and spelling regularization is done in TOKAN. The tokenization scheme can be used as parameter in machine learning for a variety of applications, such as machine translation or named-entity recognition.

TOKAN takes as input a MADA-disambiguated file and a tokenization scheme description that specifies tokenization target. Consider the following specification:

```
"w+ f+ b+ k+ l+ s+ Al+ REST + / + POS +P: +O: -DIAC"
```

This scheme separates conjunctions, prepositions, verbal particles, the definite article and pronominal clitics and it adds the basic POS tag to the form of the word. The scheme also specifies that diacritics are generated. An analysis of the word وسيكاتبها *wasayukAtibuhA* 'and he will correspond with her' would be tokenized as "wa+ sa+ yukAtibu/V +hA." A simpler scheme such as "w+ f+ REST" would simply produce "w+ sykAtbhA." See [83, 105] for a detailed description of several schemes that have become commonly followed since that work was published. TOKAN has a large number of other features that allow the user to perform different kinds of orthographic normalizations or control how the output is ordered and presented as it may fit different needs of different systems. All of the tokenization schemes shown in Figure 5.3 are supported by TOKAN.

Internally, TOKAN uses morphological generation (through ALMORGEANA) to recreate the word once different clitics are split off. This approach of back generation allows us to modify the morphological content in a word including, for instance, deleting/defaulting specific features of a word easily. This ensures that the form of the generated word is normalized and consistent with other occurrences of that word. For example, simply splitting the pronominal clitic off a word with

Ta-Marbuta (ة ħ) would keep the Ta-Marbuta in its word-internal form (regular letter Ta, ت t). With TOKAN, the Ta-Marbuta is generated as appropriate. For example, جولته jwlth 'his-visit' is tokenized into جولة+ه jwlħ+h 'visit +his', not جولت+ه jwlt+h (which is not a valid spelling).

MADA+TOKAN for NLP Applications   MADA+TOKAN has been used by numerous academic and commercial research institutes around the world. Here are some examples of it use. In the context of machine translation (MT) from Arabic to English, [83] and [105] explored the use of different preprocessing schemes and their combination. Their results have been followed by different groups of researchers working on Arabic-English MT [124, 125, 126]. [127] explored the use of MADA-generated diacritizations for MT. [107] improved automatic word alignment for Arabic-English MT using combinations of different tokenization schemes generated by MADA+TOKAN. See [97] for more details on different representations of Arabic morphology for MT. [99] used MADA in the context of English-to-Arabic MT. MADA has also been used to produce features for Named Entity Recognition (NER) [128, 129].

5.5.2   AMIRA

AMIRA is a set of tools built as a successor to the Asvmt toolkit developed at Stanford University [109] and described in detail in [117]. The toolkit includes a tokenizer, a part of speech tagger (POS) and a base phrase chunker (BPC), also known as a shallow syntactic parser. We focus in this section on AMIRA-TOK and AMIRA-POS. The technology of AMIRA is based on supervised learning with no explicit dependence on knowledge of deep morphology; hence, in contrast to MADA, it relies on surface data to learn generalizations. In general, the tools use a unified framework which casts each of the component problems as a classification problem. The underlying technology uses Support Vector Machines in a sequence modeling framework.

AMIRA-TOK   AMIRA-TOK focuses primarily on clitic tokenization. AMIRA tools do not rely on morphological analysis or generation tools in any of its processes. Hence, AMIRA-TOK learns clitic tokenization generalizations from the clitic segmentations present in the Penn Arabic Treebank (PATB), directly without relying on rules explicitly.

AMIRA-TOK segments off the following set of clitics: conjunction proclitics و +w+, ف+ f+, prepositional proclitics ك+ k+, ل+ l+, ب+ b+, future marker proclitic س+ s+, verbal particle proclitic ل +l+, definite article proclitic ال+ Al+, and pronominal enclitics indicating possessive/object pronouns.

The particular insight of the AMIRA-TOK solution is to treat tokenization of Arabic words as a character-level chunking problem. This allows using IOB syntactic chunking solutions usually used at the phrase level on the sub-word level. Here, every character (including punctuation) is annotated as: inside a chunk (I), outside a chunk (O), or beginning of a chunk (B), hence the name **IOB**. For the I and B tags, there are five possible classes: Prefix 1 (e.g., conjunction proclitic), Prefix 2 (e.g., preposition), Prefix 3 (e.g., definite article), Word, Suffix (e.g., pronominal enclitic). This leads to a total of 11 classes in the data: O, B-PRE1, I-PRE2, B-PRE2, I-PRE2, B-PRE3, I-PRE3,

B-WORD, I-WORD, B-SUFF, I-SUFF. By learning how to assign these class labels, Amira-Tok learns how to segment the words.

Amira-Tok does not produce stemmed words that are not valid Arabic words. The tool applies some heuristics to reverse the effect of morphotactics such as the loss of ‎ا *A* in the definite article ‎ال+ *Al*+ when in the context of the proclitic preposition ‎ل+ *l*+ 'for'. Most of such morphotactic restorations are deterministically applied. However, non-deterministic morphotactics such as those involving the nominal feminine marker (Ta-Marbuta) and the Alif-Maqsura are automatically determined through another layer of learning to the problem of classifying word-final letters. For Ta-Marbuta: a stem final ‎ت *t* either remains a regular ‎ت *t* or is converted to ‎ة *ħ*. And for Alif-Maqsura: a stem final ‎ا *A* either remains an ‎ا *A* or is converted to a ‎ى *ý*.

Although the primary Amira tokenization is to split off clitics and normalize the stem, the tool interface allows a limited number of variants, which include the level of clitic segmentation, and whether tokenization is indicated with spaces (changing the token count) or with a plus sign only (preserving token count). For example, the word ‎وللبلاد *wllblAd*, 'and for the countries', can have the following tokenizations among many others: *w+ l+ Al+ blAd* (Amira-Tok internal), *w+ llblAd* (Conjunction-only), *w+l+ AlblAd* (Preposition-only), *wl+Al+ blAd* (Al-only), *wllblAd* (Suffix only), and *wll+ blAd* (All Prefixes+Suffix).

Amira-Tok performs at a high F-score measure of 99.2% [117].

AMIRA-POS   Amira primarily uses the ERTS POS tag set and assumes the text is clitic tokenized. POS tagging in Amira-Pos is done through an SVM-based classification approach using character n-grams as features in the sequence models.

The user has the flexibility to input raw or tokenized text in a scheme that is consistent with one of the schemes defined by Amira-Tok. Consequently, the user may request that the POS tags be assigned to the surface forms. Internally, in case of the raw input, Amira-Pos runs Amira-Tok on the raw text and then performs POS tagging. The output can be presented as tokenized and POS tagged, or without tokenization where the POS tag is assigned to the surface words. In this latter case, the ERTS tag set is appended with the clitic POS tags to form more complex POS tags. The user can choose to either tag with ERTS or RTS (Section 5.4.2).

Interestingly, the accuracy of the ERTS tagger is 96.13% and the accuracy of the RTS tagger is 96.15%. This suggests that the choice of information to include in ERTS tag set reflects a natural division in the syntactic space. The richer tag set (ERTS) has been shown to improve the quality of downstream processing such as base phrase chunking [111, 120].

AMIRA for NLP Applications   Amira has been successfully used by several groups in the context of text MT, specifically for alignment improvement and reordering within the context of statistical MT [130], and also for identifying difficult source language text [131]. Moreover, the Amira suite was used in the context of speech MT [132]. The Amira suite was explored for the purposes of cross language information retrieval in work by [104]. Amira has been used to produce POS tag and BPC features for Arabic named entity recognition (NER) [129, 133].

5.5.3   COMPARING MADA+TOKAN WITH AMIRA

In this section, we compare and contrast MADA+TOKAN and AMIRA in terms of their design, functionality and performance.

Design As for their design, it may help to contextualize the different tools in terms of their basic use in two suites: the MADA suite and the AMIRA suite. Within the MADA suite, there is an explicit morphological analysis step handled by ALMORGEANA. The second, in fact core, component in the MADA suite, is the MADA system, which disambiguates the analyses produced by the morphological analyzers. Finally, the TOKAN component makes use of the morphological generation power of ALMORGEANA to tokenize the disambiguated analysis through regeneration. In the AMIRA suite, the two components focus on tokenization (AMIRA-TOK) and POS tagging (AMIRA-POS).

In term of their design, AMIRA-TOK and AMIRA-POS are different from the MADA suite in that they take a two-step approach to POS tagging: tokenize then tag. In comparison, MADA has a different approach that breaks the problem into three steps (analyze, disambiguate, generate), which are orthogonal to AMIRA's split. Although there are three steps in MADA, the decision for tokenization and POS tagging is done together in one-fell-swoop. One way of distinguishing these tools is in terms of the depth of linguistic knowledge needed. AMIRA is shallow in that it focuses on form-based morphology (specifically cliticization) learned from annotated data; whereas MADA has access to deeper lexically modeled functional morphology. Another difference between the current MADA suite and the AMIRA suite is that the former may produce no analysis for a given word if it does not exist in the underlying morphological tools (although typically analysis back-off is used in such cases) while the AMIRA suite always produces a hypothesized tokenization and POS tag for every word in the text.

In terms of their training needs, the MADA suite expects the presence of both a morphological analyzer and training data for supervised learning, whereas the AMIRA suite only needs annotated training data. The training data could be created through any number of ways, including the use of morphological analyzers followed by human annotation, but this is not a requirement for the AMIRA suite. These different yet similar requirements put similar limits on the kind of extensions that could be done in either approach. For example, going to an Arabic dialect would require the presence of some morphological analyzer/generator for the dialect for MADA, but not AMIRA. However, both need some amount of annotated data to train on.

Functionality In terms of functionality, we consider five applications: tokenization, diacritization, POS tagging, lemmatization and base-phrase chunking. Base-phrase chunking is only handled in the AMIRA suite, but it is in fact a separate module that can be used independently with the MADA suite. The other four applications are handled at once in MADA as part of its common morphological disambiguation process. AMIRA does not handle lemmatization or diacritization. As for tokenization and POS tagging, since MADA goes deeper than AMIRA, a wider set of possible tokenization schemes and POS tags can be output by MADA. Although AMIRA is more limited by comparison, it does handle the most commonly used tokenizations and POS tags. Researchers interested in exploring a large number of different sets of tokenizations as features in their systems should consider MADA. Researchers only interested in limited comparisons or specific applications, whose tokenizations and POS tags are supported by AMIRA, should consider AMIRA.

Performance It is hard to compare the performance of AMIRA and MADA suites. Previous attempts by [51] show that similar performance is possible on tasks that are shared: specific PATB tokenization and POS tags. AMIRA can be significantly faster than MADA; however, MADA needs to be run only once and a much larger number of tokenizations and POS tags (in addition to other outputs not supported by AMIRA) can be produced by running the fast TOKAN step.

CHAPTER 6

Arabic Syntax

Syntax is the linguistic discipline interested in modeling how words are arranged together to make larger sequences in a language. Whereas morphology describes the structure of words internally, syntax describes how words come together to make phrases and sentences.

Much of the vocabulary discussing syntax is shared across different languages, e.g., verb, verb phrase, subject and object. There are some exceptions that pertain to unique structures that are not found cross-linguistically, e.g., Idafa and Tamyiz in Arabic. We discuss specific and general terms of syntax as needed in this chapter. For a general introduction to syntax, we urge the reader to consider the numerous publications available, e.g., [134, 135] among others.

This chapter is organized as follows. We first present a sketch of Arabic syntax in Section 6.1. In Section 6.2, we present three Arabic treebanking projects and compare the different approaches they use. Finally, Section 6.3 summaries research efforts in syntactic parsing of Arabic.

6.1   A SKETCH OF ARABIC SYNTACTIC STRUCTURES

In this section, we present a general survey of Arabic syntactic phenomena. For a more complete account, consider some of the numerous Arabic grammar references [78, 7, 77, 76, 81, 82].

6.1.1   A NOTE ON MORPHOLOGY AND SYNTAX

The relationship between morphology and syntax can be complex especially for morphologically rich languages where many syntactic phenomena are expressed not only in terms of word order but also morphology. For example, Arabic subjects of verbs have a nominative case and adjectival modifiers of nouns agree with the case of the noun they modify. Arabic rich morphology allows it to have some degree of freedom in word order since the morphology can express some syntactic relations. However, as in many other languages, the actual usage of Arabic is less free, in terms of word order, than it can be in principle.

Cliticization morphology crosses various syntactic structures. As such, in Arabic treebanks, words are typically tokenized to separate all clitics (with the exception of the definite article, which happens not interfere with syntactic structure). In this chapter, all examples are tokenized in the style of the Penn Arabic Treebank [9, 136, 82].

6.1.2   SENTENCE STRUCTURE

Arabic has two types of sentences: verbal sentences (V-Sent) and nominal sentences (N-Sent). N-Sents are also called copular/equational sentences.

Verbal Sentences

The prototypical structure of a V-SENT is Verb-Subject-Object(s). This is expressed in different forms. The most basic form of the V-SENT consists of just a verb with a conjugated (pro-dropped) pronominal subject.[1] The verb expresses the person, gender and number of the subject.

(6.1) V-SENT: Verb+Subj

○   *katab+a*   كَتَبَ
    wrote+3MS

    'He wrote'

○   *katab+nA*   كَتَبْنَا
    wrote+1P

    'We wrote'

Non-pronominal subjects appear *after* the verb. The verb agrees with the subject in person (3RD) and gender (MASC or FEM) but not number, which defaults to SG. A verb with a non-pronominal subject in a V-SENT is never PL. The subject receives the NOM case.

(6.2) V-SENT: Verb Subject^{Nom}

○   *katab+a*   *Al+walad+u/Al+ÂwlAd+u*   كَتَبَ الوَلَدُ/الَاولَادُ
    wrote+3MS   the+boy+NOM/the+boys+NOM

    'The boy/boys wrote'

○   *katab+at*   *Al+bint+u/Al+banAt+u*   كَتَبَت البِنتُ/البَنَاتُ
    wrote+3FS   the+girl+NOM/the+girls+NOM

    'The girl/girls wrote'

As we saw earlier in Section 4.2.1, pronominal objects appear as part of verbal suffixes regardless of whether the subject is pronominal or not. Here are the above two constructions with pronominal objects:

(6.3) V-SENT: Verb+Subj -Obj

○   *katab+a*   *-hA*   كَتَبَ -هَا
    wrote+3MS   -it

    'He wrote it'

---

[1]Traditional Arabic grammar considers the pronominal subject affixes to be the "subject" except for the 3rd person singular masculine/feminine affixes which are used in the number-blind agreement in V-SENT. A concept of a 3rd person singular masculine/feminine *hidden pronoun* (ضمير مستتر) is introduced to explain 3rd person singular masculine/feminine pro-drop.

○ *katab+nA -hA*   كَتَبنَا -هَا
  wrote+1P -it

'We wrote it'

(6.4) V-Sᴇɴᴛ: Verb -Obj Subject^{Nom}

○ *katab+a   -hA Al+walad+u*   كَتَبَ -هَا الوَلَدُ
  wrote+3MS -it   the+boy+Nᴏᴍ

'The boy wrote it'

Non-pronominal verb objects typically follow the subject. The object receives the Acc case.

(6.5) V-Sᴇɴᴛ: Verb+Subj Object^{Acc}

○ *katab+a   Al+qiS~ah+a*   كَتَبَ القِصَّة
  wrote+3MS the+story+Acc

'He wrote the story'

(6.6) V-Sᴇɴᴛ: Verb Subject^{Nom} Object^{Acc}

○ *katab+a   Al+walad+u   Al+qiS~ah+a*   كَتَبَ الوَلَدُ القِصَّة
  wrote+3MS the+boy+Nᴏᴍ   the+story+Acc

'The boy wrote the story'

Given that case endings are not always written, there is a common ambiguity associated with the sequence [Verb+3S NounPhrase] when the Verb and NounPhrase agree in gender: (a.) the NounPhrase is the subject or (b.) the subject is pronominal (3MS or 3FS) and the NounPhrase is the object.

As in other languages, Arabic has intransitive, transitive and ditransitive verbs that take zero, one or two objects, respectively. The *direct* and *indirect* objects of a ditransitive verb both receive the Acc case.

(6.7) a. V-Sᴇɴᴛ: Verb Subject^{Nom} IObject^{Acc} DObject^{Acc}

○ *AaςTaý Al+walad+u Al+bint+a   kitAb+Aa*   اعطى الوَلَدُ البِنتَ كِتَابَا
  give+3MS the+boy+Nᴏᴍ the+girl+Acc book+Acc

'The boy gave the girl a book'

As in English, the ditransitive construction has an alternation where the indirect object appears as object of the preposition l- 'to', with a Gᴇɴ case:

(6.8) b. V-Sᴇɴᴛ: Verb Subject^{Nom} DObject^{Acc} l- IObject^{Gen}

o   *AaςTaý   Al+walad+u   kitAb+Aā   l-   Al+bint+i*   اعطى الوَلَدُ كِتَابًاً ل-البِنتِ
    give+3MS   the+boy+Nom   book+Acc   to-   the+girl+Gen

    'The boy gave a book to the girl'

    A pronominal indirect object appears as a verbal suffix:

(6.9) V-Sent: Verb+Subj -IObj DObject^{Acc}

o   *AaςTaý+nA   -hA   kitab+Aā*   اعطينَا -هَا كِتَابًاً
    give+1P   -her   book+Acc

    'We gave her a book'

(6.10) V-Sent: Verb -IObj Subject^{Nom} DObject^{Acc}

o   *AaςTaý   -hA   Al+walad+u   kitab+Aā*   اعطى -هَا الوَلَدُ كِتَابًاً
    give+3MS   -her   the+boy+Nom   book+Acc

    'The boy gave the girl a book'

However, if both direct and indirect objects are pronominal, the direct object appears as a separate non-cliticizable direct pronoun after the subject.

(6.11) V-Sent: Verb+Subj -IObj DObject

o   *AaςTaý+nA   -hA   AyA+hu*   اعطينَا -هَا إِيَّاهُ
    give+1P   -her   it

    'We gave her it'

(6.12) V-Sent: Verb -IObj Subject^{Nom} DObject

o   *AaςTaý   -hA   Al+walad+u   AyA+hu*   اعطى -هَا الوَلَدُ إِيَّاهُ
    give+3MS   -her   the+boy+Nom   it

    'The boy gave her it'

Nominal Sentences

The prototypical Nominal Sentence (N-Sent) has the form of Subject-Predicate/Topic-Complement (مبتدَأ وَخَبَر *mubtadaÂ wa+xabar*). This is sometimes referred to as a *copular construction* or *equational sentence*.

Nominal Sentence Variants   In the simplest N-Sent, the subject is typically a *definite* noun, proper noun or pronoun in the Nom case and the predicate is an *indefinite* Nom noun, proper noun or adjective that agrees with the subject in number and gender.

(6.13) N-Sent: Subject^{Nom} Predicate^{Nom}

○   *Al+kitAb+u*   *jadiyd+ū*   الكِتَابُ جَدِيدٌ
    the+book+MS+Nom+Def   new+MS+Nom+InDef

    'The book is new'

○   *hiya salmaý* هِيَ سَلمَى
    she   Salma

    'She is Salma'

○   *Al+rajul+Ani*   *kAtib+Ani*   الرَّجُلانِ كَاتِبَانِ
    the+man+DU+Nom+Def   author+DU+Nom+InDef

    'The two men are authors'

   For the rest of this section, we will limit the glossing of morphological features to the minimum needed. In addition to the basic nominal predicate form, the predicate can be a prepositional phrase (PP):

(6.14) N-Sent: Subject^{Nom} PP-Predicate

○   *Al+rajul+u*   *fiy Albayt+i*   الرَّجُلُ فِي البَيتِ
    the+man+Nom   in the+house+Gen

    'The man is in the house'

   The predicate can also be another N-Sent. In this construction, the subject of the top N-Sent serves as a *topic*. The predicate of the top N-Sent will typically reference the *topic* using some pronominal reference.

(6.15) N-Sent: Subject$_1^{Nom}$ [N-Sent Subject$_2^{Nom}$ Predicate$_2^{Nom}$]$_1$

○   *Al+bayt+u*   *bAb+u -hu*   *jadiyd+ū*   البيتُ بَابُ -هُ جَدِيدٌ
    the+house+Nom   door+Nom -its   new+Nom

    'The house, its door is new'

   However, perhaps the most interesting predicate structure involves a V-Sent. Most commonly, this construction produces a Subject-Verb-Object look-alike order in Arabic when the subject of the embedded predicating V-Sent refers back to the subject of the main N-Sent. Here, the subject and verb agree in full (gender, number and person) as opposed to agreeing in gender and person as in a normal V-Sent. This construction is sometimes referred to as a "complex sentence." Contrast this following example with its base V-Sent variant.

(6.16) N-Sent: Subject$_1^{Nom}$ [V-Sent Verb+Subj$_1^{Nom}$ Object^{Acc}]*predicate*

○   *Al+AwlAd+u*   *katab+uwA*   *Al+qiSaS+a*   الَاولَادُ كَتَبُوا القِصَصَ
    the+boys+Nom   wrote+3MP   the+stories+Acc

'The boys wrote the stories' (lit. 'The boys, they wrote the stories')

○   *katab+a*   *Al+AwlAd+u*   *Al+qiSaS+a*   كَتَبَ الَاولَادُ القِصَصَ
    wrote+3MS   the+boys+Nom   the+stories+Acc

'The boys wrote the stories'

As a result, there are three types of verbal constructions when it comes to how the subject is expressed in Arabic: Verb-Subject, Subject-Verb and Verb+Subj.

The subject of the main N-Sent can be also referred to by other arguments and adjuncts inside the predicating V-Sent, such as the V-Sent object or object of one of its prepositions.

(6.17) N-Sent: Subject$_1^{Nom}$ [V-Sent Verb SubjectNom Object$_1$]*predicate*

○   *Al+kitAb+u*   *katab+a*   *-hu Al+kAtib+u*   الكِتَابُ كَتَبَ -هُ الكَاتِبُ
    the+book+Nom   wrote+3MS   -it   the+author+Nom

'The author wrote the book' (lit. 'The book, the author wrote it')

(6.18) N-Sent: Subject$_1^{Nom}$ [V-Sent Verb Subject^{Nom} Prep Object$_1$]*predicate*

○   *háða Al+bayt+u katab+a Al+kAtib+u çan   -hu*   هذَا البيتُ كَتَبَ الكَاتِبُ عَن -هُ
    this   the+house   write   the+author   about   -it

'The author wrote about this house' (lit. 'This house, the author wrote about it')

Note how in the above example, the top N-Sent subject, *the topic*, is in Nom case regardless of its co-reference inside the V-Sent. Arabic allows a variant construction of the example above where the verb object is topicalized, *moved*, without change in its case. In this construction, no pronominal reference in the V-Sent is needed. This is not a common construction.

(6.19) V-Sent: object^{Acc} Verb Subject^{Nom}

○   *Al+kitAb+a*   *katab+a*   *Al+kAtibu*   الكِتَابَ كَتَبَ الكَاتِبُ
    the+book+Acc   wrote+3MS   the+author+Nom

'The author wrote the book'

A final note: if the subject is indefinite, the order of subject and predicate is reversed. This often happens with prepositional phrase predicates.

(6.20) N-Sent: PP-Predicate Subject^{Nom}

○ *fiy Albayti*   *rajul+ū*   فِي البَيتِ رَجُلٌ
   in the+house+GEN   man+InDef+Nom

   'There is a man in the house' (lit. 'a man is in the house')

○ *ςind -y kitAb+ū*   عِند-ي كِتَابٌ
   at -me   book+InDef+Nom

   'I have a book' (lit. 'a book is at me')

6.1.3 NOMINAL PHRASE STRUCTURE

The most basic nominal phrase (N-Phrase) is a noun or an adjective with or without the definite article:

(6.21) N-Phrase: Noun

○ *kitAb+ū*   كِتَابٌ
   book+InDef

   'a book'

(6.22) N-Phrase: DET+Noun

○ *Al+kitAb+u*   الكِتَابُ
   the+book+Def

   'the book'

   We distinguish several types of nominal modifiers, which we present next.

Adjectival Modification

Arabic adjectives follow the nouns they modify. Adjectives and nouns always agree in definiteness and case. Adjectives of rational (Human) nouns agree in gender and number also. Broken plural adjectives are form-wise singular and with ad hoc form-based gender, but they are functionally plural (see Section 4.2.2). For example, the word أَلَمَهَرَةُ *Al+maharaħ+u* is feminine and singular by form but masculine and plural functionally.

(6.23) N-Phrase: RATIONAL-NOUN ADJECTIVE

a. *kAtibū*   *mAhirū*   كَاتِبٌ مَاهِرٌ
    author+MS   clever+MS

    'a clever author'

b. *kAtibaħū   mAhiraħū*   كَاتِبَةٌ مَاهِرَةٌ
    author+FS   clever+FS

    'a clever author'

c. *kAtibAni   mAhirAni*   كَاتِبَانِ مَاهِرَانِ
    author+MD   clever+MD

    'two clever authors'

d. *AlkAtibAtu   AlmAhirAtu*   الكَاتِبَاتُ المَاهِرَاتُ
    the+authors+FP   the+clever+FP

    'the clever authors'

e. *Alkut~Abu   Almaharaħu*   الكُتَّابُ المَهَرَةُ
    the+authors+MP   the+clever+MP

    'the clever authors'

f. *Alkut~Abu   AlmAhiruwna*   الكُتَّابُ المَاهِرُونَ
    the+authors+MP   the+clever+MP

    'the clever authors'

While adjectives of irrational (non-human) nouns agree with the nouns in gender and number when the nouns are singular or dual; adjectives of plural irrational nouns are oddly feminine singular.

(6.24) N-Phrase: IRRATIONAL-NOUN ADJECTIVE

a. *maktabū   jadiydū*   مَكْتَبٌ جَدِيدٌ
    office+MS   new+MS

    'a new office'

b. *maktabaħū jadiydaħū*   مَكْتَبَةٌ جَدِيدَةٌ
    library+FS   new+FS

    'a new library'

c. *maktbAni   jadiydAni*   مَكْتَبَانِ جَدِيدَانِ
    offices+MD   new+MD

    'two new offices'

d. *makAtibu   jadiydaħū*   مَكَاتِبُ جَدِيدَةٌ
    offices+MP   new+FS

    'new offices'

e. *maktbAtū   jadiydaħū* مَكْتَبَاتٌ جَدِيدَةٌ
    libraries+FP new+FS

    'new libraries'

Idafa Construction

The Idafa construction is a possessive/genitive construction relating two nouns: the first noun, the possessor (مضاف *muDAf*), grammatically heads, and semantically possesses the second noun, the possessed (مضَاف اليه *muDAf Ăilayhi*). The possessor is in the construct state. And the possessed has a genitive case. This construction has many comparables in English: $Noun_1$ $Noun_2$ can translate into $Noun_1$ *of* $Noun_2$, $Noun_2$ *'s* $Noun_1$ or a compound $Noun_2$ $Noun_1$.

(6.25) N-Phrase: NOUN1^{construct} NOUN2^{Gen}

o *mafAtiyHu Al+say~Araħi* مَفَاتِيحُ السَّيَّارَةِ
   keys   the+car

   'the keys of the car' or 'the car's keys' or 'the car keys'

The two nouns together form a noun phrase which can be the second part of a different Idafa construction. This can be extended recursively creating what is called an **Idafa chain**. All the words in an Idafa chain except for the first word must be genitive. And all the words except for the last word must be in construct state.

(6.26) N-Phrase: Idafa Chain

o إِبْنُ عَمِّ جَارِ رَئِيسِ مَجْلِسِ إِدَارَةِ الشَّرِكَةِ

   Aibonu Eam~i jAri   raŷiysi majlisi ĂidAraħi   Alš~arikaħi
   son   uncle neighbor chief   committee management the-company
   'the cousin of the CEO's neighbor'

Adjectives modifying the head of an Idafa construction agree with it in case, but they agree with its dependent in definiteness:

(6.27) N-Phrase: NOUN1^{construct} NOUN2^{Gen} ADJ1

o *bAb+u Al+say~Araħi Al+jadiyd+u* بَابُ السَّيَّارَةِ الجَدِيدُ
   door the+car+Gen   the+new+Nom

   'the car's new door'

o *bAb+u say~Araħī jadiyd+ū* بَابُ سَيَّارَةٍ جَدِيدٌ
   door car+Gen   new+Nom

   'a car's new door'

In addition to basic possessive constructions, the Idafa construction is used in many linguistic constructions in Arabic:

- Quantification constructions such as كل الكتب *kul~u Alkutubi* 'all [of] the books' and خمسة كُتُب *xamsaħu kutubī* 'five books'.

- Preposition-like adverbial constructions such as قرب البيت *qurba Albayti* 'near the house'.

- Adjectival Idafa, also known as false Idafa إضافة غير حقيقية, such as طويل القامة *Tawiylu AlqAmaħi* 'tall of stature'.

Tamyiz Construction

The Tamyiz (تمييز *tamyiyz* or *accusative of specification*) construction relates two nouns. The first noun, the *specified* (المُمَيَّز *Almumay~az*) heads and governs the second noun, the *specifier* (المُمَيِّز *Almumay~iz*), which qualifies the first noun. The specifier is always singular in number and accusative in case. Tamyiz is used in variety of linguistic constructions in Arabic:

- comparatives and superlatives such as أَكثَرُ بَيَاضاً *Akθaru bayADAā* [lit. more as to whiteness] 'whiter'.

- measurement specification such as كيلو لحماً *kylw laHmAā* [lit. a kilo as in meat] 'a kilo of meat', or the common interrogative كم كتَاباً؟ *kam kitAbAā?* [lit. how many as in book?] 'how many books?'

- some number constructions such as خَمسُونَ كِتَاباً *xamsuwna kitAbAā* [lit. fifty as of book] 'fifty books'.

- type specification such as خَاتِمٌ فِضَّةً *xAtimū fiD~aħā* [lit. a ring as in silver] 'a sliver ring'.

Apposition

An apposition construction (بدل *badal*) relates two noun phrases that refer to the same entity. The heads of the two noun phrases agree in case, e.g., الرئيس الأَمريكي، باراك اوباما *Alrŷiysu AlÂmriykiy~u, bArAk AwbAmA* the 'American President, Barack Obama'. A very common appositional construction in Arabic involves the demonstrative pronoun, which typically precedes the noun it modifies although it can also follow: هذَا الكِتَاب *hâðA AlkitAb* '[lit. this the-book] this book'.

Relative Clauses

Relative clauses modify the noun that heads them. If the heading noun is definite, the relative clause (جملة وصل 'Sila/linking sentence') is introduced and headed with a relative pronoun (اسم موصول, RELPRO). When prsent, the relative pronoun agrees with noun it modifies in gender and number following Adjectival agreement rules (irrationality gets exceptional agreement).

(6.28) N-Phrase: NOUN^{definite} RELPRO SENTENCE

○   *AlkitAbu   Al~ðiy   [ÂuHib~u   -hu]*   الكِتَابُ الّذي أُحِبّ -هُ
   the-book   which   [I+love   -it]

   'the book [which] I love'

If the heading noun is indefinite, the relative clause (called جملة صفة 'Sifa/adjectival sentence' in this case) is not introduced with a relative pronoun.

(6.29) N-Phrase: NOUN^{indefinite} SENTENCE

○   *kitAbū   [ÂuHib~u   -hu]*   كِتَابٌ أُحِبّ -هُ
   book   [I+love   -it]

   'a book [which] I love'

The definite relative clause headed with a relative pronoun can stand on its own in Arabic as a noun phrase.

(6.30) N-Phrase: RELPRO SENTENCE

○   *Al~ðiy*   *[ÂuHib~u   -hu]*   الّذي أُحِبّ -هُ
   who/which   [I+love   -it]

   'the one/thing [whom/which] I love'

Nominal Arguments

Verbal nouns in Arabic such as deverbal nouns (مصدر *maSdar*) and active participles (اسم فَاعل) behave like verbs in that they can take an accusative object argument and other verbal modifiers. Their nominal form allows them to additionally participate in some of the nominal constructions discussed earlier, such as Idafa.

(6.31) N-Phrase: MASDAR^{construct} NOUN1^{Gen} NP-OBJ^{Acc}

○   *maʕrifaħu*   *Alrajuli*   *AlHaqiyqaħa*   مَعرِفَةُ الرّجُلِ الحَقِيقَةَ
   knowning+Nom   the+man+Gen   the+truth+Acc

   'the man's knowledge of the truth'

6.1.4   PREPOSITIONAL PHRASES

Arabic prepositional phrases consist of a preposition followed by a noun phrase. The head of the noun phrase is in the genitive case.

(6.32) P-PHRASE: PREP NOUN^{Gen}

○   *fiy Al+bayt+i* في البَيتِ
   in   the-house

   'in the house'

6.2   ARABIC TREEBANKS

Collections of manually checked syntactic analyses of sentences, or treebanks, are an important resource for building statistical parsers and evaluating parsers, in general. Rich treebank annotations have also been used for a variety of applications such as tokenization, diacritization, part-of-speech (POS) tagging, morphological disambiguation, base phrase chunking, and semantic role labeling. Under time restrictions, the creation of a treebank faces a tradeoff between linguistic richness and treebank size. This is especially the case for morpho-syntactically complex languages such as Arabic or Czech. Linguistically rich representations provide many (all) linguistic features that may be useful for a variety of applications. This comes at the cost of slower annotation as a result of longer guidelines and more intense annotator training. As a result, the richer the annotation, the slower the annotation process and the smaller the size of the treebank. Consequently, there is less data to train tools.

In the case of Arabic, two important rich-annotation treebanking efforts exist: the Penn Arabic Treebank (PATB) [9, 136, 82] and the Prague Arabic Dependency Treebank (PADT) [137, 138]. Both of these efforts employ complex and very rich linguistic representations that require a lot of human training. The amount of details specified in the representations is impressive. The PATB not only provides tokenization, complex POS tags, and syntactic structure; it also provides empty categories, diacritizations, lemma choices and some semantic tags. This information allows for important research in general NLP applications; however, much of this rich annotation is currently unused in Arabic parsing research [119] since it is generally considered to be derivative of the output of parsing itself. For example, nominal case, which can be determined for gold syntactic analyses at high accuracy [79], cannot be predicted well in a pre-parsing POS tagging step [116, 35]. To address this issue, a third treebank, the Columbia Arabic Treebank (CATiB), was recently introduced with the goal of speeding up annotation through representation simplification [112, 121].

In this section, we present a brief discussion of each of these three resources and compare them to each other.

Figure 6.1: The phrase structure representation in the Penn Arabic Treebank (PATB) for the sentence خمسون الف سائح زاروا لبنان وسوريا في ايلول الماضي *xmswn Alf sAŷH zArwA lbnAn wswryA fy Aylwl AlmADy* '50 thousand tourists visited Lebanon and Syria last September.'

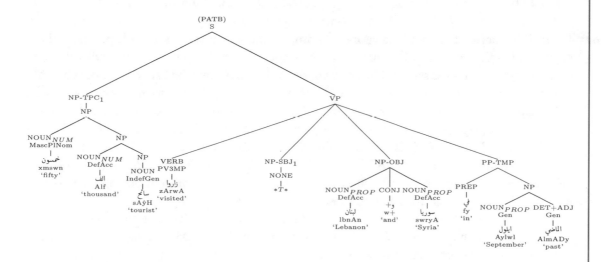

6.2.1 THE PENN ARABIC TREEBANK

The Penn Arabic Treebank (PATB)[2] project started in 2001 at the Linguistic Data Consortium (LDC) and the University of Pennsylvania, the birthplace of treebanks for English, Chinese, and Korean [139, 9, 71, 47, 136, 82]. As of the time of writing this book, three parts of the PATB have been released publicly through the LDC (almost 650K words) and four other parts, including a Levantine Arabic Treebank [140], have been developed for DARPA-funded projects.[3] Each PATB part was released in different versions with different degrees of improvements.

The PATB is annotated for morphological information, English gloss, and for syntactic structure in the phrase-structure style of the Penn (English) Treebank (PTB) [118]. The PTB guidelines are modified to handle Arabic. For example, Arabic verbal subjects are analyzed as verb phrase (VP) internal, following the verb.

An example of a tree in the PATB is presented in Figure 6.1. For the actual format of the PATB trees, see Figure 6.4. Phrase structure labels in PATB are extended with *dashtags* that specify syntactic or semantic roles, such as TPC (topic), SBJ (subject) or TMP (time). Some phrases are also co-indexed using an index number extension to the phrase label. The whole tree represents

---

[2]Being the first treebank for Arabic, the PATB is often referred to as simply the *Arabic Treebank* (ATB).
[3]Some of these resources could be made available to the general public in the future.

a sentence (label S), which consists of two phrases: a noun phrase (NP) functioning as a topic (NP-TPC) and a verb phrase (VP). The topic consists of numeral followed by an NP, which itself consists of a numeral followed by an NP. The deepest NP contains a single noun. The PATB uses the configuration (NP NOUN NP) to mark Idafa and Tamyiz constructions. The two constructions can only be distinguished using the morphological case of the noun in the embedded NP. The VP contains a subject (NP-SBJ), an object (NP-OBJ) and a temporal prepositional phrase (PP-TMP). The subject is an empty category (pro-drop), indicating that the subject is pronominal and conjugated in the verb form. The subject is also coindexed with the topic, indicating that the topic in this construction is the same as the subject of the verb. This is how the PATB represents nominal sentences with verbal sentence predicates. The object consists of two proper nouns conjoined with the conjunction +و $w+$ 'and'. The prepositional phrase (PP) contains a preposition (PREP) followed by an object of preposition NP. The NP consists of a proper noun that is modified by an adjective. Full form-based morphology is indicated for all the words in the tree. A full description of the PATB is available as part of the PATB annotation manual [82]. Most of the PATB sentences have been translated to English or had translations associated with them already. Some have also been treebanked in English, creating a unique resource, a parallel treebank.

The creation of the PATB is a great achievement for Arabic NLP. This resource has been crucial for so much research in morphological analysis, disambiguation, POS tagging and tokenization, not to mention of course parsing. Every other treebank, created since PATB, has used it or some of the tools developed for it. For instance, both the Prague Arabic Dependency Treebank and the Columbia Arabic Treebank converted the PATB to their own representation in addition to annotating additional data. Another example of the importance of the PATB is that its tokenization is the de facto standard for most Arabic treebanking efforts.

6.2.2   THE PRAGUE ARABIC DEPENDENCY TREEBANK

The Prague Arabic Dependency Treebank (PADT) is maintained by the Institute of Formal and Applied Linguistics, Charles University in Prague. PADT contains a multi-level description comprising functional morphology, analytical dependency syntax, and tectogrammatical representation of linguistic meaning. These linguistic annotations are based on the Functional Generative Description theory [141] and the Prague Dependency Treebank project [142].

The morphological and syntactic annotations in PADT differs considerably from the Penn Arabic Treebank. The POS annotations are in a functional morphology tag set developed as part of ELIXIRFM [143] (Section 5.2.5). The syntactic annotations are in a particular dependency structure representation with two levels of information: the analytical and the tectogrammatical. We will not discuss the tectogrammatical representation here.

An example of a sentence in the PADT representation is in Figure 6.2. In this example, the head of the sentence is the verb زاروا $zArwA$ 'visited'. It has three children, a subject (Sb), a coordinating (Coord) conjunction +و $w+$ 'and', and an auxiliary prepositional phrase (AuxP). The subject contains a number word modified by another number word in an attributive (Atr) relation. The second number

Figure 6.2: The dependency representation in PADT for the sentence خمسون الف سائح زاروا لبنان وسوريا في ايلول الماضي *xmswn Alf sAŷH zArwA lbnAn wswryA fy Aylwl AlmADy* '50 thousand tourists visited Lebanon and Syria last September.'

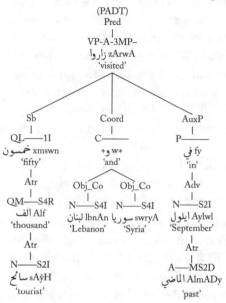

word is also modified by a noun in an attributive relation. The PADT does not distinguish between Idafa, Tamyiz and adjectival modification – they are all called *Atr*. The second child of the verb heads two proper nouns with the composite relation Obj_Co, which indicates at once that the two proper nouns are coordinated (Co) by their parent and that they both are objects (Obj) of their grandparent verb. The last child of the verb, the preposition في *fy* 'in' heads a proper noun ايلول *Aylwl* 'September' with the relation Adv (adverbial), which heads an adjective in an attribute (Atr) relation. The relation Adv indicates how the month name modifies the main verb despite the presence of the preposition in between the two. This highlights an important aspect of the analytical syntactic representation in the PADT, namely that it is deeper and more semantically (specifically propositionally) aware than other treebanks. For more information on PADT, see [144, 145, 143, 67, 138].

The initial version of PADT [145] contained around one hundred thousand words. PADT was used in the CoNLL 2006 and CoNLL 2007 shared tasks on dependency parsing [146] and its morphological data has been used for training automatic taggers [114]. The current version of PADT (2.0) contains over one million tokens of PATB-converted trees and trees annotated for PADT directly.

6.2.3   COLUMBIA ARABIC TREEBANK

The Columbia Arabic Tree Bank (CATiB) project started at Columbia University in 2008. It contrasts with previous Arabic treebanking approaches in putting an emphasis on faster production with some constraints on linguistic richness [112, 121]. Two ideas inspire the CATiB approach. First, CATiB avoids annotation of redundant linguistic information. For example, nominal case and state in Arabic are determined automatically from syntax and morphological analysis of the words and need not be annotated by humans. Of course, some information in CATiB is not easily recoverable, such as phrasal co-indexation and full lemma disambiguation. Second, CATiB uses an intuitive dependency structure representation and relational labels inspired by traditional Arabic grammar such as Tamyiz and Idafa in addition to the well-recognized labels of subject, object and modifier. This makes it easier to train annotators, who need not have degrees in linguistics.

There are eight syntactic relations used to label the dependency attachments in CATiB: subject (SBJ), object (OBJ), predicate (PRD), topic (TPC), Idafa (IDF), Tamyiz (TMZ), modifier (MOD) and flat (—). SBJ marks the explicit syntactic subjects of verbs (active or passive), regardless of whether they appear before or after the verb and subjects of nominal sentences. TPC is restricted to the subject/topic (مبتدأ) of a complex nominal sentence whose complement is a verb with a *different* subject. Typically, there is an object pronoun that refers back to the topic. The use of SBJ and TPC is different in CATiB from PATB. MOD is the most common relation used to mark all modifications such as adjectival modifications of nouns, adverbial modification and prepositional phrase modification of nouns and verbs. The flat relation marks multi-word structures that cannot be explained using any of the above relations. The most common case is the different parts of a proper name, e.g., a last name is in a flat relation to a first name.

CATiB includes almost 1 million tokens: 270K tokens of annotated newswire text in addition to converted PATB trees (parts 1, 2 and 3). Since the PATB has more information, conversion to CATiB is feasible at a good degree of correctness [112]. All CATiB annotated sentences are taken from a parallel Arabic-English corpus, so the sentences have translations associated with them.

Figure 6.3 presents and example of a sentence in CATiB. For the actual format of the CATiB trees, see Figure 6.4. To some degree, the dependency representation is similar to that used in PADT but with some very important differences (which we discuss in the next section). The head of the sentence is the verb زاروا *zArwA* 'visited'. It has three children, a subject (SBJ), an object (OBJ) and a prepositional modifier (MOD). The subject contains a complex number expression containing an Idafa and Tamyiz relations. The object heads a coordinating conjunction particle, which heads a coordinated conjunct. The third verb child, the preposition, governs an object (OBJ), which itself is modified by an adjectival nominal. This simplicity and coarse-grained nature of the relations used is the distinguishing mark of CATiB annotation compared to the other treebanking approaches.

6.2.4   COMPARISON: PATB, PADT AND CATIB

When comparing PATB, PADT and CATiB, we can distinguish two high-level aspects: syntactic representation and linguistic content. In terms of syntactic representation, PABT uses phrase struc-

Figure 6.3: The dependency representation in CATiB for the sentence خمسون الف سائح زاروا لبنان وسوريا في ايلول الماضي *xmswn Alf sAŷH zArwA lbnAn wswryA fy Aylwl AlmADy* '50 thousand tourists visited Lebanon and Syria last September.'

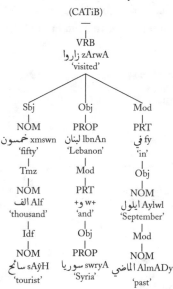

ture (PS) and both CATiB and PADT use dependency structure (DS). See Figures 6.1, 6.2 and 6.3. PS is a tree representation in which words in a sentence appear as leaves and internal nodes are syntactic categories such as *noun phrase* (NP) or *verb phrase* (VP). DS is also a tree except that the words in the sentence are the nodes on the tree [147]. In terms of linguistic content, we can further distinguish the following categories of content.

Syntactic Structure PADT and CATiB annotate heads explicitly and spans of phrases/clauses implicitly; whereas PATB annotates spans explicitly and heads implicitly. PATB uses intermediate projections, such as VP, to represent certain syntactic facts. The DS treebanks, PADT and CATiB, use other devices, such as attachment labels, to represent the same facts. PADT and CATiB approach some structures differently. For example, in PADT, the coordination conjunction heads over the different elements it coordinates as opposed to the way it is done in CATiB. See how لبنان و+سوريا *lbnAn w+ swryA* 'Lebanon and Syria' is represented in PADT and CATiB in Figures 6.2 and 6.3.

Syntactic and Semantic Functions PATB uses about 20 *dashtags* that are used for marking syntactic and semantic functions. Syntactic dashtags include -TPC and -OBJ and semantic tags includes -TMP (time) and -LOC (location). Some dashtags serve a dual semantic/syntactic purpose such

Figure 6.4: The internal representation of a syntactic tree in phrase structure (specifically PATB release format) and dependency structure (specifically CATiB release format). These examples are paired with the examples in Figures 6.1 and 6.3. The PATB trees are typically printed on a single line. The CATiB trees are represented in five columns indicating *word index*, *word*, *POS*, *parent word index* and *relation*. The Arabic words are represented in the Buckwalter transliteration scheme [88]. All glosses are additional.

Penn Arabic Treebank Example

```
(S (NP-TPC-1 (NOUN_NUM+NSUFF_MASC_PL_NOM xmswn)        fifty
             (NP (NOUN_NUM+CASE_DEF_ACC Alf)            thousand
                 (NP (NOUN+CASE_INDEF_GEN sA}H))))      tourist
   (VP (PV+PVSUFF_SUBJ:3MP zArwA)                       visited
       (NP-SBJ-1 (-NONE- *T*))
       (NP-OBJ (NOUN_PROP+CASE_DEF_ACC lbnAn)           Lebanon
               (CONJ w+)                                and
               (NOUN_PROP+CASE_DEF_ACC swryA))          Syria
       (PP-TMP (PREP fy)                                in
               (NP NOUN_PROP+CASE_DEF_GEN Aylwl         September
                  (DET+ADJ+CASE_DEF_GEN AlmADy)))))     past
```

Columbia Arabic Treebank Example

```
1    xmswn    NOM    4    SBJ    fifty
2    Alf      NOM    1    IDF    thousand
3    sA}H     NOM    2    IDF    tourist
4    zArwA    VRB    0    ---    visited
5    lbnAn    PROP   4    OBJ    Lebanon
6    w+       PRT    5    MOD    and
7    swryA    PROP   6    OBJ    Syria
8    fy       PRT    4    MOD    in
9    Aylwl    PROP   8    OBJ    September
10   AlmADy   NOM    9    MOD    past
```

as -SBJ which can mark syntactic subject of a verb and the semantic subject of a deverbal noun. PATB does not explicitly annotate dashtags in some cases such as objects of prepositions or the Idafa/Tamyiz constructions. These are implicitly marked through the syntactic structure. Idafa and Tamyiz are identical in PATB except for the morphological case information, which can be used to distinguish them. CATiB's relation labels mark syntactic function only. The use of the syntactic labels SBJ and TPC is different between CATiB and PATB. In PATB, TPC is used to mark the subject or object when they appear before the verb. Further co-indexation is used to specify the role of the TPC inside the verb phrase. See how the subject is handled in Figure 6.1 and 6.3. The subject of a verbless (non-complex) nominal sentence is marked as SBJ in both PATB and CATiB. PADT uses around 20 labels, although with different functionality from PATB and CATiB. In general, PADT analytical labels are deeper than CATiB since they are intended to be a stepping stone towards the

PADT tectogrammatical level. For instance, dependents of prepositions are marked with the relation they have to the node governing the preposition (the grandparent node). For example, in Figure 6.2, ايلول *Aylwl* 'September' is marked Adv (Adverbial) *of the main verb* زاروا *zArwA* 'visited'. Similarly, the coordinated elements لبنان و+ سوريا *lbnAn w+ swryA* 'Lebanon and Syria' are marked as both Co (coordinated) and with their relationship to the governing verb, Obj (object). PADT does not distinguish different types of nominal modifiers, i.e., adjectives, Idafa and Tamyiz (in numbers) are all marked as Atr (Attribute).

Empty Pronouns   Empty pronouns are annotated in PATB but not PADT nor CATiB. Verbs with no explicit subjects in CATiB (and PADT) can be assumed to pro-drop (implicit annotation).

Coreference   Coreference indices are annotated in PATB for traces and explicit pronouns. PADT only annotates coreference between explicit pronouns and what they corefer with. CATiB does not annotate any coreference indices.

Word Morphology   CATiB uses the same basic tokenization scheme used by PATB and PADT. As for parts-of-speech, PATB uses over 400 tags specifying every aspect of Arabic word morphology such as definiteness, gender, number, person, mood, voice and case. PADT morphology is more complex than PATB. For instance, it makes more sophisticated distinctions on nominal and adjectival definiteness/state, number, and gender. In contrast, CATiB uses six POS tags only. It is important to point out that in most Arabic parsing work, a much smaller POS tag set is used, reducing the 400 or so tags in PATB to a set between 20 and 40 tags [119]. [110] reports on simple regular-expression-based extension to CATiB's tag set that produces competitive results. Some of the rich morphology information not included in reduced POS tag sets, such as nominal case, can also be retrieved from the tree structure because they are defined syntactically [79].

Despite the many differences, conversion between these different representation can be done with a good degree of success given that the information is available in the tree although represented differently. Since CATiB has less content than PATB and PADT, it is perhaps much easier to convert from these two representations into CATiB's than the other way around.

6.2.5   A FOREST OF TREEBANKS

There are numerous extensions to the work on treebanks, in general. We present here pointers to efforts in Arabic treebanking extending in three dimensions: genre, representation, and depth.

- The team behind the PATB has been extending its profile to include additional genres such as Arabic used in broadcast news and conversation, telephone conversations and blogs. One example of this is the Levantine Arabic treebank [140, 148].

- The Quran Corpus project at the University of Leeds includes a treebanking effort targeting the Quran (QuranTree). The representation used in this project is a hybrid of phrase and dependency structures and is the closest to descriptions of traditional Arabic grammar [10, 149].

- A version of the PATB at Dublin University uses a lexical functional grammar (LFG) representation. This treebank was automatically converted and does not include additional annotations [150].

- The Arabic Propbank (Propositional Bank) [151] and the OntoNotes project [152] annotate for Arabic semantic information. We discuss the Arabic Propbank further in the next Chapter.

6.3   SYNTACTIC APPLICATIONS

The most obvious syntactic application is syntactic parsing, whose goal is to assign a syntactic structure to a sequence of words. This enabling technology can be and have been used for a variety of higher-order NLP applications such as machine translation and automatic summarization. Much work has been done on parsing, in general. There are several state-of-the-art parsers used for parsing Arabic: Bikel parser (phrase structure) [153, 119, 154], Malt parser (dependency) [146, 112, 110] and Stanford parser [155, 156], among others. All of the parsers mentioned above require the presence of a treebank. This is not a problem for MSA; however, Arabic dialects are rather impoverished in terms of treebanks. A recent Johns Hopkins Summer workshop demonstrated how Arabic dialects could be parsed using resources for MSA [148]. Among other (rule-based) efforts to MSA parsing, see [157, 158].

   A task related to syntactic parsing but shallower is base phase chunking (BPC). BPC is the process by which a sequence of adjacent words are grouped together to form syntactic phrases such as NPs and VPs [117, 120]. Different researchers have studied the utility of BPC for different applications such as MT [130] and named entity recognition (NER) [129].

6.4   FURTHER READINGS

Arabic faces similar challenges to other morphologically rich languages when it comes to parsing. A very recent workshop focused on such challenges: Workshop on Statistical Parsing of Morphologically Rich Languages (SPMRL – NAACL 2010). Other resources and tools relevant to syntax are mentioned in Appendix D.

CHAPTER 7

A Note on Arabic Semantics

Semantics is the study of the meaning of linguistic expressions. The amount of research in computational models of semantics is much smaller than other areas of NLP. This is perhaps due to its higher complexity and subtlety. Research on semantics in Arabic NLP is no different.

In this chapter, we start with a brief note on terminology. This is followed by a presentation of a set of resources developed for computational semantic modeling of Arabic and some of their associated applications. We leave discussions of various theories and representations of semantics out of this book.

7.1   A BRIEF NOTE ON TERMINOLOGY

The terminology used in discussing semantics tends to be more language independent than, say, morphology or orthography. For example, the basic concepts of homonymy,[1] synonymy[2] and semantic roles,[3] among others, are pretty much the same when used for Arabic or English. For more information, see [159, 160, 161].

That said, obviously, Arabic particulars, such as morphological richness and orthographic ambiguity due to optional diacritization, may lead to a larger number of homographs and as such more ambiguity than may be found in English. In addition, no different from other languages, Arabic words represent and distinguish different aspects of meaning idiosyncratically. For example, the Arabic word قلم *qalam* is used for both 'pen' and 'pencil,' yet the word صلاة *SlAħ* is used for 'prayer' only in the worship (*pray to*) sense not the request (*pray for*) sense.[4] Fantastic cliches of Arabic having a large number of words for *camel* (among others) are true. However, most Arabic speakers won't know more than a couple, particularly جمل *jamal* 'male camel', ناقة *nAqaħ* 'female camel' and إبل *Ăibil* 'camels (collective plural)'. Other words for *camel* are part of the jargon of camel breeders and specialists, e.g., حوار *HuwAr* 'a baby camel still at its mother's side', لبون *labuwn* 'lactating camel' or

---

[1]Homonymy is the state of two words having identical form (same spelling and same pronunciation) but different meaning, e.g., بيت *bayt* is both 'house' and 'poetic verse'. If these words have the same spelling but not same pronunciation, they are called homographs, e.g., the undiacritized word حب *Hb* can be pronounced /Hubb/ 'love' or /Habb/ 'seed'. If the two words have same pronunciation but different spelling, they are called homophones, e.g., عصى *ςaSaý* 'to disobey' and عصا *ςaSA* 'a stick' are both pronounced /ςaSa/. A homonym must be both a homograph and a homophone.

[2]Synonymy is the state of two words having identical meaning but different form, e.g., بيت *bayt* and دار *dAr* are both 'house'.

[3]Semantic role is the underlying relationship between a predicate and its argument regardless of the argument's syntactic expression. Semantic roles are also called thematic roles or theta roles. For example, in كتب علي كتابا *kataba ςaliy~ū kitAbAā* 'Ali wrote a book', *wrote* is the predicating verb, *Ali* is its agent/doer and *book* is its patient/theme/object.

[4]Word sense is a technical term referring to a specific meaning of a word.

خلوج *xaluwj* 'a female camel whose baby died'. This situation is comparable to the numerous words for 'horse' in the English jargon of horse breeders, e.g., *foal* 'a baby horse still at its mother's side' or *gelding* 'a castrated male horse'. In that respect, Arabic is no different again from other languages.

7.2   ARABIC PROPBANK

A Proposition Bank (propbank) is a type of semantically annotated corpus. Propbanks annotate propositions and their arguments in the form of predicate-argument information and semantic role labels on top of an existing syntactic treebank [162]. Other important semantically annotated corpora include Framenet [163]. An Arabic Propbank (APB) is currently under development at the University of Colorado following an approach similar to that used in the development of the English and Chinese propbanks [162, 164]. The APB is built on top of the PATB's syntactic structure and abides by it [151]. The APB also has access to the semantic dashtags and lemma annotations present in the PATB.

Propbanks crucially define an inventory of framesets for every verb. A frameset specifies the meaning of the predicating verb and the number and role of its arguments.[5] Adjuncts, which extend the meaning of the sentence but are not essential for the predicate verb, are not typically included in a frameset. Figure 7.1 illustrates with examples the five framesets associated with the Arabic verb قام *qAm*.

Figure 7.1: The various framesets associated with the Arabic verb قام *qAm* with examples.

F#	Frameset Definition	Example
F1	to carry out or to undertake Arg0: implementer Arg1: implemented	[قام]$_{Pred}$ [الفنان]$_{Arg0}$ [ب+ رسم الصورة]$_{Arg1}$ [qAm]$_{Pred}$ [AlfnAn]$_{Arg0}$ [b+ rsm AlSwrh]$_{Arg1}$ [The artist]$_{Arg0}$ [undertook]$_{Pred}$ [the painting of the picture]$_{Arg1}$
F2	to start or to happen Arg1: event	[قامت]$_{Pred}$ [الحرب]$_{Arg1}$ [qAmt]$_{Pred}$ [AlHrb]$_{Arg1}$ [The war]$_{Arg1}$ [started]$_{Pred}$
F3	to stand or be located Arg1: thing standing Arg2: location	[يقوم]$_{Pred}$ [المسجد]$_{Arg1}$ [ب+ جانب الكنيسة]$_{Arg2}$ [yqwm]$_{Pred}$ [Almsjd]$_{Arg1}$ [b+ jAnb Alknysh]$_{Arg2}$ [The mosque]$_{Arg1}$ [is located]$_{Pred}$ [next to the church]$_{Arg2}$
F4	to stand up Arg1: person standing	[قام]$_{Pred}$ [الرجل]$_{Arg1}$ [qAm]$_{Pred}$ [Alrjl]$_{Arg1}$ [The man]$_{Arg1}$ [stood up]$_{Pred}$
F5	to consist of Arg1: whole Arg2: parts	[يقوم]$_{Pred}$ [المشروع]$_{Arg1}$ [على أربع مراحل]$_{Arg2}$ [yqwm]$_{Pred}$ [Almšrwς]$_{Arg1}$ [ςlý Árbς mrAHl]$_{Arg2}$ [The project]$_{Arg1}$ [consists]$_{Pred}$ [of four phases]$_{Arg2}$

The APB also defines 24 argument types, which include five primary numbered arguments (ARG0, ARG1, ARG2, ARG3, ARG4) and 19 adjunctive arguments, which include ARGM-TMP

---

[5]http://verbs.colorado.edu/propbank/framesets-arabic/

(temporal adjunct) and ARGM-NEG (negation adjunct). The use of numbered arguments allows a propbank to capture generalizations about framesets of a particular verb without having to select from a restricted set of named thematic/semantic roles. An example of a fully annotated tree is presented in Figure 7.2.[6]

Figure 7.2: The Arabic Propbank annotation of the Penn Arabic Treebank (PATB) for the sentence خمسون الف سائح زاروا لبنان وسوريا في ايلول الماضي *xmswn Alf sÂŷH zArwA lbnAn wswryA fy Aylwl AlmADy* '50 thousand tourists visited Lebanon and Syria last September.' The main verb predicate, زار *zAr* 'visit' has only one frameset with two arguments: ARG0 (entity visiting) and ARG1 (entity visited). The NP-TPC in this example is indirectly assigned the ARG0 label through its common index with NP-SBJ.

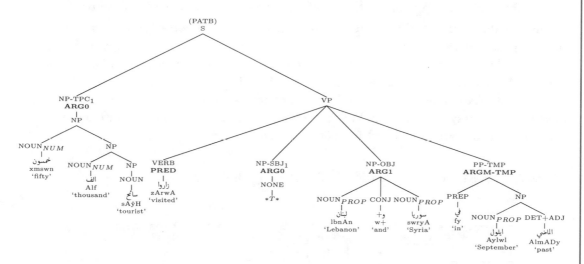

The Arabic Propbank has already been used by researchers in the task of Semantic Role Labeling (SRL) [165, 166].

7.3 ARABIC WORDNET

A wordnet is a machine-readable lexical database that groups words into clusters of synonyms called *synsets*. Every synset can be thought of as representing a unique word sense (meaning or concept). A wordnet typically provides general definitions and examples for the synsets and includes semantic relations between them. The semantic relations, which include among others, hyponymy[7] and hypernymy,[8] allow for a wordnet to be interpreted hierarchically as a lexical ontology/taxonomy.

---

[6] APB annotations are stored in separate files from the PATB trees they extend. The figure we use here is intended to be illustrative.
[7] A hyponym is a word whose semantic range is included in another word, e.g., *woman* is a hyponym of *human being*.
[8] A hypernym is a word whose semantic range includes another word, e.g., *human being* is a hypernym of *woman*.

The Princeton English WordNet is the first wordnet created [167]. It has been followed by many similar efforts and extensions, most notable amongst which is EuroWordNet [168]. Many of the wordnet efforts have been coordinated to include cross links. This allows them to be used not only as sophisticated computational monolingual thesauri but also as dictionaries.

The Arabic WordNet (AWN) effort started in 2006 through a collaboration of several universities and companies [169, 170]. AWN is based on the design and contents of the Princeton WordNet. Arabic synsets are paired with synsets in the Princeton WordNet and are mappable to synsets in EuroWordNet. Arabic words in AWN are represented in terms of their lemmas, abstracting away from morphological inflections. Figure 7.3 presents the various synsets involving the Arabic verb زار *zAr* and its English translation *visit*. Every row in the figure represents two synsets that have been paired up (Arabic and English). The English WordNet, which is bigger than AWN, includes three additional synsets that have no current mapping in the AWN. The pairing in Figure 7.3 highlights some important differences between the two words. The Arabic verb زار *zAr* does not include the sense of inflicting/imposing possible with the verb *visit*. زار *zAr* can also be said to be more general in that it maps to the synset (tour), which happens to be a hypernym of the synset (visit, see). The hypernymy relation is not shown in Figure 7.3. Both the Arabic WordNet and the English WordNet are publicly available and browsable online.

The AWN has been used as the lexical reference for evaluating Arabic word sense disambiguation (WSD) systems [166]. In WSD, words are tagged with their specific meaning in context using meaning definitions in a predefined lexical resource.

Figure 7.3: Paired synsets from Arabic WordNet and English WordNet.

Arabic WordNet Synset	English WordNet Synset
زار zAr, تجول tjwl, جال jAl, جاب jAb, دار dAr, طاف TAf	tour
زار zAr, رأى rÂý, شاهد šAhd	visit, see
زار zAr, سافر إلى sAfr ÂlY	visit, travel to
زار zAr	visit, call in, call
وجه wjh, فرض frD, صب Sb, ابتلى Abtlý, أنزل Ânzl, أصاب ÂSAb, أزعج ÂzEj	visit, inflict, bring down, impose
تسامر tsAmr, تحادث tHAdθ, دردش drdš	visit, chew the fat, shoot the breeze, chat, confabulate

7.4 ARABIC RESOURCES FOR INFORMATION EXTRACTION

The goal of Information Extraction (IE) is to automatically extract structured and semantically well-defined information from unstructured raw text documents, e.g., identifying names of geographical locations in text. IE subtasks typically include mention detection, coreference resolution and relation extraction. The mention detection task includes identifying three classes of entity mentions: named (e.g., باراك اوباما *bArAk AwbAmA* 'Barack Obama'), nominal (e.g., الرئيس الأمريكي *Alrŷys AlÂmryky* 'the American President') and pronominal (e.g., هو *hw* 'he'). Each mention can be classified into one of five types: person (PER), organization (ORG), location (LOC), geo-political entity (GPE) and facility (FAC). The task of Named Entity Recognition (NER) focuses on mention detection and classification of named entities only. The task of coreference resolution relates different mentions in text to each other, e.g., identifying that a particular هو *hw* 'he' is indeed باراك اوباما *bArAk AwbAmA* 'Barack Obama' as opposed to someone else. Relation extraction specifies the kind of relation between two different entities, e.g., a specific PER is located at a specific GPE.

Arabic resources for IE have been developed as part of the Automatic Content Extraction (ACE) program [171].[9] This includes annotated text for various IE tasks, which can be used for developing and testing IE systems [172, 128, 129, 173]. An example of the output of an NER system is presented in Figure 7.4.

Figure 7.4: An example of a sentence in Arabic and English with named entity recognition tags in XML.

زار <PER>الملك حسين</PER> <GPE>لبنان</GPE> في العام الماضي.

zAr <PER>*Almlk Hsyn*</PER> <GPE>*lbnAn*</GPE> *fy AlٵAm AlmADy.*

<PER>King Hussein</PER> visited <GPE>Lebanon</GPE> last year.

7.5   FURTHER READINGS

In this section, we present a brief listing of pointers to noteworthy efforts on Arabic semantic modeling. Pointers to lexica, thesauri and dictionaries are presented in Appendix B and C.

- [174] described and evaluated an approach for developing resources and a system for Arabic word sense disambiguation.

- OntoNotes is an effort for annotating English, Arabic and Chinese texts in various genres for syntax, predicate argument structure, word sense and coreference [152].

- The Interlingual Annotation for Multilingual Text Corpora (IAMTC) project explored a common representation for annotating increasingly semantic phenomena in seven languages (Arabic, Hindi, English, Spanish, Korean, Japanese and French) [175].

- The Prague Arabic Dependency Treebank includes some annotation of tectogrammatics, the underlying syntax reflecting the linguistic meaning of utterances [138].

[9]The ACE annotation guidelines for English, Arabic and Chinese are available at http://projects.ldc.upenn.edu/ace/data/.

- The Conceptual Interlingua, a resource for information retrieval based on the Princeton English WordNet was extended with Arabic terms in [176].

- The Language Understanding Annotation Corpus is an experimental corpus of English and Arabic text annotated for committed belief, event and entity coreference, dialog acts and temporal relations.

- [14] constructed a corpus with annotations for naturally occurring numerical expressions and used it to evaluate a system for automatic detection of these expressions.

CHAPTER 8

A Note on Arabic and Machine Translation

The previous chapters in this book discusses Arabic from a monolingual point of view. By contrast, this chapter addresses the multilingual issues of working with Arabic. We specifically consider one application, Machine Translation (MT). Since some of the readers may not be familiar with this application, a short introduction is provided in the following section to define basic terms and concepts. We recommend that readers consider some of the numerous books, articles and websites offering far more thorough introductions to the field of MT. The rest of the chapter offers a discussion of Arabic linguistic features from a comparative point of view and with MT in mind. This is followed by a survey of available resources and a presentation of the state of the field of Arabic MT (from Arabic and to Arabic).

8.1   BASIC CONCEPTS OF MACHINE TRANSLATION

MT is basically an application for mapping from one human language (source language) to another (target language). The various approaches to MT can be grouped into two camps: the symbolic/rule-based (RBMT) and the statistical/corpus-based (SMT) approaches.

RBMT is characterized with the explicit use of linguistically informed rules and representations. In its pure form, RBMT includes techniques such as Transfer MT, which relates languages at some syntactic level, and Interlingual MT, which attempts to model semantics. RBMT solutions require the creation of specialized linguistic translation dictionaries that model the languages and their mapping lexically and syntactically. Typically, these resources are created manually or semi-automatically [177].

In its pure form, SMT is corpus based, i.e., learned from examples of translations called parallel/bilingual corpora. The following is a simplistic account of what SMT systems do. The source and target sides of parallel texts are automatically word aligned [178]. See Figure 8.1. The word alignments are used to learn translation models that relate words and sequences of words in the source language to those in the target language [179]. When translating (aka decoding) a source language sentence, a statistical decoder combines the information in the translation model with a language model of the target language to produce a ranked list of optimal sentences in the target language.

In the last two decades, the success of SMT approaches has changed the face of the field, which was previously dominated by RBMT approaches. It should be noted that the distinction between,

Figure 8.1: A pair of word-aligned Arabic and English sentences.

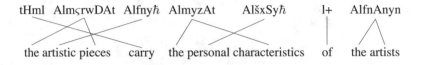

and nomenclature of, the SMT and RBMT camps can be deceptive since explicit linguistic rules can be probabilistic and can be learned automatically. The last few years have witnessed an increased interest in hybridizing the two approaches to create systems that exploit the advantages of both linguistic rules and statistical techniques. The most successful of such attempts so far are solutions that build on statistical corpus-based approaches by strategically using linguistics constraints or features.

8.2   A MULTILINGUAL COMPARISON

Since MT is essentially about relating two languages to each other, the challenges for MT are different when the languages share some characteristics [180] than when they are different. The direction of the translation, translation modality (speech or text) and availability of monolingual and bilingual resources are also important factors to consider. In this section, we compare Arabic, in terms of its orthography, morphology and syntax, to three other languages with rather different linguistic characteristics: Chinese, English and Spanish.[1] See the comparison summary in Figure 8.2.

8.2.1   ORTHOGRAPHY

In terms of orthography, Arabic's reduced alphabet with optional diacritics and common cliticizations falls in between Spanish and English (both alphabets) on one hand and Chinese (complex system with around 10,000 logographic characters) on the other. Arabic tokenization is far easier than Chinese segmentation. But the two languages start to pose similar challenges when translating from OCRed text. Arabic diacritic absence adds to the ambiguity of translating from Arabic, in general, but it is especially problematic for proper name transliteration [21, 45, 50, 22]. The good news is that when translating into Arabic, as opposed from Arabic, the absent diacritics in the output may render some translation errors irrelevant.

---

[1]The four languages we discuss here are all resource-rich high-density languages. It is important to point out that Arabic dialects, which are not part of this book, are technically resource-poor or low-density languages. The issue of resource density will not be discussed here.

Figure 8.2: A comparison of Arabic, Spanish, English and Chinese across six linguistic aspects. Table legend: V=Verb, Subj=Subject, V_{Subj}=Pro-dropped Verb, N=Noun, Adj=Adjective, Poss=Possessor, Rel=Relative Clause.

	Arabic	Spanish	English	Chinese
Orthography	optionally-reduced alphabet	alphabet	alphabet	logographic characters
Morphology	very rich	rich	poor	very poor
Subject-Verb order	V Subj V_{Subj} Subj V	V_{Subj} Subj V	Subj V	Subj V
Adjectival Modifier	N Adj	N Adj	Adj N	Adj 的 N
Possessive Modifier	N Poss	N de Poss	N of Poss Poss 's N Poss N	Poss 的 N
Relative Modifier	N Rel	N Rel	N Rel	Rel 的 N

8.2.2   MORPHOLOGY

Arabic stands as the most morphologically complex language compared. Arabic is followed by Spanish, then English and finally Chinese, which is an isolating language with no morphology to talk of. Arabic morphological complexity leads to a large number of possible word forms, which results into the computational problems of increased sparsity and high degree of Out-of-Vocabulary (OOV) terms. In a study by [50], almost 60% of OOV words in an Arabic to English MT system were found to involve verbs, nouns and adjectives, many of which are unseen morphological variants of infrequently seen words.

Arabic morphological complexity and its consequences are typically handled through automatic tokenization to break up words into smaller units with less sparsity. The question of what is an optimal tokenization has been explored by various researchers mostly working on Arabic-English MT. Lee [108] investigated the use of automatic alignment of POS-tagged English and affix-stem segmented Arabic to determine appropriate tokenizations of Arabic. [83, 105] conducted a large set of experiments including multiple preprocessing schemes reflecting different levels of morphological representation and multiple techniques for disambiguation/tokenization. Other results were reported using specific preprocessing schemes and techniques by [181, 182, 183, 98]. Improvements for word alignment was also shown using different morphological tokenizations [107]. In principle, different optimal tokenizations can be used for different parts of an MT system so long they are coordinated.

For example, lemmas can be used for automatic alignment, but some inflected decliticized form can be used in the translation model. Various tokenization schemes are discussed in Section 5.3.

Translation into Arabic from other languages faces an added problem: the output needs to be in a morphologically complex form even if some simplified form is used in the translation models or dictionaries. Arabic *detokenization* or *recombination* has been demonstrated successfully by [99, 13, 106].

8.2.3 SYNTAX

Figure 8.3: A pair of word-aligned Arabic and English sentences. The Arabic syntactic representation, provided for illustrative purposes, is in CATiB style annotation.

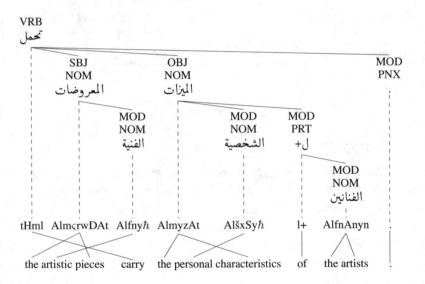

Arabic is a morphosyntactically complex language with many differences from Spanish, English and Chinese. We describe here four syntactic phenomena: subject-verb order, adjectival modification, possessive modification, and relative modification. Figure 8.3 illustrates some of these phenomena in an Arabic to English context.

Arabic verb subjects may be: (a.) pro-dropped (verb conjugated), (b.) pre-verbal, or (c.) post-verbal. Each situation comes with its own morphosyntactic restrictions. Spanish also allows pro-drop in similar contexts to Arabic, but unlike Arabic, Spanish does not have an option for a Verb-Subject order. English and Chinese are both generally Subject-Verb languages. Given the three possibilities for where the subject can go, when translating from Arabic, the challenge is to determine whether there is an explicit subject and, if so, whether it is pre- or post-verbal. Since Arabic objects also

Figure 8.4: An example of long distance reordering of Arabic VSO order into English SVO order

---

[**V**اعلن] [NP-SBJ] المنسق العام لمشروع السكة الحديد بين دول مجلس التعاون الخليجي] [SUB ان ...]

[**V Aςln**] [NP-SBJ Almnsq AlςAm lmšrwς Alskħ AlHdyd byn dwl mjls AltςAwn Alxlyjy] *[SUB An ...]*

[NP-SBJ The general coordinator of the railroad project among the countries of the Gulf Cooperation Council]
[**V announced**] *[SUB that ...]*

---

follow the verb, a sequence of Verb and a noun phrase may be a Verb-Subject or a pro-dropped Verb-Object. The problem is exacerbated with very long subjects that can themselves be split mistakenly into smaller noun phrases. This is a challenge to both SMT systems (with possible limited phrase window size) and RBMT systems, which may make syntactic parsing errors. See Figure 8.4 for a ten-word subject example.

Translating from any of the other languages to Arabic may in principle be easier since maintaing the original word order is acceptable in Arabic. This may be true syntactically, but it will have some consequences on perceived fluency and textual flow in Arabic.

Arabic and Spanish nominal modifiers of all types (adjectival, possessive and relative) follow the noun they modify. Chinese is consistent also, but in the opposite order. Chinese uses the function particle 的 *de* for marking all modification structures. Spanish also uses function words: a preposition (coincidentally also *de*) for marking possessive structures and relative pronouns, e.g., *que*, for relative modification. Arabic, however, depends more on subtle coordination of definite articles to distinguish adjectival and possessive (Idafa) modification. As for relative structures, indefinite relative modification in Arabic forbids the presence of a relative pronoun, which leads to structural ambiguity comparable to the English: *the man wanted (by Mary)/(to go)*. While English's Verb-Subject order is simple, English nominal modification phenomena are all over the place. In some cases, English is closer to Arabic or Spanish and in others it is closer to Chinese. In particular, English has a lot of variety in its possessive construction. For example, the English phrases *the car keys*, *the car's keys* and *the keys of the car* all translate into the Arabic مفاتيح السيارة *mfAtyH AlsyArħ* '[lit.] keys the-car.' In contrast, Arabic has a lot of variety in Verb-Subject order, but not in nominal modification order.

Much work is going on in terms of syntactic modeling for MT, in general, and for Arabic-English [184, 130, 185, 186, 156, 187] and English-Arabic [188, 189], in particular.

8.3   STATE OF THE FIELD OF ARABIC MT

Arabic-English MT has received a lot of attention in recent years. This has led to significant progress in terms of created resources and built systems. There are several very large parallel corpora and numerous dictionaries for Arabic-English, and other languages, e.g., the UN corpus has parallel documents in Arabic, English, Chinese, Spanish, French and Russian (See Appendix C).

There are several competitive MT evaluation campaigns that include Arabic as one of their languages. Most notable is the NIST MT Eval (Arabic-English) and also the recently inaugurated MEDAR MT evaluation (English-Arabic). Some USA governmental funded programs such as GALE (text/speech-text), MADCAT (OCR for text-text) and TRANSTAC (speech-speech) also focus heavily on evaluation of Arabic-English MT.

The majority of Arabic MT research is on Arabic-English; however, there are some published efforts in English-Arabic[99, 188, 13, 106] Arabic-French[190] and even Arabic-Chinese [191], Danish-Arabic [192] and Hebrew-Arabic [193]. Various companies have different MT systems for different language pairs; most notable among these is Google Translate which allows bidirectional translation across 50+ languages including Arabic. Other important public systems include Microsoft's Bing Trasnslator and Sakhr's Tarjim.

Finally, although a majority of the published research on Arabic MT is in SMT, we are aware of the following published research on Arabic RBMT: [194, 195] (within the transfer approach) and [196, 197, 198] (within the interlingua approach). Two of the top Arabic MT companies using RBMT or hybrid systems are Apptek and Sakhr.

8.4   FURTHER READINGS

Although this chapter focused on MT, an important related application deserves a few words. Cross-language information retrieval (CLIR) is a type of information retrieval where the language of the query and the language of the searched text are different, e.g., searching Arabic text using an English query. Given the increasing amount of digital text, CLIR can allow a user to do some triage to sub-select documents for MT or human translation. Arabic was one of the languages considered in the Text Retrieval Conference (TREC) tracks in 2001 [199] and 2002 [200]. The Arabic TREC corpus has been used as a testbed by many researchers [201, 202, 203].

APPENDIX A

Arabic NLP Repositories and Networking Resources

A.1 REPOSITORIES

A.1.1 RESOURCE DISTRIBUTORS

- Linguistic Data Consortium (LDC)

- Evaluation and Language Resource Distribution Agency (ELDA)

- European Language Resources Association (ELRA)

A.1.2 RESEARCH PAPER REPOSITORIES

- Anthology of the Association for Computational Linguistics (ACL Anthology)

- Machine Translation Archive (MT Archive)

- Proceedings of some of the Language Resources and Evaluation Conferences (LREC)

A.1.3 COLLECTIONS OF LINKS

- The Arabic WordNet Project's webpage on Arabic NLP Resources

- Arabic Information Retrieval and Computational Linguistics Resources

- Elsnet's List of pointers to Arabic and other Semitic NLP and Speech sites

- **MEDAR**: 2009 Arabic HLT Survey, 2005 Arabic HLT Survey, BLARK and Archive

- Latifa Al-Sulaiti's webpage on Arabic Resources

- ELRA's *Universal Catalog* (search for Arabic)

- Linguistlist on Arabic

- Stanford's webpage on Resources for NLP

- Arabic Language Directory

- Columbia's Arabic Dialect Modeling Group

- Ajeeb – links to different sites related to Sakhr's Arabic solutions

- The Perseus Project's collection of Arabic materials

- NLP-4-Arabic webpage

A.2 NETWORKING AND CONFERENCES

A.2.1 PROFESSIONAL NETWORKS

- Network for Euro-Mediterranean LAnguage Resources (NEMLAR)

- Mediterranean Arabic Language and Speech Technology (MEDAR)

- European Network of Excellence in Human Language Technologies (ELSNET)

- The Arabic Language Academies

- ARABIC-L: Arabic Language and Linguistics Mailing List

- Semitic Mailing List

- Linguist List

- Corpora Mailing List

A.2.2 CONFERENCES AND WORKSHOPS

- Workshop on Computational Approaches to Semitic Languages (LREC 2010, EACL 2009, ACL 2007, ACL 2005, ACL 2002, ACL 1998)

- Workshop on Statistical Parsing of Morphologically Rich Languages (SPMRL – NAACL 2010)

- Georgetown University Round Table on Arabic Language and Linguistics (GURT 2010)

- Workshop on Computational Approaches to Arabic Script-based Languages (MTSummit XII 2009, LSA 2007, COLING 2004)

- Conference on Arabic Language Resources and Tools (MEDAR-2009, NEMLAR-2004)

- International Symposium on Computer and Arabic Language (ISCAL 2009, ISCAL 2007)

- Workshop on HLT & NLP within the Arab World (LREC 2008)

- NLP track in the International Conference on Informatics and Systems (INFOS 2010, INFOS 2008)

- Colloque International sur le Traitement Automatique de la Langue Arabe (CITALA) (Rabat, 2007)

- The Challenge of Arabic for NLP/MT Conference (British Computer Society 2006)

- Parsing Arabic Dialects (Johns Hopkins University summer workshop 2005)

- Special session on Arabic Processing in Traitement Automatique du Langage Naturel (TALN 2004)

- Workshop on Machine Translation for Semitic Languages (MT Summit 2003)

- Novel Approaches to Arabic Speech Recognition (Johns Hopkins University summer workshop 2002)

- International Symposium on Processing of Arabic (Tunisia 2002)

- Workshop on Arabic Language Resources and Evaluation (LREC 2002)

- Workshop on Arabic Language Processing (ACL/EACL-2001)

- Arabic Translation and Localization Symposium (ATLAS 1999)

APPENDIX B

Arabic NLP Books and References

B.1 LINGUISTICS

- Badawi, E., M. G. Carter, and A. Gully. 2004. Modern Written Arabic: A Comprehensive Grammar. Routledge, London.

- Bateson, Mary Catherine. 2003. Arabic Language Handbook. Georgetown University Press.

- Brustad, Kristen E. 2000. The Syntax of Spoken Arabic: A Comparative Study of Moroccan, Egyptian, Syrian, and Kuwaiti Dialects. Georgetown University Press.

- Fischer, W. 2001. A Grammar of Classical Arabic. Yale Language Series. Yale University Press. Translated by Jonathan Rodgers.

- Holes, Clive. 2004. Modern Arabic: Structures, Functions, and Varieties. Georgetown University Press.

- Georgetown Classics in Arabic Language/Linguistics. Karin C. Ryding and Margaret Nydell, eds. (several excellent titles)

- Ryding, Karin C. 2006. A Reference Grammar of Modern Standard Arabic. Cambridge University Press.

- Schulz, Eckehard. 2008. A Student Grammar of Modern Standard Arabic. Cambridge University Press.

- Buckley, Ron. 2004. Modern Literary Arabic: A Reference Grammar. Librairie du Liban.

- Wright, W. 1896. A Grammar of the Arabic Language. Cambridge University Press. (a classic grammar book)

- Bohas, G., J. Guillaume and D. Kouloughli. 2006. The Arabic Linguistic Tradition. Georgetown University Press.

- Almulla Traditional Arabic Grammar Rules (800+ slides in Arabic)

B.2   PAPER/SCANNED DICTIONARIES

- List of dictionaries (in Arabic) from Dar Al-Ilm lil-Malayin (monolingual, bilingual and multilingual dictionaries)

- Wehr, Hans. 1979. Dictionary of Modern Written Arabic (Arabic-English). Ithaca: Spoken Language Services.

- Lane, Edward William. 1968. Arabic-English Lexicon. Beirut: Librarie du Liban.

- Hinds, Martin and El-Said Badawi. 1986. A Dictionary of Egyptian Arabic. Beirut: Librarie du Liban.

- Stowasser, Karl and Moukhtar Ani. 2004. A Dictionary of Syrian Arabic. Georgetown University Press.

- Clarity, B. E., Karl Stowasser, Ronald G. Wolfe, D. R. Woodhead, and Wayne Beene. 2003. A Dictionary of Iraqi Arabic. Georgetown University Press.

- Harrell, Richard S. and Harvey Sobelman. 2004. A Dictionary of Moroccan Arabic. Georgetown University Press.

- Qafisheh, Hamdi. 1999. NTC's Gulf Arabic - English Dictionary. NTC Publishing Group.

- Qafisheh, Hamdi. 1999. NTC's Yemeni Arabic - English Dictionary. NTC Publishing Group.

B.3   COMPUTATIONAL LINGUISTICS

- Kiraz, George. 2001. Computational Nonlinear Morphology with Emphasis on Semitic Languages. Studies in Natural Language Processing. Cambridge University Press.

- Van den Bosch, A. and A. Soudi. 2007. Arabic Computational Morphology: Knowledge-based and Empirical Methods. Springer.

- Farghaly, Ali. 2010. Arabic Computational Linguistics. The University of Chicago Press.

- Farghaly, Ali and Khaled Shaalan. 2009. Arabic Natural Language Processing: Challenges and Solutions. A Special Issue of the ACM Transactions on Asian Language Information Processing (TALIP).

- Wintner, Shuly. 2009. Language Resources for Semitic Languages – Challenges and Solutions. In Sergei Nirenburg (ed.) Language Engineering for Lesser-Studied Languages. Amsterdam: IOS Press.

- United Nations Report. 2003. Harmonization of ICT standards related to Arabic Language use in information society applications. (A very informative report on information and communication technology in the Arab World).

B.4   TUTORIALS AND LECTURES

- Habash, Nizar. Introduction to Arabic Natural Language Processing.

- Smrž, Otakar. Yet Another Introduction to Arabic Natural Language Processing.

- Diab, Mona and Nizar Habash. Arabic Dialect Processing.

- Habash, Nizar. Semitic Linguistic Phenomena and Variations.

APPENDIX C

Arabic NLP Corpora and Lexica

C.1 SPEECH CORPORA

- Arabic Broadcast News (Audio) (Transcripts)

- CALLHOME Egyptian Arabic Speech (Audio) (Transcripts) (Audio Supplement) (Transcripts Supplement)

- Egyptian Arabic telephone conversations: 1997 HUB5 Arabic Evaluation (Audio) (Transcripts)

- Appen's Gulf Arabic Conversational Telephone Speech (Audio) (Transcripts)

- Appen's Iraqi Arabic Conversational Telephone Speech (Audio) Transcripts

- Appen's Levantine Arabic Conversational Telephone Speech (Audio) (Transcripts)

- Levantine Arabic QT Training Data Set 5 (Audio) (Transcripts) *A combination of four training data sets totaling 250 hours of telephone conversation in Levantine Arabic*

- BBN/AUB DARPA Babylon Levantine Arabic Speech and Transcripts

- West Point Arabic Speech (scripted speech, native and non-native)

- CALLFRIEND Egyptian Arabic (Audio only, intended for language identification)

- Saudi Accented Arabic Voice Bank (SAAVB)

- KACST Arabic Phonetics Database (KAPD)

- NetDC Arabic Broadcast News Speech Corpus (Audio and Transcriptions) – ELRA Catalog S0157

- GlobalPhone Arabic (Audio and Transcriptions) – ELRA Catalog S0192

- Arabic Transcription Guidelines in EARS

- AMADAT: Arabic Multi-Dialectal Transcription tool

- NEMLAR Broadcast News Speech Corpus – ELRA Catalog S0219

- NEMLAR Speech Synthesis Corpus – ELRA Catalog S0220

- Appen has a number of speech corpora and lexica for different dialects. Appen Catalogue – search for Arabic

- OrienTel is a European project focusing on the development of language resources for speech-based applications (Website):

  - OrienTel Morocco Modern Colloquial Arabic – ELRA Catalog S0183
  - OrienTel Morocco Modern Standard Arabic – ELRA Catalog S0184
  - OrienTel Tunisia Modern Colloquial Arabic – ELRA Catalog S0186
  - OrienTel Tunisia Modern Standard Arabic – ELRA Catalog S0187
  - OrienTel Egypt Modern Colloquial Arabic – ELRA Catalog S0221
  - OrienTel Egypt MSA Modern Standard Arabic – ELRA Catalog S0222
  - OrienTel Jordan Modern Colloquial Arabic – ELRA Catalog S0289
  - OrienTel Jordan Modern Standard Arabic – ELRA Catalog S0290
  - OrienTel Arabic as spoken in Israel – ELRA Catalog S0190
  - Orientel United Arab Emirates Modern Colloquial Arabic – ELRA Catalog S0258
  - Orientel United Arab Emirates Modern Standard Arabic – ELRA Catalog S0259

C.2 ARABIC HANDWRITING RECOGNITION CORPORA AND EVALUATIONS

- LDC Resources for Arabic Handwriting Recognition

- Applied Media Analysis dataset for handwritten Arabic

- The 2010 NIST Open Handwriting Recognition and Translation Evaluation (OpenHaRT 2010)

C.3 TEXT CORPORA

C.3.1 MONOLINGUAL TEXT

- Arabic Gigaword

- Corpus of Contemporary Arabic

- ArabiCorpus

- Quranic Arabic Corpus (Annotations for POS tags and Syntax)

- Almeshkat collection of free Arabic books (some in text form)

- Al-Eman collection of free Arabic books (some in text form)

- Al-Hayat Arabic Corpus – ELRA Catalog W0030

- An-Nahar Newspaper Text Corpus – ELRA Catalog W0027

- *Le Monde Diplomatique* Text corpus in Arabic – ELRA Catalog W0036-04

- Qamus.org's corpora webpage

C.3.2   PARALLEL TEXT

- Arabic Broadcast News Parallel Text: GALE Phase 1 (Part 1) (Part 2)

- Arabic Newsgroup Parallel Text: GALE Phase 1 (Part 1) (Part 2)

- Arabic Blog Parallel Text: GALE Phase 1

- ISI Arabic-English Automatically Extracted Parallel Text (newswire)

- Arabic English Parallel News Part 1

- Arabic News Translation Text Part 1

- Arabic Newswire English Translation Collection (PATB data)

- English-Arabic Treebank v 1.0 (Treebank of English translation of portions of Penn Arabic Treebank Part 1 version 3.0)

- Multiple-Translation Arabic (MTA) (Part 1) (Part 2)

- MEEDAN: A web forum with Arabic-English parallel postings

- Official Document System of the United Nations (English, French, Spanish, Arabic, Russian, Chinese)

- Arabic Wikipedia with many terms paired with other languages (not strictly parallel)

- Egyptian Arabic Wikipedia

- The Qur'an in Arabic with four translations

- The Bible in Arabic, English [KJV] and other languages

- A fully diacritized modern Arabic translation of the Bible (by Biblica).

- The STRAND Arabic-English Bilingual Database (automatically collected pairs of URLs)

C.3.3   POS TAGGED AND/OR DIACRITIZED TEXT

- "Le Monde Diplomatique" Arabic tagged corpus: raw, diacritized, POS tagged – ELRA Catalog W0049

- NEMLAR Written Corpus: raw text, fully vowelized text, text with Arabic lexical analysis, text with Arabic POS-tags –ELRA Catalog W0042

- Khoja POS tagged corpus

- Part 4 v 1.0 (only morphology and POS tags)

- University of Haifa Morphologically Tagged Qur'an

C.3.4   ANNOTATIONS FOR INFORMATION EXTRACTION AND RETRIEVAL

- Automatic Content Extraction Evaluation   (ACE)   Multilingual   Training   Corpus (2003)(2004) (2005)

- GALE Phase 1 Distillation Training data

C.3.5   TREEBANKS

- Penn Arabic Treebank (LDC) Part 1 v 3.0 Part 2 v 2.0 Part 3 v 2.0

  – Penn Arabic Treebank Morphological and Syntactic Guidelines

- Prague Arabic Dependency Treebank 1.0: (through LDC) (114K tokens) – PADT 2.0.

- CATiB: Columbia Arabic Treebank 1.0 (Website) (available through LDC - LDC2009E06 - by request ldc@ldc.upenn.edu)

- Dublin City University LFG Arabic Treebank

- University of Leeds' Quran Treebank

- Levantine Arabic Treebank (available through LDC - LDC2005E78 - by request ldc@ldc.upenn.edu)

- Arabic Proposition Bank (Propbank)

- OntoNotes Release 3.0 (English, Arabic and Chinese texts annotated for syntax, predicate argument structure, word sense and coreference). (BBN's webpage)

- Syddansk Universiteit's Visual Interactive Syntax Learning Site

C.4 EVALUATION CORPORA

- NIST's Language Recognition Evaluation (LRE) webpage (LRE-2003 data, LRE-2007 test set and supplemental training)

- 2008 NIST Metrics for Machine Translation (MetricsMATR08) Development Data

- NIST's Machine Translation Evaluation

- CESTA Evaluation Package: Campagne d'Evaluation de Systèmes de Traduction Automatique (Machine Translation Evaluation Campaign) – (French initiative; Arabic-French MT) – ELRA Catalog E0020

- ARCADE II Evaluation Package: Action de Recherche Concertée sur l'Alignement de Documents et son Evaluation (Evaluation of parallel text alignment systems) – (French initiative; Arabic-French MT) – ELRA Catalog E0018

- OpenHaRT 2010: NIST Open Handwriting Recognition and Translation Evaluation

C.5 LEXICAL DATABASES

C.5.1 MONOLINGUAL DICTIONARIES

- Al-Baheth Al-Arabi – Online search of a collection of classic Arabic dictionaries, such as Lisan Al-Arab and Al-Qamus Al-Muheet (in Arabic)

C.5.2 MULTILINGUAL DICTIONARIES

- UNTERM United Nations Terminology Database

- UNESCO Term database

- Unified Medical Dictionary of the World Health Organization

- UN Bibliographical Information System Thesaurus

- Google Online dictionary (multilingual)

- Webster's Online Dictionary (multilingual)

- Multilingual Dictionary of Sports (English-French-Greek-Arabic-German-Spanish-Portuguese) database – ELRA Catalog T0372-01

- Sakhr's English-Arabic dictionary (Arabic ⇔ English/French/Trukish/German)

- Ectaco English-Arabic Dictionary

- CRL New Mexico Arabic-English Dictionary

- Effel Arabic-English Dictionary

- Arabeyes Arabic-English QaMoose Dictionary

- Almisbar Arabic-English dictionary

- Salmoné's Advanced Learner's Arabic-English Dictionary

- The Nijmegen Dutch-Arabic Dictionary Project

- Bilingual Dictionary French Arabic, Arabic French (DixAF) – ELRA Catalog M0040

- Ayelon-Shin'ar Arabic-Hebrew online dictionary

- Lexicool: A directory of online dictionaries and glossaries – numerous Arabic entries

C.5.3   MORPHOLOGICAL LEXICA

- Egyptian Colloquial Arabic Lexicon

- DIINAR (DIctionnaire INformatisé de l'ARabe) Monolingual Arabic Lexicon – ELRA Catalog L0073 – 120,000 lemmas. [204]

- (see also lexicons of morphological analyzers)

C.5.4   ROOT LISTS

- Buckwalter's list of Arabic roots

- Project Root List

- Root list inside the morphological analyzer Sebawai (Contact Dr. Kareem Darwish)

C.5.5   PHONETIC DATABASES

- LC-STAR Standard Arabic Phonetic Lexicon ELRA Catalog S0247

- Egyptian Colloquial Arabic Lexicon (contains phonetic and phonemic representations)

C.5.6   GAZETTEERS

- FAOTERM: United Nations' Food and Agriculture Organization of the Terminology reference for country names (six languages including Arabic)

- Foreignword.com's country names in 16 languages including Arabic

- Geonames.de's multilingual resource for names of geographical entities (and other things)

- U.S. Board on Geographic Names (including Arab countries) – uses SATTS Arabic transliteration

- ANERGazet: a collection of 3 Gazetteers for names of geographical entities, people and organizations

- 10001 Arabic Names (through LDC by request LDC2005G02)

- Databases for names in Arabic at the CJK Dictionary Institute

C.5.7 SEMANTIC ONTOLOGIES

- Arabic Wordnet

APPENDIX D

Arabic NLP Tools

D.1   STEMMING

- Khoja Arabic Stemmer

- Arabic Stemmers: Sebawai and Al-Stem (Contact Dr. Kareem Darwish)

- Larkey's L-stem (contact authors)

D.2   MORPHOLOGICAL ANALYSIS AND GENERATION

- Buckwalter Arabic Morphological Analyzer (BAMA) versions 1.0, 1.2 and 2.0

- Standard Arabic Morphological Analyzer (SAMA, version 3.0 of BAMA)

- ELIXIRFM: *Functional Arabic Morphology* online interface (download)

- Xerox Arabic Morphological Analysis and Generation

- NMSU's Arabic Morphological Analyzer

- MAGEAD: *Morphological Analysis and Generation for Arabic and its Dialects*

- ALMORGEANA: *Arabic Lexeme-based Morphological Generation and Analysis* is distributed as part of the MADA system.

- Alkhalil Morphological Analyzer (Manual)

D.3   MORPHOLOGICAL DISAMBIGUATION AND POS TAGGING

- Khoja Arabic Tagger

- AMIRA: *Toolkit for Arabic tokenization, POS tagging and base phrase chunking*

- MADA: *Morphological Analysis and Disambiguation for Arabic* – a tool for tokenization, lemmatization, diacritization and POS tagging

D.4   PARSERS

- The Stanford Parser

- The Bikel Parser

- MALTParser

- Mohammed Attia's Rule-based Parser for MSA

D.5   TYPSETTING

- ArabTEX (L*A*TEX support for Arabic)

D.6   NAMED ENTITY RECOGNITION

- Yassine Benajiba's ANER (Arabic Named Entity Recognition) system

- BBN's Identifinder (English, Arabic, Chinese)

D.7   TREE EDITING

- Tred for Arabic - **Tree Editor with Arabic support**

D.8   LEXICOGRAPHY

- aConCorde: **A concordance generation program for Arabic**

D.9   TEXT ENTRY

- Yamli.com

- Google's Ta3reeb

- Mircorosft's Maren

D.10 MACHINE TRANSLATION

- Google Translate – bidirectional translation for over 50 languages including Arabic

- Microsoft's Bing Translator – bidirectional translation for over 30 languages including Arabic

- Sakhr's Tarjim (Arabic-English and English-Arabic)

- Almisbar Arabic-English translation

- Statistical MT public resources: **Giza alignment, Pharaoh and Moses decoders, etc.**

APPENDIX E

Important Arabic NLP Acronyms

- ACE: Automatic Content Extraction
- ACL: Association for Computational Linguistics
- ACM: Association for Computing Machinery
- AMTA: Association for Machine Translation in the Americas
- ANLP: Applied Natural Language Processing
- BC: Broadcast Conversations
- BLARK: Basic Language Resource Kit – a minimal set of language resources necessary to do research.
- BN: Broadcast News
- CLIR: Cross-Language Information Retrieval
- COLABA: Cross-lingual Arabic Blogging Alerts (TSWG funded)
- COLING: Computational Linguistics Conference
- COTS: Commercial-Off-The-Shelf systems (e.g., commercial Machine Translation systems)
- CTS: Conversational Telephone Speech
- DARPA: Defense Advanced Research Projects Agency (USA)
- EACL: European ACL
- EAMT: European Association for Machine Translation
- EARS: Efficient, Affordable, Reusable Speech-to-Text (DARPA program)
- ELDA: Evaluations and Language resources Distribution Agency
- ELRA: European Language Resources Association

- ELSNET: European Network of Excellence in Human Language Technologies

- EMNLP: Empirical Methods to Natural Language Processing Conference

- EuRADic: European and Arabic Dictionaries and Corpora

- GALE: Global Autonomous Linguistic Exploitation (DARPA program)

- HARD: High Accuracy Retrieval from Documents

- HDL: High-Density Language (i.e., with rich NLP resources)

- HLT: Human Language Technology

- ICASSP:International Conference on Acoustics, Speech and Signal Processing

- ICSLP: International Conference on Spoken Language Processing

- LCTL: Less Commonly Taught Languages

- LDC: Linguistic Data Consortium, University of Pennsylvania

- LDL: Low-Density Language (i.e., with poor NLP resources)

- LRE: Language Recognition Evaluation

- LREC: Language Resources and Evaluation Conference

- LSA: Linguistic Society of America

- MADCAT: Multilingual Automatic Document Classification Analysis and Translation (DARPA program)

- MCA: Modern Colloquial Arabic

- MEDAR: Mediterranean Arabic Language and Speech Technology,a consortium consisting of 15 partners from European and Arabic - Mediterranean countries

- MSA: Modern Standard Arabic

- MTS: Machine Translation Summit

- NAACL: North American ACL

- NACAL: North America Conference on Afro-asiatic Languages

- NAPLUS: Natural Arabic Processing for Language Understanding Systems (European-funded Project)

- NEMLAR: Network for Euro-Mediterranean LAnguage Resources

- NIST: National Institute of Standards and Technology (USA)

- NSF: National Science Foundation (USA)

- NW: Newswire

- RANLP:Recent Advances in Natural Language Processing

- STT: Speech-to-Text

- SATTS: Standard Arabic Technical Transliteration System

- TALN: Traitement Automatique du Langage Naturel

- TDT: Topic Detection and Tracking evaluation

- TIDES: Translingual Information Detection Extraction and Summarization (DARPA program)

- TRANSTAC: Translation for Tactical Use (DARPA program)

- TREC: Text Retrieval Conference

- TSWG: Technical Support Working Group (a US interagency research and development program)

- TTS: Text-to-Speech

- WB: Weblogs

Bibliography

[1] El-Said M. Badawi. *Mustawayat al-'Arabiyya al-mu'asira fi Misr (The Levels of Modern Arabic in Egypt)*. Cairo: Dar al-Ma'arif, 1973. 1, 2

[2] Reem Bassiouney. *Arabic Sociolinguistics: Topics in Diglossia, Gender, Identity, and Politics.* Georgetown University Press, 2009. 2

[3] Charles F Ferguson. Diglossia. *Word*, 15(2):325–340, 1959. 2

[4] Nizar Habash, Abdelhadi Soudi, and Tim Buckwalter. On Arabic Transliteration. In A. van den Bosch and A. Soudi, editors, *Arabic Computational Morphology: Knowledge-based and Empirical Methods*. Springer, 2007. 4, 21, 27, 31

[5] Tim Buckwalter. Issues in Arabic Morphological Analysis. In A. van den Bosch and A. Soudi, editors, *Arabic Computational Morphology: Knowledge-based and Empirical Methods*. Springer, 2007. 7, 13, 33

[6] Kam-Fai Wong, Wenji Li, Ruifeng Xu, and Zheng sheng Zhang. *Introduction to Chinese Natural Language Processing*. Synthesis Lectures on Human Language Technologies. Morgan and Claypool, 2010. 8

[7] Elsaid Badawi, Mike G. Carter, and Adrian Gully. *Modern Written Arabic: A Comprehensive Grammar*. Routledge, 2004. 10, 63, 93

[8] Nizar Habash and Owen Rambow. Morphophonemic and Orthographic Rules in a Multi-Dialectal Morphological Analyzer and Generator for Arabic Verbs. In *International Symposium on Computer and Arabic Language (ISCAL)*, Riyadh, Saudi Arabia, 2007. 10, 32, 59

[9] Mohamed Maamouri, Ann Bies, Tim Buckwalter, and Wigdan Mekki. The Penn Arabic Treebank: Building a Large-Scale Annotated Arabic Corpus, 2004. 11, 53, 79, 93, 104, 105

[10] Kais Dukes and Nizar Habash. Morphological Annotation of Quranic Arabic. In *Proceedings of the Language Resources and Evaluation Conference (LREC)*, Malta, 2010. 12, 112

[11] Rani Nelken and Stuart Shieber. Arabic Diacritization Using Weighted Finite-State Transducers. In *Proceedings of the Workshop on Computational Approaches to Semitic Languages at 43rd Meeting of the Association for Computational Linguistics (ACL'05)*, pages 79–86, Ann Arbor, Michigan, 2005. DOI: 10.3115/1621787.1621802 13, 24

[12] Imed Zitouni, Jeffrey S. Sorensen, and Ruhi Sarikaya. Maximum Entropy Based Restoration of Arabic Diacritics. In *Proceedings of the 21st International Conference on Computational Linguistics and 44th Annual Meeting of the Association for Computational Linguistics*, pages 577–584, Sydney, Australia, 2006. DOI: 10.3115/1220175.1220248 13, 24

[13] Ahmed El Kholy and Nizar Habash. Techniques for Arabic Morphological Detokenization and Orthographic Denormalization. In *Workshop on Language Resources and Human Language Technology for Semitic Languages in the Language Resources and Evaluation Conference (LREC)*, Valletta, Malta, 2010. 13, 36, 69, 77, 78, 122, 124

[14] Nizar Habash and Ryan Roth. Identification of Naturally Occurring Numerical Expressions in Arabic. In *Proceedings of the Language Resources and Evaluation Conference (LREC)*, Marrakech, Morocco, 2008. 14, 118

[15] Alan Kaye. Adaptations of Arabic Script. In P.T. Daniels and W. Bright, editors, *The World's Writing Systems*. Oxford University Press, 1996. 14

[16] Klaus Lagally. ArabTEX: Typesetting Arabic and Hebrew, User Manual Version 4.00. Technical Report 2004/03, Fakultät Informatik, Universität Stuttgart, March 11 2004. 16, 76

[17] Nizar Habash. Nuun: A System for Developing Platform and Browser Independent Arabic Web Applications. In *Proceedings of the Arabic Translation and Localization Conference (ATLAS-99)*, Tunis, Tunisia, 1999. 17

[18] United Nations Report. *HARMONIZATION OF ICT STANDARDS RELATED TO ARABIC LANGUAGE USE IN INFORMATION SOCIETY APPLICATIONS*. United Nations Publication, http://unpan1.un.org/intradoc/groups/public/documents/unescwa/unpan030581.pdf, 2003. 18

[19] Gina Engström. Internationalisation and Localisation Problems in the Chinese and Arabic Scripts. Master's thesis, Uppsala University, 2008. 18, 19

[20] Kenneth R. Beesley. Romanization, Transcription and Transliteration, 1997. http://www.xrce.xerox.com/Research-Development/Historical-projects/Linguistic-Demos/Arabic-Morphological-Analysis-and-Generation/Romanization-Transcription-and-Transliteration. 20

[21] Y. Al-Onaizan and K. Knight. Machine Transliteration of Names in Arabic Text. In *Proceedings of the ACL Workshop on Computational Approaches to Semitic Languages*, 2002. DOI: 10.3115/1118637.1118642 21, 36, 120

[22] Ulf Hermjakob, Kevin Knight, and Hal Daumé III. Name Translation in Statistical Machine Translation - Learning When to Transliterate. In *Proceedings of ACL-08: HLT*, Columbus, Ohio, 2008. 21, 36, 120

[23] Tim Buckwalter. Buckwalter Arabic Morphological Analyzer Version 2.0, 2004. Linguistic Data Consortium, University of Pennsylvania. LDC Cat alog No.: LDC2004L02, ISBN 1-58563-324-0. 20, 32, 36, 41, 47, 67, 68, 69, 70, 71

[24] Fadi Biadsy, Jihad El-Sana, and Nizar Habash. Online Arabic handwriting recognition using Hidden Markov Models. In *The 10th International Workshop on Frontiers in Handwriting Recognition (IWFHR'10)*, La Baule, France, 2006. 23

[25] Volker Märgner and Haikal El Abed. Arabic Word and Text Recognition - Current Developments. In Khalid Choukri and Bente Maegaard, editors, *Proceedings of the Second International Conference on Arabic Language Resources and Tools*, Cairo, Egypt, April 2009. The MEDAR Consortium. 23

[26] Liana M. Lorigo and Venu Govindaraju. Offline Arabic Handwriting Recognition: A Survey. *IEEE Transactions on Pattern Analysis and Machine Intelligence*, 28(5):712–724, 2006. DOI: 10.1109/TPAMI.2006.102 23

[27] Kareem Darwish and Douglas W. Oard. Term Selection for Searching Printed Arabic. In *SIGIR '02: Proceedings of the 25th annual international ACM SIGIR conference on Research and development in information retrieval*, pages 261–268, New York, NY, USA, 2002. ACM. DOI: 10.1145/564376.564423 23

[28] Walid Magdy and Kareem Darwish. Arabic OCR Error Correction Using Character Segment Correction, Language Modeling, and Shallow Morphology. In *Proceedings of 2006 Conference on Empirical Methods in Natural Language Processing (EMNLP 2006)*, pages 408–414, Sydney, Austrailia, 2006. DOI: 10.3115/1610075.1610132 23

[29] Prem Natarajan, Shirin Saleem, Rohit Prasad, Ehry MacRostie, and Krishna Subramanian. *Arabic and Chinese Handwriting Recognition*, volume 4768 of *Lecture Notes in Computer Science*, pages 231–250. Springer, Berlin, Germany, 2008. 23

[30] Shirin Saleem, Huaigu Cao, Krishna Subramanian, Marin Kamali, Rohit Prasad, and Prem Natarajan. Improvements in BBN's HMM-based Offline Handwriting Recognition System. In Khalid Choukri and Bente Maegaard, editors, *10th International Conference on Document Analysis and Recognition (ICDAR)*, Barcelona, Spain, July 2009. 23

[31] Zhidong Lu, Issam Bazzi, Andras Kornai, John Makhoul, Premkumar Natarajan, and Richard Schwartz. A Robust, Language-Independent OCR System. In *the 27th AIPR Workshop: Advances in Computer Assisted Recognition, SPIE*, 1999. DOI: 10.1117/12.339811 23

[32] Stephanie Strassel. Linguistic Resources for Arabic Handwriting Recognition. In Khalid Choukri and Bente Maegaard, editors, *Proceedings of the Second International Conference on Arabic Language Resources and Tools*, Cairo, Egypt, April 2009. The MEDAR Consortium. 23

[33] Dimitra Vergyri and Katrin Kirchhoff. Automatic Diacritization of Arabic for Acoustic Modeling in Speech Recognition. In Ali Farghaly and Karine Megerdoomian, editors, *COLING 2004 Workshop on Computational Approaches to Arabic Script-based Languages*, pages 66–73, Geneva, Switzerland, 2004. DOI: 10.3115/1621804 24, 37

[34] S. Ananthakrishnan, S. Narayanan, and S. Bangalore. Automatic Diacritization of Arabic Transcripts for ASR. In *Proceedings of ICON*, Kanpur, India, 2005. 24

[35] Nizar Habash and Owen Rambow. Arabic Diacritization through Full Morphological Tagging. In *Proceedings of the 8th Meeting of the North American Chapter of the Association for Computational Linguistics/Human Language Technologies Conference (HLT-NAACL07)*, 2007. DOI: 10.3115/1614108.1614122 24, 86, 88, 104

[36] Daniel Jurafsky and James H. Martin. *Speech and Language Processing*. Prentice Hall, New Jersey, USA, 2000. 27

[37] Eugene E. Loos, Susan Anderson, Jr. Dwight H., Day, Paul C. Jordan, and J. Douglas Wingate. Glossary of Linguistic Terms, 2004. 27, 41

[38] Clive Holes. *Modern Arabic: Structures, Functions, and Varieties*. Georgetown Classics in Arabic Language and Linguistics. Georgetown University Press, 2004. 29, 30, 33, 42, 51, 52, 59, 63

[39] Janet C. E. Watson. *The Phonology and Morphology of Arabic*. Oxford University Press, 2002. 29, 30, 33

[40] Nizar Habash. On Arabic and its Dialects. *Multilingual Magazine*, 17(81), 2006. 30

[41] Fadi Biadsy, Nizar Habash, and Julia Hirschberg. Improving the Arabic Pronunciation Dictionary for Phone and Word Recognition with Linguistically-Based Pronunciation Rules. In *Proceedings of Human Language Technologies: The 2009 Annual Conference of the North American Chapter of the Association for Computational Linguistics*, pages 397–405, Boulder, Colorado, June 2009. Association for Computational Linguistics. DOI: 10.3115/1620754.1620812 30, 37

[42] Y. A. El-Imam. Phonetization of Arabic: Rules and Algorithms. In *Computer Speech and Language 18*, pages 339–373, 2004. DOI: 10.1016/S0885-2308(03)00035-4 31, 37

[43] Hany Hassan and Jeffrey Sorensen. An Integrated Approach for Arabic-English Named Entity Translation. In *Proceedings of the ACL Workshop on Computational Approaches to Semitic Languages*, pages 87–93, Ann Arbor, Michigan, June 2005. Association for Computational Linguistics. DOI: 10.3115/1621787.1621803 36

[44] Bing Zhao, Nguyen Bach, Ian Lane, and Stephan Vogel. A Log-Linear Block Transliteration Model based on Bi-Stream HMMs. In *Human Language Technologies 2007: The Conference of the North American Chapter of the Association for Computational Linguistics; Proceedings of the Main Conference*, pages 364–371, Rochester, New York, April 2007. Association for Computational Linguistics. 36

[45] A. Freeman, S. Condon, and C. Ackerman. Cross Linguistic Name Matching in English and Arabic. In *Proceedings of the Human Language Technology Conference of the NAACL, Main Conference*, pages 471–478, New York City, USA, June 2006. Association for Computational Linguistics. DOI: 10.3115/1220835.1220895 36, 120

[46] Bassam Haddad and Mustafa Yaseen. Detection and Correction of Non-Words in Arabic: A Hybrid Approach. *International Journal of Computer Processing Of Languages (IJCPOL)*, 2007. DOI: 10.1142/S0219427907001706 36

[47] Mohamed Maamouri, Ann Bies, and Seth Kulick. Enhancing the Arabic Treebank: a Collaborative Effort toward New Annotation Guidelines. In European Language Resources Association (ELRA), editor, *Proceedings of the Sixth International Language Resources and Evaluation (LREC'08)*, Marrakech, Morocco, May 2008. 36, 105

[48] Chiraz Ben Othmane Zribi and Mohammed Ben Ahmed. Efficient Automatic Correction of Misspelled Arabic Words Based on Contextual Information. In *Proceedings of the Knowledge-Based Intelligent Information and Engineering Systems Conference*, Oxford, UK, 2003. 36

[49] Khaled Shaalan, Amin Allam, and Abdallah Gomah. Towards Automatic Spell Checking for Arabic. In *Conference on Language Engineering, ELSE*, Cairo, Egypt, 2003. 36

[50] Nizar Habash. Four Techniques for Online Handling of Out-of-Vocabulary Words in Arabic-English Statistical Machine Translation. In *Proceedings of ACL-08: HLT, Short Papers*, pages 57–60, Columbus, Ohio, June 2008. Association for Computational Linguistics. DOI: 10.3115/1557690.1557706 36, 120, 121

[51] Nizar Habash and Owen Rambow. Arabic Tokenization, Part-of-Speech Tagging and Morphological Disambiguation in One Fell Swoop. In *Proceedings of the 43rd Annual Meeting of the Association for Computational Linguistics (ACL'05)*, pages 573–580, Ann Arbor, Michigan, June 2005. Association for Computational Linguistics. DOI: 10.3115/1219840.1219911 36, 66, 80, 86, 88, 92

[52] Linguistic Data Consortium. Egyptian Colloquial Arabic Lexicon. LDC catalog number LDC99L22, ISBN 1-58563-155-8, 1999. 36, 68

[53] David Graff, Tim Buckwalter, Hubert Jin, and Mohamed Maamouri. Lexicon Development for Varieties of Spoken Colloquial Arabic. In *LREC 2006: Fifth International Conference on Language Resources and Evaluation*, pages 999–1004, Genova, Italy, 2006. 36

[54] Mona Diab, Nizar Habash, Owen Rambow, Mohamed Altantawy, and Yassine Benajiba. CO-LABA: Arabic Dialect Annotation and Processing. In *Proceedings of the seventh International Conference on Language Resources and Evaluation (LREC)*, Valletta, Malta, 2010. 36

[55] Fred Jelinek. Large Vocabulary Continuous Speech Recognition. Technical report, CLSP, JohnsHopkins University, Baltimore, MD, 1997. Summer Research Workshop Technical Reports. 37

[56] Katrin Kirchhoff, Jeff Bilmes, Sourin Das, Nicolae Duta, Melissa Egan, Gang Ji, Feng He, John Henderson, Daben Liu, Mohamed Noamany, Pat Schone, Richard Schwartz, and Dimitra Vergyri. Novel Approaches to Arabic Speech Recognition: Report from the 2002 Johns-Hopkins Summer Workshop. In *Proceedings of ICASSP 2003*, 2003. DOI: 10.1109/ICASSP.2003.1198788 37

[57] Katrin Kirchhoff, Dimitra Vergyri, Jeff A. Blimes, Kevin Duh, and Andreas Stolcke. Morphology-based Language Modeling for Conversational Arabic Speech Recognition. *Computer Speech and Language*, 20:589–608, 2006. DOI: 10.1016/j.csl.2005.10.001 37

[58] D. Vergyri, A. Mandal, W. Wang, A. Stolcke, J. Zheng, M. Graciarena, D. Rybach, C. Gollan, R. Schlüter, K. Kirchhoff, A. Faria, and N. Morgan. Development of the SRI/Nightingale Arabic ASR System. In *In Proceedings of Interspeech 2008*, 2008. 37

[59] R. Sproat, editor. *Multilingual Text-to-Speech Synthesis: The Bell Labs Approach*. Kluwer, Boston, MA, 1997. 37

[60] M. Afify, R. Sarikaya, H. Kuo, L. Besacier, and Y. Gao. On the Use of Morphological Analysis for Dialectal Arabic Speech Recognition. In *Proceedings of Interspeech 2006*, Pittsburgh PA., 2006. 37

[61] F. Diehl, M.J.F. Gales, M. Tomalin, and P.C. Woodland. Morphological Analysis and Decomposition for Arabic Speech-to-Text Systems. In *Proceedings of InterSpeech*, 2009. 37, 69

[62] Roger Hsiao, Ashish Venugopal, Thilo Köhler, Ying Zhang, Paisarn Charoenpornsawat, Andreas Zollmann, Stephan Vogel, Alan W Black, Tanja Schultz, and Alex Waibel. Optimizing Components for Handheld Two-way Speech Translation for an English-Iraqi Arabic System. In *INTERSPEECH*, Pittsburgh, PA, 2006. 37

[63] Fawzi Alorfi. *Automatic Identification Of Arabic Dialects Using Hidden Markov Models*. PhD thesis, University of Pittsburgh, 2008. 37

[64] Fadi Biadsy, Julia Hirschberg, and Nizar Habash. Spoken Arabic Dialect Identification Using Phonotactic Modeling. In *Proceedings of the EACL 2009 Workshop on Computational Approaches to Semitic Languages*, pages 53–61, Athens, Greece, March 2009. Association for Computational Linguistics. DOI: 10.3115/1621774.1621784 37

[65] Fadi Biadsy and Julia Hirschberg. Using Prosody and Phonotactics in Arabic Dialect Identification. In *Proceedings of Interspeech*, Brighton, UK, 2009. 37

[66] Fadi Biadsy, Andrew Rosenberg, Rolf Carlson, Julia Hirschberg, and Eva Strangert. A Cross-Cultural Comparison of American, Palestinian, and Swedish Perception of Charismatic Speech. In *Speech Prosody*, Campinas, Brazil, 2008. 37

[67] Otakar Smrž. *Functional Arabic Morphology. Formal System and Implementation*. PhD thesis, Charles University in Prague, Prague, Czech Republic, 2007. 39, 67, 69, 72, 75, 84, 107

[68] Georges Bohas. *Matrices, Étymons, Racines: Éléments d'une théorie lexicographique du vocabulaire arabe*. Peeters, Leuven, 1997. 41

[69] Z. Harris. Linguistic structure of Hebrew. *Journal of the American Oriental Society*, 62:143–67, 1941. DOI: 10.2307/594501 43

[70] John J. McCarthy. A Prosodic Theory of Nonconcatenative Morphology. *Linguistic Inquiry*, 12:373–418, 1981. 43

[71] Mohamed Maamouri and Ann Bies. Developing an Arabic Treebank: Methods, Guidelines, Procedures, and Tools. In *Proceedings of the COLING 2004 Workshop on Computational Approaches to Arabic Script-based Languages*, pages 2–9, 2004. DOI: 10.3115/1621804.1621808 47, 105

[72] Mark W. Cowell. *A Reference Grammar of Syrian Arabic*. Georgetown University Press, 1964. 50

[73] Wallace Erwin. *A Short Reference Grammar of Iraqi Arabic*. Georgetown University Press, 1963. 50

[74] Ernest T. Abdel-Massih, Zaki N. Abdel-Malek, and El-Said M. Badawi. *A Reference Grammar of Egyptian Arabic*. Georgetown University Press, 1979. 50

[75] Richard Harrell. *A Short Reference Grammar of Moroccan Arabic*. Georgetown University Press, 1962. 50

[76] Eckehard Schulz. *A Student Grammar of Modern Standard Arabic*. Cambridge University Press, New York, 2005. 51, 63, 93

[77] Ron Buckley. *Modern Literary Arabic: A Reference Grammar*. Librairie du Liban, 2004. 52, 57, 61, 63, 93

[78] William Wright. *A Grammar of the Arabic Language*. Cambridge University Press, reprint of third revised edition, 1991. Translated from the German of Caspari and edited with numerous additions and corrections by W. Wright, revised by W. Robertson Smith and M. J. de Goeje, preface and addenda et corrigenda by Pierre Cachia. 55, 63, 93

[79] Nizar Habash, Ryan Gabbard, Owen Rambow, Seth Kulick, and Mitch Marcus. Determining Case in Arabic: Learning Complex Linguistic Behavior Requires Complex Linguistic Features. In *Proceedings of the 2007 Joint Conference on Empirical Methods in Natural Language Processing and Computational Natural Language Learning (EMNLP-CoNLL)*, pages 1084–1092, 2007. 57, 104, 111

[80] Nizar Habash and Owen Rambow. MAGEAD: A Morphological Analyzer and Generator for the Arabic Dialects. In *Proceedings of the 21st International Conference on Computational Linguistics and 44th Annual Meeting of the Association for Computational Linguistics*, pages 681–688, Sydney, Australia, July 2006. Association for Computational Linguistics. DOI: 10.3115/1220175.1220261 59, 67, 69, 75

[81] Karin C Ryding. *A Reference Grammar of Modern Standard Arabic*. Reference Grammars. Cambridge University Press, New York, 2006. 63, 93

[82] Mohamed Maamouri, Ann Bies, Sondos Krouna, Fatma Gaddeche, and Basma Bouziri. *Penn Arabic Treebank Guidelines*. Linguistic Data Consortium, 2009. 63, 80, 93, 104, 105, 106

[83] Nizar Habash and Fatiha Sadat. Arabic Preprocessing Schemes for Statistical Machine Translation. In *Proceedings of the Human Language Technology Conference of the NAACL, Companion Volume: Short Papers*, pages 49–52, New York City, USA, June 2006. Association for Computational Linguistics. DOI: 10.3115/1614049.1614062 66, 76, 77, 88, 89, 121

[84] Muhammed Aljlayl and Ophir Frieder. On Arabic Search: Improving the Retrieval Effectiveness via a Light Stemming Approach. In *Proceedings of ACM Eleventh Conference on Information and Knowledge Management, Mclean, VA*, pages 340–347, 2002. DOI: 10.1145/584792.584848 67

[85] Imad Al-Sughaiyer and Ibrahim Al-Kharashi. Arabic Morphological Analysis Techniques: A Comprehensive Survey. *Journal of the American Society for Information Science and Technology*, 55(3):189–213, 2004. DOI: 10.1002/asi.10368 67

[86] Kenneth Beesley. Arabic Finite-State Morphological Analysis and Generation. In *Proceedings of the 16th International Conference on Computational Linguistics (COLING-96)*, pages 89–94, Copenhagen, Denmark, 1996. DOI: 10.3115/992628.992647 67, 69, 73

[87] Mohamed Attia Mohamed Elaraby Ahmed. A Large-Scale Computational Processor of the Arabic Morphology and Applications. Master's thesis, Faculty of Engineering, Cairo University, 2000. 67

[88] Tim Buckwalter. Buckwalter Arabic Morphological Analyzer Version 1.0, 2002. Linguistic Data Consortium, University of Pennsylvania. LDC Catalog No.: LDC2002L49. 67, 70, 71, 75, 110

[89] Kareem Darwish. Building a Shallow Morphological Analyzer in One Day. In *Proceedings of the workshop on Computational Approaches to Semitic Languages in the 40th Annual Meeting of the Association for Computational Linguistics (ACL-02)*, pages 47–54, Philadelphia, PA, USA, 2002. DOI: 10.3115/1118637.1118643 67, 68

[90] Jim Yaghi and Sane Yagi. Systematic Verb Stem Generation for Arabic. In *COLING 2004 Computational Approaches to Arabic Script-based Languages*, pages 23–30, Geneva, Switzerland, 2004. DOI: 10.3115/1621804.1621812 67

[91] George Kiraz. Multi-tape Two-level Morphology: A Case study in Semitic Non-Linear Morphology. In *Proceedings of Fifteenth International Conference on Computational Linguistics (COLING-94)*, pages 180–186, Kyoto, Japan, 1994. DOI: 10.3115/991886.991917 67

[92] Nizar Habash, Owen Rambow, and George Kiraz. Morphological Analysis and Generation for Arabic Dialects. In *Proceedings of the Workshop on Computational Approaches to Semitic Languages at 43rd Meeting of the Association for Computational Linguistics (ACL'05)*, pages 17–24, Ann Arbor, Michigan, 2005. DOI: 10.3115/1621787.1621791 67, 75

[93] Mohammed Attia. An Ambiguity-Controlled Morphological Analyzer for Modern Standard Arabic Modelling Finite State Networks. In *The Challenge of Arabic for NLP/MT Conference*, London, 2006. The British Computer Society. 67

[94] Violetta Cavalli-Sforza, Abdelhadi Soudi, and Teruko Mitamura. Arabic Morphology Generation Using a Concatenative Strategy. In *Proceedings of the 6th Applied Natural Language Processing Conference (ANLP 2000)*, pages 86–93, Seattle, Washington, USA, 2000. 67

[95] Abdelhadi Soudi, Violetta Cavalli-Sforza, and Abderrahim Jamari. A Computational Lexeme-Based Treatment of Arabic Morphology. In *Proceedings of the Arabic Natural Language Processing Workshop, Conference of the Association for Computational Linguistics (ACL 2001)*, pages 50–57, Toulouse, France, 2001. 67, 69

[96] Nizar Habash. Large Scale Lexeme Based Arabic Morphological Generation. In *Proceedings of Traitement Automatique des Langues Naturelles (TALN-04)*, pages 271–276, 2004. Fez, Morocco. 67, 69, 71

[97] Nizar Habash. Arabic Morphological Representations for Machine Translation. In A. van den Bosch and A. Soudi, editors, *Arabic Computational Morphology: Knowledge-based and Empirical Methods*. Springer, 2007. 67, 72, 88, 89

[98] Franz Josef Och. Google System Description for the 2005 NIST MT Evaluation. In *MT Eval Workshop (unpublished talk)*, 2005. 68, 78, 121

[99] Ibrahim Badr, Rabih Zbib, and James Glass. Segmentation for English-to-Arabic Statistical Machine Translation. In *Proceedings of ACL-08: HLT, Short Papers*, pages

153–156, Columbus, Ohio, June 2008. Association for Computational Linguistics. DOI: 10.3115/1557690.1557732 69, 77, 79, 89, 122, 124

[100] George Anton Kiraz. Multi-Tiered Nonlinear Morphology Using Multi-Tape Finite Automata: A Case Study on Syriac and Arabic. *Computational Linguistics*, 26(1):77–105, 2000. DOI: 10.1162/089120100561647 73

[101] Mohamed Altantawy, Nizar Habash, Owen Rambow, and Ibrahim Saleh. Morphological Analysis and Generation of Arabic Nouns: A Morphemic Functional Approach. In *Proceedings of the seventh International Conference on Language Resources and Evaluation (LREC)*, Valletta, Malta, 2010. 75

[102] Viktor Bielický and Otakar Smrž. Enhancing the ElixirFM Lexicon with Verbal Valency Frames. In Khalid Choukri and Bente Maegaard, editors, *Proceedings of the Second International Conference on Arabic Language Resources and Tools*, Cairo, Egypt, April 2009. The MEDAR Consortium. 75

[103] Markus Forsberg and Aarne Ranta. Functional Morphology. In *Proceedings of the Ninth ACM SIGPLAN International Conference on Functional Programming, ICFP 2004*, pages 213–223. ACM Press, 2004. DOI: 10.1145/1016850.1016879 75

[104] Leah S. Larkey, Lisa Ballesteros, and Margaret E. Connell. *Arabic Computational Morphology: Knowledge-based and Empirical Methods*, chapter Light Stemming for Arabic Information Retrieval. Springer Netherlands, kluwer/springer edition, 2007. 77, 90

[105] Fatiha Sadat and Nizar Habash. Combination of Arabic Preprocessing Schemes for Statistical Machine Translation. In *Proceedings of the 21st International Conference on Computational Linguistics and 44th Annual Meeting of the Association for Computational Linguistics*, pages 1–8, Sydney, Australia, July 2006. Association for Computational Linguistics. DOI: 10.3115/1220175.1220176 77, 79, 88, 89, 121

[106] Hassan Al-Haj and Alon Lavie. The Impact of Arabic Morphological Segmentation on Broad-coverage English-to-Arabic Statistical Machine Translation. In *Proceedings of the Conference of the Association for Machine Translation in the Americas (AMTA)*, Denver, Colorado, 2010. 77, 122, 124

[107] Jakob Elming and Nizar Habash. Combination of Statistical Word Alignments Based on Multiple Preprocessing Schemes. In *Human Language Technologies 2007: The Conference of the North American Chapter of the Association for Computational Linguistics; Companion Volume, Short Papers*, pages 25–28, Rochester, New York, April 2007. Association for Computational Linguistics. DOI: 10.3115/1614108.1614115 77, 89, 121

[108] Young-Suk Lee. Morphological Analysis for Statistical Machine Translation. In *Proceedings of the 5th Meeting of the North American Chapter of the Association for Computational Linguistics/Human Language Technologies Conference (HLT-NAACL04)*, pages 57–60, Boston, MA, 2004. DOI: 10.3115/1613984.1613999 79, 121

[109] Mona Diab, Kadri Hacioglu, and Daniel Jurafsky. Automatic Tagging of Arabic Text: From Raw Text to Base Phrase Chunks. In *Proceedings of the 5th Meeting of the North American Chapter of the Association for Computational Linguistics/Human Language Technologies Conference (HLT-NAACL04)*, pages 149–152, Boston, MA, 2004. DOI: 10.3115/1613984.1614022 79, 80, 89

[110] Yuval Marton, Nizar Habash, and Owen Rambow. Improving Arabic Dependency Parsing with Lexical and Inflectional Morphological Features. In *Proceedings of the NAACL HLT 2010 First Workshop on Statistical Parsing of Morphologically-Rich Languages*, pages 13–21, Los Angeles, CA, USA, June 2010. Association for Computational Linguistics. 79, 83, 111, 112

[111] Mona Diab. Towards an Optimal POS tag set for Modern Standard Arabic Processing. In *Proceedings of Recent Advances in Natural Language Processing (RANLP)*, Borovets, Bulgaria, 2007. 79, 83, 90

[112] Nizar Habash and Ryan Roth. CATiB: The Columbia Arabic Treebank. In *Proceedings of the ACL-IJCNLP 2009 Conference Short Papers*, pages 221–224, Suntec, Singapore, August 2009. Association for Computational Linguistics. DOI: 10.3115/1667583.1667651 79, 83, 104, 108, 112

[113] Shereen Khoja. APT: Arabic Part-of-Speech Tagger. In *Proceedings of Student Research Workshop at NAACL 2001*, pages 20–26, Pittsburgh, 2001. Association for Computational Linguistics. 80, 84

[114] Jan Hajič, Otakar Smrž, Tim Buckwalter, and Hubert Jin. Feature-based Tagger of Approximations of Functional Arabic Morphology. In Ma. Antonia Martí Montserrat Civit, Sandra Kübler, editor, *Proceedings of Treebanks and Linguistic Theories (TLT)*, pages 53–64, Barcelona, Spain, 2005. 80, 84, 107

[115] Noah Smith, David Smith, and Roy Tromble. Context-Based Morphological Disambiguation with Random Fields. In *Proceedings of the 2005 Conference on Empirical Methods in Natural Language Processing (EMNLP05)*, pages 475–482, Vancouver, Canada, 2005. DOI: 10.3115/1220575.1220635 80

[116] Ryan Roth, Owen Rambow, Nizar Habash, Mona Diab, and Cynthia Rudin. Arabic Morphological Tagging, Diacritization, and Lemmatization Using Lexeme Models and Feature Ranking. In *Proceedings of ACL-08: HLT, Short Papers*, pages 117–120, Columbus, Ohio, June

2008. Association for Computational Linguistics. DOI: 10.3115/1557690.1557721 80, 86, 88, 104

[117] Mona Diab, Kadri Hacioglu, and Daniel Jurafsky. *Arabic Computational Morphology: Knowledge-based and Empirical Methods*, chapter Automated Methods for Processing Arabic Text: From Tokenization to Base Phrase Chunking. Springer Netherlands, kluwer/springer edition, 2007. 80, 89, 90, 112

[118] Mitchell M. Marcus, Beatrice Santorini, and Mary Ann Marcinkiewicz. Building a Large Annotated Corpus of English: The Penn Treebank. *Computational Linguistics*, 19.2:313–330, June 1993. 80, 105

[119] Seth Kulick, Ryan Gabbard, and Mitch Marcus. Parsing the Arabic Treebank: Analysis and Improvements. In *Proceedings of the Treebanks and Linguistic Theories Conference*, pages 31–42, Prague, Czech Republic, 2006. 80, 82, 104, 111, 112

[120] Mona Diab. Improved Arabic Base Phrase Chunking with a New Enriched POS Tag Set. In *Proceedings of the 2007 Workshop on Computational Approaches to Semitic Languages: Common Issues and Resources*, pages 89–96, Prague, Czech Republic, June 2007. Association for Computational Linguistics. DOI: 10.3115/1654576.1654592 82, 90, 112

[121] Nizar Habash, Reem Faraj, and Ryan Roth. Syntactic Annotation in the Columbia Arabic Treebank. In *Proceedings of MEDAR International Conference on Arabic Language Resources and Tools*, Cairo, Egypt, 2009. 83, 104, 108

[122] Shereen Khoja, Roger Garside, and Gerry Knowles. A tagset for the morphosyntactic tagging of Arabic. In *Proceedings of Corpus Linguistics 2001*, pages 341–353, Lancaster, UK, 2001. 84

[123] Otakar Smrž and Petr Zemánek. Sherds from an Arabic Treebanking Mosaic. *Prague Bulletin of Mathematical Linguistics*, 78:63–76, 2002. 84

[124] Marta R. Costa-jussà, Josep M. Crego, Adrià de Gispert, Patrik Lambert, Maxim Khalilov, José A.R. Fonollosa, José B. Mariño, and Rafael Banchs. TALP Phrase-Based System and TALP System Combination for IWSLT 2006. In *Proc. of the International Workshop on Spoken Language Translation*, pages 123–129, Kyoto, Japan, 2006. 89

[125] Josep M. Crego, Adrià de Gispert, Patrik Lambert, Maxim Khalilov, Marta R. Costa-jussà, José B. Mariño, Rafael Banchs, and José A.R. Fonollosa. The TALP Ngram-based SMT System for IWSLT 2006. In *Proc. of the International Workshop on Spoken Language Translation*, pages 116–122, Kyoto, Japan, 2006. 89

[126] David Vilar, Daniel Stein, Yuqi Zhang, Evgeny Matusov, Arne Mauser, Oliver Bender, Saab Mansour, and Hermann Ney. The RWTH Machine Translation System for IWSLT 2008. In *Proc. of the International Workshop on Spoken Language Translation*, pages 108–115, Hawaii, USA, 2008. 89

[127] Mona Diab, Mahmoud Ghoneim, and Nizar Habash. Arabic Diacritization in the Context of Statistical Machine Translation. In *Proceedings of Machine Translation Summit (MT-Summit)*, Copenhagen, Denmark, 2007. 89

[128] Benjamin Farber, Dayne Freitag, Nizar Habash, and Owen Rambow. Improving NER in Arabic Using a Morphological Tagger. In *Proceedings of the Language Resources and Evaluation Conference (LREC)*, Marrakech, Morocco, 2008. 89, 117

[129] Yassine Benajiba, Mona Diab, and Paolo Rosso. Arabic Named Entity Recognition using Optimized Feature Sets. In *Proceedings of the 2008 Conference on Empirical Methods in Natural Language Processing*, pages 284–293, Honolulu, Hawaii, October 2008. Association for Computational Linguistics. DOI: 10.3115/1613715.1613755 89, 90, 112, 117

[130] Josep M. Crego and Nizar Habash. Using Shallow Syntax Information to Improve Word Alignment and Reordering for SMT. In *Proceedings of the Third Workshop on Statistical Machine Translation*, pages 53–61, Columbus, Ohio, June 2008. Association for Computational Linguistics. DOI: 10.3115/1626394.1626401 90, 112, 123

[131] Behrang Mohit and Rebecca Hwa. Localization of Difficult-to-Translate Phrases. In *Proceedings of the Second Workshop on Statistical Machine Translation*, pages 248–255, Prague, Czech Republic, June 2007. Association for Computational Linguistics. DOI: 10.3115/1626355.1626392 90

[132] Nicolas Stroppa and Andy Way. MATREX: DCU Machine Translation System for IWSLT 2006. In *Proc. of the International Workshop on Spoken Language Translation*, pages 31–36, Kyoto, Japan, 2006. 90

[133] David Farwell, Jesús Giménez, Edgar González, Reda Halkoum, Horacio Rodríguez, and Mihai Surdeanu. The UPC System for Arabic-to-English Entity Translation. In *Proceedings of ACE 2007*, 2007. 90

[134] Robert D. Van Valin. *An Introduction to Syntax*. Cambridge University Press, 2001. 93

[135] Beatrice Santorini and Anthony Kroch. The Syntax of Natural Language: An Online Introduction using the Trees Program, 2007. 93

[136] Mohamed Maamouri, Ann Bies, and Seth Kulick. Creating a Methodology for Large-Scale Correction of Treebank Annotation: The Case of the Arabic Treebank. In *Proceedings of MEDAR International Conference on Arabic Language Resources and Tools*, Cairo, Egypt, 2009. 93, 104, 105

[137] Otakar Smrž and Jan Hajič. The Other Arabic Treebank: Prague Dependencies and Functions. In Ali Farghaly, editor, *Arabic Computational Linguistics: Current Implementations*. CSLI Publications, 2006. 104

[138] Otakar Smrž, Viktor Bielický, Iveta Kouřilová, Jakub Kráčmar, Jan Hajič, and Petr Zemánek. Prague Arabic Dependency Treebank: A Word on the Million Words. In *Proceedings of the Workshop on Arabic and Local Languages (LREC 2008)*, pages 16–23, Marrakech, Morocco, 2008. 104, 107, 117

[139] Mohamed Maamouri and Christopher Cieri. Resources for Natural Language Processing at the Linguistic Data Consortium. In *Proceedings of the International Symposium on Processing of Arabic*, pages 125–146, Manouba, Tunisia, 2002. 105

[140] Mohamed Maamouri, Ann Bies, Tim Buckwalter, Mona Diab, Nizar Habash, Owen Rambow, and Dalila Tabessi. Developing and Using a Pilot Dialectal Arabic Treebank. In *Proceedings of the Fifth International Conference on Language Resources and Evaluation, LREC'06*, Genoa, Italy, 2006. 105, 111

[141] Petr Sgall, Eva Hajičová, and Jarmila Panevová. *The Meaning of the Sentence in Its Semantic and Pragmatic Aspects*. D. Reidel & Academia, 1986. 106

[142] Jan Hajič, Barbora Hladká, and Petr Pajas. The Prague Dependency Treebank: Annotation Structure and Support. In *Proceedings of the IRCS Workshop on Linguistic Databases*, pages 105–114, Philadelphia, 2001. University of Pennsylvania. 106

[143] Otakar Smrž. ElixirFM — Implementation of Functional Arabic Morphology. In *Proceedings of the 2007 Workshop on Computational Approaches to Semitic Languages: Common Issues and Resources*, pages 1–8, Prague, Czech Republic, June 2007. ACL. DOI: 10.3115/1654576.1654578 106, 107

[144] Zdeněk Žabokrtský and Otakar Smrž. Arabic Syntactic Trees: from Constituency to Dependency. In *Proceedings of the Eleventh Conference of the European Chapter of the Association for Computational Linguistics (EACL'03) – Research Notes*, Budapest, Hungary, 2003. DOI: 10.3115/1067737.1067779 107

[145] Jan Hajič, Otakar Smrž, Petr Zemánek, Jan Šnaidauf, and Emanuel Beška. Prague Arabic Dependency Treebank: Development in Data and Tools. In *NEMLAR International Conference on Arabic Language Resources and Tools*, pages 110–117. ELDA, 2004. 107

[146] Joakim Nivre, Johan Hall, Jens Nilsson, Atanas Chanev, Gulsen Eryigit, Sandra Kubler, Svetoslav Marinov, and Erwin Marsi. MaltParser: A Language-independent System for Data-driven Dependency Parsing. *Natural Language Engineering*, 13(2):95–135, 2007. DOI: 10.1017/S1351324906004505 107, 112

[147] Fei Xia, Owen Rambow, Rajesh Bhatt, Martha Palmer, and Dipti Misra Sharma. Towards a Multi-Representation Treebank. In *Proceedings of Treebanks and Linguistic Theories (TLT 7)*, Groningen, Netherlands, 2009. 109

[148] David Chiang, Mona Diab, Nizar Habash, Owen Rambow, and Safiullah Shareef. Parsing Arabic Dialects. In *Proceedings of the European Chapter of ACL (EACL)*, 2006. 111, 112

[149] Kais Dukes and Tim Buckwalter. A Dependency Treebank of the Quran using Traditional Arabic Grammar. In *Proceedings of the 7th international conference on Informatics and Systems (INFOS 2010)*, Cairo, Egypt, 2010. 112

[150] Lamia Tounsi, Mohammed Attia, and Josef van Genabith. Automatic Treebank-Based Acquisition of Arabic LFG Dependency Structures. In *Proceedings of the EACL 2009 Workshop on Computational Approaches to Semitic Languages*, pages 45–52, Athens, Greece, 2009. DOI: 10.3115/1621774.1621783 112

[151] Martha Palmer, Olga Babko-Malaya, Ann Bies, Mona Diab, Mohamed Maamouri, Aous Mansouri, and Wajdi Zaghouani. A Pilot Arabic Propbank. In *Proceedings of LREC*, Marrakech, Morocco, May 2008. 112, 114

[152] Eduard Hovy, Mitchell Marcus, Martha Palmer, Lance Ramshaw, and Ralph Weischedel. OntoNotes: The 90% Solution. In *NAACL '06: Proceedings of the Human Language Technology Conference of the NAACL, Companion Volume: Short Papers on XX*, pages 57–60, Morristown, NJ, USA, 2006. Association for Computational Linguistics. DOI: 10.3115/1614049.1614064 112, 117

[153] Daniel Bikel. Design of a Multi-lingual, Parallel-processing Statistical Parsing Engine. In *Proceedings of International Conference on Human Language Technology Research (HLT)*, pages 24–27, 2002. DOI: 10.3115/1289189.1289191 112

[154] Ryan Gabbard and Seth Kulick. Construct State Modification in the Arabic Treebank. In *Proceedings of ACL-08: HLT, Short Papers*, pages 209–212, Columbus, Ohio, June 2008. Association for Computational Linguistics. DOI: 10.3115/1557690.1557750 112

[155] Dan Klein and Christopher D. Manning. Accurate Unlexicalized Parsing. In *Proceedings of the 41st Meeting of the Association for Computational Linguistics (ACL'03)*, 2003. DOI: 10.3115/1075096.1075150 112

[156] Spence Green, Conal Sathi, and Christopher D. Manning. NP Subject Detection in Verb-initial Arabic Clauses. In *Proceedings of the Third Workshop on Computational Approaches to Arabic Script-based Languages (CAASL3)*, 2009. 112, 123

[157] Michael C. McCord and Violetta Cavalli-Sforza. An Arabic Slot Grammar Parser. In *Proceedings of the 2007 Workshop on Computational Approaches to Semitic Languages*, pages 81–88, Morristown, NJ, USA, 2007. Association for Computational Linguistics. DOI: 10.3115/1654576.1654591 112

[158] Eman Othman, Khaled Shaalan, and Ahmed Rafea. A Chart Parser for Analyzing Modern Standard Arabic Sentence. In *Proceedings of the MT Summit IX Workshop on Machine Translation for Semitic Languages: Issues and Approaches*, pages 37–44, 2003. 112

[159] D. Cruse. *Lexical Semantics*. Cambridge University Press, 1986. 113

[160] R. Jackendoff. *Semantic Structures*. MIT Press, Boston, Mass, 1990. 113

[161] G. Chierchia and S. McConell-Ginet. *Meaning and Grammar: An Introduction to Semantics*. The MIT Press, Cambridge, MA, 1990. 113

[162] M. Palmer, D. Gildea, and P. Kingsbury. The Proposition Bank: An Annotated Corpus of Semantic Roles. *Computational Linguistics*, 31(1):71–106, 2005. DOI: 10.1162/0891201053630264 114

[163] Collin F. Baker, Charles J. Fillmore, and John B. Lowe. The Berkeley FrameNet Project. In *COLING-ACL '98: Proceedings of the Conference, held at the University of Montréal*, pages 86–90, 1998. DOI: 10.3115/980845.980860 114

[164] Nianwen Xue and Martha Palmer. Adding Semantic Roles to the Chinese Treebank. *Nat. Lang. Eng.*, 15(1):143–172, 2009. DOI: 10.1017/S1351324908004865 114

[165] Mona Diab, Alessandro Moschitti, and Daniele Pighin. Semantic Role Labeling Systems for Arabic using Kernel Methods. In *Proceedings of ACL-08: HLT*, pages 798–806, Columbus, Ohio, June 2008. Association for Computational Linguistics. 115

[166] Mona Diab, Musa Alkhalifa, Sabry ElKateb, Christiane Fellbaum, Aous Mansouri, and Martha Palmer. SemEval-2007 Task 18: Arabic Semantic Labeling. In *Proceedings of the Fourth International Workshop on Semantic Evaluations (SemEval-2007)*, pages 93–98, Prague, Czech Republic, June 2007. Association for Computational Linguistics. DOI: 10.3115/1621474.1621491 115, 116

[167] Christiane Fellbaum. *WordNet: An Electronic Lexical Database*. MIT Press, 1998. http://www.cogsci.princeton.edu/~wn [2000, September 7]. 116

[168] Piek Vossen. *EuroWordNet: A Multilingual Database with Lexical Semantic Networks*. Kluwer Academic Publishers, Dordrecht, 1998. 116

[169] W. Black, S. Elkateb, H. Rodriguez, M. Alkhalifa, P. Vossen, A. Pease, and C. Fellbaum. Introducing the Arabic WordNet Project. In *Proceedings of the Third International WordNet Conference*, Jeju Island, Korea, 2006. 116

[170] S. Elkateb, W. Black, H. Rodriguez, M. Alkhalifa, P. Vossen, A. Pease, and C. Fellbaum. Building a WordNet for Arabic. In *Proceedings of The fifth international conference on Language Resources and Evaluation (LREC 2006)*, Genoa, Italy, 2006. 116

[171] G. Doddington, A. Mitchell, M. Przybocki, L. Ramshaw, S. Strassel, and R. Weischedel. The Automatic Content Extraction (ACE) Program–Tasks, Data, and Evaluation. *Proceedings of LREC 2004*, pages 837–840, 2004. 117

[172] Imed Zitouni, Jeffrey Sorensen, Xiaoqiang Luo, and Radu Florian. The impact of morphological stemming on Arabic mention detection and coreference resolution. In *Proceedings of the ACL Workshop on Computational Approaches to Semitic Languages*, pages 63–70, Ann Arbor, Michigan, June 2005. 117

[173] Yassine Benajiba and Imed Zitouni. Morphology based Segmentation Combination for Arabic Mention Detection. *Special issue on Arabic Natural Processing of the ACM Transactions on Asian Language Information Processing (TALIP)*, 2010. DOI: 10.1145/1644879.1644883 117

[174] Mona T. Diab. An Unsupervised Approach for Bootstrapping Arabic Sense Tagging. In Ali Farghaly and Karine Megerdoomian, editors, *COLING 2004 Computational Approaches to Arabic Script-based Languages*, pages 43–50, Geneva, Switzerland, August 28th 2004. COLING. 117

[175] David Farwell, Stephen Helmreich, Florence Reeder, Bonnie Dorr, Nizar Habash, Eduard Hovy, Lori Levin, Keith Miller, Teruko Mitamura, Owen Rambow, and Advaith Siddharthan. Interlingual Annotation of Multilingual Text Corpus. In *Proceedings of the NAACL/HLT Workshop: New Frontiers in Corpus Annotation*, 2004. 117

[176] Nizar Habash, Clinton Mah, Sabiha Imran, Randy Calistri-Yeh, and Páraic Sheridan. Design, Construction and Validation of an Arabic-English Conceptual Interlingua for Cross-lingual Information Retrieval. In *LREC-2006: Fifth International Conference on Language Resources and Evaluation*, pages 107–112, Genoa, Italy, 2006. 118

[177] Bonnie J. Dorr, Pamela W. Jordan, and John W. Benoit. A Survey of Current Research in Machine Translation. In M. Zelkowitz, editor, *Advances in Computers, Vol. 49*, pages 1–68. Academic Press, London, 1999. 119

[178] Franz Josef Och and Hermann Ney. A Systematic Comparison of Various Statistical Alignment Models. *Computational Linguistics*, 29(1):19–52, 2003. DOI: 10.1162/089120103321337421 119

[179] Philipp Koehn. Pharaoh: a Beam Search Decoder for Phrase-based Statistical Machine Translation Models. In *Proceedings of the Association for Machine Translation in the Americas*, pages 115–124, 2004. 119

[180] Jan Hajič, Jan Hric, and Vladislav Kubon. Machine Translation of Very Close Languages. In *Proceedings of the 6th Applied Natural Language Processing Conference (ANLP'2000)*, pages 7–12, Seattle, 2000. DOI: 10.3115/974147.974149 120

[181] Andreas Zollmann, Ashish Venugopal, and Stephan Vogel. Bridging the Inflection Morphology Gap for Arabic Statistical Machine Translation. In *Proceedings of the Human Language Technology Conference of the NAACL, Companion Volume: Short Papers*, pages 201–204, New York City, USA, 2006. Association for Computational Linguistics. DOI: 10.3115/1614049.1614100 121

[182] Jason Riesa and David Yarowsky. Minimally Supervised Morphological Segmentation with Applications to Machine Translation. In *Proceedings of the 7th Conference of the Association for Machine Translation in the Americas (AMTA06)*, pages 185–192, Cambridge,MA, 2006. 121

[183] Anas El Isbihani, Shahram Khadivi, Oliver Bender, and Hermann Ney. Morpho-syntactic Arabic Preprocessing for Arabic to English Statistical Machine Translation. In *Proceedings on the Workshop on Statistical Machine Translation*, pages 15–22, New York City, June 2006. Association for Computational Linguistics. DOI: 10.3115/1654650.1654654 121

[184] Nizar Habash. Syntactic Preprocessing for Statistical MT. In *Proceedings of the Machine Translation Summit (MT SUMMIT XI)*, Copenhagen, Denmark, 2007. 123

[185] Nizar Habash, Bonnie Dorr, and Christof Monz. Challenges in Building an Arabic-English GHMT System with SMT Components. In *Proceedings of the 7th Conference of the Association for Machine Translation in the Americas (AMTA06)*, pages 56–65, Cambridge, MA, 2006. 123

[186] Steve DeNeefe and Kevin Knight. Synchronous Tree Adjoining Machine Translation. In *Proceedings of the 2009 Conference on Empirical Methods in Natural Language Processing*, pages 727–736, Singapore, August 2009. Association for Computational Linguistics. DOI: 10.3115/1699571.1699607 123

[187] Marine Carpuat, Yuval Marton, and Nizar Habash. Improving Arabic-to-English Statistical Machine Translation by Reordering Post-Verbal Subjects for Alignment. In *Proceedings of the ACL 2010 Conference Short Papers*, pages 178–183, Uppsala, Sweden, July 2010. Association for Computational Linguistics. 123

[188] Ibrahim Badr, Rabih Zbib, and James Glass. Syntactic Phrase Reordering for English-to-Arabic Statistical Machine Translation. In *Proceedings of the 12th Conference of the European Chapter of the ACL (EACL 2009)*, pages 86–93, Athens, Greece, March 2009. Association for Computational Linguistics. DOI: 10.3115/1609067.1609076 123, 124

[189] Jakob Elming and Nizar Habash. Syntactic Reordering for English-Arabic Phrase-Based Machine Translation. In *Proceedings of the EACL 2009 Workshop on Computational Approaches to Semitic Languages*, pages 69–77, Athens, Greece, March 2009. Association for Computational Linguistics. DOI: 10.3115/1621774.1621786 123

[190] Saša Hasan, Anas El Isbihani, and Hermann Ney. Creating a Large-Scale Arabic to French Statistical Machine Translation System . In *Proceedings of Language Resources and Evaluation Conference (LREC)*, pages 855–858, Genoa, Italy, 2006. 124

[191] Nizar Habash and Jun Hu. Improving Arabic-Chinese Statistical Machine Translation using English as Pivot Language. In *Proceedings of the Fourth Workshop on Statistical Machine Translation*, pages 173–181, Athens, Greece, March 2009. Association for Computational Linguistics. DOI: 10.3115/1626431.1626467 124

[192] Mossab Al-Hunaity, Bente Maegaard, and Dorte Hansen. Using English as a Pivot Language to Enhance Danish-Arabic Statistical Machine Translation. In *Workshop on Language Resources and Human Language Technology for Semitic Languages in the Language Resources and Evaluation Conference (LREC)*, Valletta, Malta, 2010. 124

[193] Reshef Shilon, Nizar Habash, Alon Lavie, and Shuly Wintner. Machine Translation between Hebrew and Arabic: Needs, Challenges and Preliminary Solutions. In *Proceedings of the Student Research Workshop in the Conference of the Association for Machine Translation in the Americas (AMTA)*, Denver, Colorado, 2010. 124

[194] Haytham Alsharaf, Sylviane Cardey, Peter Greenfield, and Yihui Shen. Problems and Solutions in Machine Translation Involving Arabic, Chinese and French. In *Proceedings of the International Conference on Information Technology*, pages 293–297, Las Vegas, Nevada, 2004. DOI: 10.1109/ITCC.2004.1286649 124

[195] Mohammed Sharaf. Implications of the Agreement Features in (English to Arabic) Machine Translation. Master's thesis, Al-Azhar University, 2002. 124

[196] Abdelhadi Soudi, Violetta Cavalli-Sforza, and Abderrahim Jamari. A Prototype English-to-Arabic Interlingua-based MT system. In *Proceedings of the Third International Conference on Language Resources and Evaluation: Workshop on Arabic language resources and evaluation*, Las Palmas, Spain, 2002. 124

[197] Abdelhadi Soudi. Challenges in the Generation of Arabic from Interlingua. In *Proceedings of Traitement Automatique des Langues Naturelles (TALN-04)*, pages 343–350, 2004. Fez, Morocco. 124

[198] Azza Abdel-Monem, Khaled Shaalan, Ahmed Rafea, and Hoda Baraka. A Proposed Approach for Generating Arabic from Interlingua in a Multilingual Machine Translation System. In *Proceedings of the 4th Conference on Language Engineering*, pages 197–206, 2003. Cairo, Egypt. 124

[199] F. Gey and D. Oard. The TREC-2001 Cross-Language Information Retrieval Track: Searching Arabic Using English, French or Arabic Queries. In *The 10th Text Retrieval Conference (TREC-10)*, 2001. 124

[200] F. Gey and D. Oard. The TREC-2002 Arabic/English Cross-Language Information Retrieval Track. In *The 11th Text Retrieval Conference (TREC-11)*, 2002. 124

[201] Jinxi Xu, Alexander Fraser, and Ralph Weischedel. Empirical Studies in Strategies for Arabic Retrieval. In *SIGIR '02: Proceedings of the 25th annual international ACM SIGIR conference on Research and development in information retrieval*, pages 269–274, New York, NY, USA, 2002. ACM. DOI: 10.1145/564376.564424 124

[202] Leah S. Larkey, Lisa Ballesteros, and Margaret E. Connell. Improving Stemming for Arabic Information Retrieval: Light Stemming and Co-occurrence Analysis. In *Proceedings of the 25th Annual International Conference on Research and Development in Information Retrieval (SIGIR 2002), Tampere, Finland*, pages 275–282, 2002. DOI: 10.1145/564376.564425 124

[203] K. Darwish and D. Oard. CLIR Experiments at Maryland for TREC 2002: Evidence Combination for Arabic-English Retrieval. In *The 11th Text Retrieval Conference (TREC-11)*, 2002. 124

[204] Ramzi Abbès, Joseph Dichy, and Mohamed Hassoun. The Architecture of a Standard Arabic Lexical Database. Some Figures, Ratios and Categories from the DIINAR.1 Source Program. In Ali Farghaly and Karine Megerdoomian, editors, *COLING 2004 Computational Approaches to Arabic Script-based Languages*, pages 15–22, Geneva, Switzerland, August 28th 2004. COLING. 138

Author's Biography

NIZAR HABASH

Nizar Habash is a research scientist at the Center for Computational Learning Systems in Columbia University, where he has worked since 2004. He received a B.Sc. in Computer Engineering and a B.A. in Linguistics and Languages from Old Dominion University in 1997. He received his Ph.D. in 2003 from the Computer Science Department, University of Maryland College Park. His Ph.D. thesis is titled *Generation-Heavy Hybrid Machine Translation*. In 2005, he co-founded the Columbia Arabic Dialect Modeling (CADIM) group with Mona Diab and Owen Rambow. Nizar's research includes work on machine translation, natural language generation, lexical semantics, morphological analysis, generation and disambiguation, syntactic parsing and annotation, and computational modeling of Arabic and its dialects.

Nizar currently serves as secretary of the board of AMTA (Association for Machine Translation in the Americas) and of IAMT (International Association for Machine Translation). He served as vice-president of the Semitic Language Special Interest Group in the Association of Computational Linguistics (ACL) (2006-2009). He also served as the research community representative on the AMTA board (2006-2008). He previously served as a research program co-chair for the AMTA 2006 conference, the Workshop on Computational Approaches to Semitic Languages (ACL 2005) and the Workshop on Machine Translation for Semitic Languages (MT Summit 2003).

Nizar has published over 80 papers in international conferences and journals and has given numerous lectures and tutorials for academic and industrial audiences.

Nizar's website is located at http://www.nizarhabash.com/.